HUMANS, COMPUTERS AND WIZARDS

Computers are increasingly able to mimic abilities we often think of as exclusively human – memory, decision-making, vision and now, speech. A new generation of speech recognition systems can make at least some attempt at understanding what is said to them and can respond accordingly. These systems are coming into daily use in areas such as home banking, airline flight enquiries and telephone shopping services, and are fast becoming more powerful and more pervasive.

Using data from the SUNDIAL project, a major European Commission funded project on speech understanding, this book shows how such data may be analysed to yield important conclusions about the organisation of both human–human and human–computer information dialogues. It describes the Wizard of Oz method of collecting spoken dialogues, which monitors people who believe they are interacting with a speech understanding system before that system has been fully designed or built, and shows how the resulting dialogues may be analysed to guide further design. This book provides detailed and comparative empirical studies of human–human and human–computer speech dialogues, including analyses of opening and closing sequences, turn-taking, and the organisation of overlap and repair strategies to overcome troubles in verbal interaction.

Humans, Computers and Wizards considers current perspectives on human–computer interaction and stresses the value of a sociological approach based on conversation analysis. This breaks away from the individualistic, cognitivist approach of much HCI research and takes seriously the idea that a human–computer dialogue, like a human–human dialogue, is an instance of emergent social order.

Robin Wooffitt is Lecturer in Sociology at the University of Surrey, **Norman M. Fraser** is Lecturer in Linguistics at the University of Surrey, **Nigel Gilbert** is Professor of Sociology at the University of Surrey and **Scott McGlashan** is Senior Research Scientist at the Swedish Institute of Computer Science.

HUMANS, COMPUTERS AND WIZARDS

Analysing human (simulated) computer interaction

Robin Wooffitt, Norman M. Fraser, Nigel Gilbert and Scott McGlashan

Routledge
Taylor & Francis Group
LONDON AND NEW YORK

First published 1997
by Routledge

Published 2013
by Routledge
2 Park Square, Milton Park, Abingdon, Oxfordshire OX14 4RN

Simultaneously published in the USA and Canada
by Routledge
711 Third Avenue, New York, NY 10017

First issued in paperback 2014
Routledge is an imprint of the Taylor and Francis Group, an informa business

Typeset in Garamond by
Ponting–Green Publishing Services, Chesham,
Buckinghamshire

British Library Cataloguing in Publication Data
A catalogue record for this book is available from the British Library

Library of Congress Cataloguing in Publication Data
A catalogue record for this book has been requested

ISBN 978-0-415-06948-9 (hbk)
ISBN 978-0-415-86772-6 (pbk)

CONTENTS

FIGURES AND TABLES

FIGURES

TABLES

ACKNOWLEDGEMENTS

The authors would like to acknowledge the support and influence of all their colleagues from the UK, France, Germany, Italy and Sweden who worked on the SUNDIAL Project. Special thanks also to those colleagues who have worked in the Social and Computer Sciences research group without whose encouragement and advice this book would have been much harder to write: Anne Ankrah, Sarah Buckland, Andrew Fordham, David Frohlich, Ian Hutchby, Marina Jirotka, Carol Lee, Paul Luff, Catriona MacDermid, Alison Mill-Ingen, Andrew Simpson and Ave Wrigley.

1

SOCIOLOGY AND HUMAN–MACHINE DIALOGUE

As technology advances, we see an increasing number of machines that can mimic sophisticated human abilities. The past fifty years have seen computers with memory, with vision, with the ability to make complex decisions based on access to large quantities of information, and now, computers that can apparently talk to us and listen to our replies with at least some pretence at understanding what we say. These developments open up interesting practical possibilities for designing more useful and powerful machines, and rich opportunities for examining some basic questions about human action and human society.

The chance to investigate fundamental issues about human action arises because in human–machine interaction the conventional distinctions between person and object, human and machine, and intelligence and mere reaction seem to be threatened. As Suchman notes, it is possible to investigate

> the apparent challenge that computational artifacts pose to the long-standing distinction between the physical and the social, in the special sense of those things that one designs, builds and uses, on the one hand, and those things with which one communicates, on the other. While this distinction has been relatively non-problematic to date, now for the first time the term 'interaction' – in a sense previously reserved for describing a uniquely interpersonal activity – seems appropriately to characterise what goes on between people and certain machines as well.
> (Suchman, 1987: 6)

This book is particularly concerned with attempts to develop machines that speak and hear when we talk to them. Such machines, albeit with rather crude and unsophisticated abilities, are moving out of research laboratories and into ordinary life. For example, some banks now have services that customers can telephone to request the balance of their accounts or pay bills. The agent at the other end of the line is not a person, but a speech understanding system that asks questions using synthesised or pre-recorded speech and that responds to the customers' single word answers. The technology is changing rapidly and while the current capabilities of such 'home banking' systems could not be mistaken for the speech abilities of humans, much more powerful systems are on their way.

However, this is not a book about the technology of speech recognition systems themselves;[1] rather, it is concerned with what we can learn about human behaviour in interaction with such machines. The focus is on the human side, not on the machine side of human–machine interaction. There are several reasons for this focus. First, until now, analyses of human interaction have, naturally, been confined to data in which people are talking to other people. Data on human–machine interaction open up a new range of possibilities for the analysis of human dialogue, examples of which can be found in later chapters of this book.

Second, research based on human–machine interaction data could lead to recommendations about how speech understanding machines can be designed to be more easily usable and more effective. That is, the research could provide practical guidelines for designers of human computer interaction. However, such guidelines are only likely to be helpful if they are based on a prior careful and thorough analysis of the structure and organisation of human–machine interaction.

Third, the availability of data on speech interactions between humans and machines raises the possibility of exploring new approaches to the understanding of human–computer interaction (HCI) based on sociological, rather than psychological and cognitive perspectives. We can draw on a substantial body of sociological work on the analysis of verbal interaction between people in examining human–computer dialogues, and this is the approach that we take in this book.

In this introductory chapter, we begin by plotting the likely future of speech systems and explain a little of the technical and research background, in particular, the 'SUNDIAL' project that formed the basis of the work reported in later chapters. We then review the currently prevalent paradigm in the field of human–computer interaction, one which takes an individualistic and cognitivist stance to understanding interaction, and contrast it with a sociological approach. Finally, we outline the contents of the remaining chapters of the book.

SPEECH UNDERSTANDING SYSTEMS

While computers are now ubiquitous, by far the most common means of interacting with them remains the keyboard and screen, despite the disadvantages of these devices. Using a computer by means of typed text input is slow, requires the user to have good manual dexterity and their hands free, and ideally demands the ability to type. Monitor screens are bulky, heavy and therefore not portable, difficult to read unless one is near them, and only able to convey a limited amount of information at any time. Other forms of computer media have different kinds of advantages and disadvantages for users (Chapanis, 1981). In particular, speech has a quite different range of strong and weak points from that of the screen and keyboard combination. For example, most people can talk very much more quickly than they can type. Close physical proximity of speaker and hearer is not needed; over long distances telephones can be used. No prior training in how to use the interaction medium is required, for, with the exception of some hearing impaired people, and people with severe mental disabilities, everyone knows how to talk. On the other hand, speech is a linear medium: once a word has been spoken, it has gone and cannot be retrieved later, as one might look back to an earlier passage on a page or screen.

The advantages of speech mean that although the technology at present is still very crude, speech interfaces are already being used for some special applications. The home banking systems that allow telephone callers to interrogate their accounts were mentioned above. Such systems provide remote access by telephone to banking databases for users drawn from the general public. There are other information services available to the public where similar speech interfaces are being used or considered. For instance, airline information on flight arrivals and departures can already be obtained by calling a telephone number and interacting with a computer system linked to the airlines' plane movements database. Other domains where similar facilities are available or planned include notification of drug side-effects, weather reports and forecasts, and train information. The common characteristic of these applications is a large, central database of changing information that needs to be accessed by many geographically distributed people who have no prior training in using the system. For such applications, the fact that speech interfaces can be used by anyone without equipment other than a telephone and without prior training gives them great advantages over other means of communication with computers.

Another, related application of speech interfaces, one with more controversial consequences for employment and for service to customers, is the sale of goods over the telephone. For example, mail order companies, insurance companies and maintenance organisations employ large teams of people to take orders over the telephone. The agents' dialogues with customers are more or less standardised, requiring the collection of a number of pre-specified items of information (the make, model and quantity of the goods required and payment details). These calls could be handled directly by a computer through a speech interface, rather than as at present, having a person doing little more than reading prompts from a computer screen down the telephone to the customer and typing in the customer's replies.

A quite different domain of application for speech interfaces is command and control. These are applications where the user issues instructions to a computer, a control system or a robot. A speech interface has an advantage over other interface media when the operator has his or her hands full with other tasks and so cannot type, or when the operator has to be mobile. For example, there are experimental speech systems designed for use by pilots in aircraft cockpits and commercially available systems for stock control by warehouse workers who record stock levels by speaking into a portable microphone connected to a speech understanding system.

In future, we shall probably also see speech systems being used in the leisure industry, to control games and as a means of interaction in virtual reality environments. The fact that the user does not need to be trained to interact with the system is obviously important. There are also attractions to players in having a truly interactive dialogue with a computer game.

The use of speech systems in these application areas is possible because they represent limited domains, in which users can interact with the computer using constrained and standardised dialogues. As we explain in Appendix A, understanding human speech is still a very difficult technical problem and therefore practical systems have to limit their scope very severely.

Nevertheless, the promise of these various applications of speech interface technology was sufficient to persuade a number of research agencies worldwide to invest heavily in the development of speech understanding systems over the last twenty years. In the United States, the Department of Defense has funded research (through the DARPA programme) on speech understanding since the early 1970s. Notable examples of US systems are HEARSAY (Erman, 1974; Erman, 1977), HARPY (Lowerre and Reddy, 1980) and HWIM (Wolf, 1977), all of which achieved some success in recognising continuous speech with vocabularies of about 1000 words. In the UK, the military and the research councils have put money into speech research: for example, the VODIS project was supported by the Alvey Programme to develop a train information service available over the telephone. Similar research has been conducted elsewhere in Europe and in the United States. More recently, the ATIS project in the US, funded by the Department of Defense, has set research laboratories in competition with each other to develop the best speech understanding system able to handle enquiries about a limited domain of aircraft information. In Europe, there have been national research programmes in the UK and Germany and the Commission of the European Communities has supported a number of large projects on speech understanding under its ESPRIT programme, one of which is the SUNDIAL project.

The SUNDIAL project (the name comes from a contraction of *S*peech *Un*derstanding and *Dial*ogue) was a five-year (1988–93) project involving partners from five European countries: Logica, Vocalis and the University of Surrey in the UK, CNET, CAP Gemini Innovation and IRISA/University of Rennes in France, CSELT, Saritel and the Politechnico di Torino in Italy, Daimler Benz, Siemens and the University of Erlangen in Germany, and Infovox in Sweden. The project developed four similar speech understanding systems, one for each of the English, French, German and Italian languages, to enable users to inquire about information such as flight times, flight reservations and train schedules. In all, the project involved 170 person-years of work. By the end, demonstration systems using large (1000 word) vocabularies were able to hold successful dialogues with members of the public calling the systems over the public telephone network.

The results of all these research projects have begun to emerge as commercial products. Boards with the hardware and software for speech recognition for fitting inside personal computers can be purchased 'off the shelf'. Apple Computer sell personal computers complete with a sophisticated speech recognition and synthesis system that can be customised by the user to recognise computer commands, developed directly from US Department of Defense funded research at Carnegie-Mellon University (Lee *et al.*, 1990). And an increasing range of information services is now available commercially by telephone, taking advantage of current speech recognition systems. The experience of designing and developing these basic systems has emphasised the importance of taking account of how people – most of whom are likely never to have spoken to a computer speech system before – manage to interact with such systems, that is, their 'usability'.

PERSPECTIVES ON HUMAN–COMPUTER INTERACTION

For the last twenty years, ever since computers achieved widespread use, there has been a concern with increasing their usability. The dominant perspective used to examine usability issues has been informed by psychology, in particular cognitive psychology. Indeed, the link between work on human–computer interaction (HCI) and cognitive psychology has been so strong that HCI has sometimes been regarded as merely a branch of applied cognitive psychology (Norman, 1988).

Cognitive psychology provided a way of defining the topic of HCI (the factors influencing the interaction between a computer and an individual user), a method of investigation (the experimental method, with users exposed to stimuli from the computer under controlled conditions), and a theory for understanding the reactions of users under these experimental conditions (a computational view of the mind). We shall examine each of these in turn.

The cognitive emphasis of HCI has focused attention on the cognitive capacities of users and how these affect users' ability to carry out specific tasks with computer systems. In contrast to behaviourism, which argued that action must be understood solely in terms of observable relationships between the organism and its environment, cognitive psychology and more generally, cognitive science, admit the possibility of explanations couched in terms of mental processes, but with the proviso that these processes are expressed in computational terms. An often cited and influential example of such work is Card, Moran and Newell's (1983) 'GOMS' (Goals, Operations, Methods and Selection) model of performance. In a GOMS analysis, the user's task is described in terms of the user's goals, a set of operators, that is, low-level actions that users perform to use the system, methods, consisting of sequence of operators, and selections, the choices the user makes between alternative methods of achieving a goal. A typical GOMS analysis of a task involves decomposing an overall goal (that is, to complete the task successfully) into sub-goals, each of which is in turn decomposed into further sub-goals until ultimately these are reduced to basic operators. Thus the action required to complete the task is analysed into a hierarchical network of goals, sub-goals and operators. The assumption is that users' cognitive processing mirrors this network. GOMS analysis has been used to predict the time taken by typical users to complete tasks, by finding the time taken to perform each basic operator under experimental conditions and then aggregating the operator times for all operators involved in the task.

GOMS was one of the first attempts to infer a cognitive model to describe how users performed tasks. More recently, rather more complex models have been proposed, using variations on linguistic grammar theory (for example, task-action grammar (Payne and Green, 1986)) and production systems and the SOAR cognitive architecture (for example, programmable user models (Young *et al.*, 1989). It is characteristic of all this work that it abstracts users' actions into 'tasks' (for example, editing, or even typing a single character) in order to explore the computational processes assumed to lie behind their achievement. The abstraction into tasks means that the analyst does not have to deal at the same time with the situation or context in which the task is actually embedded. This analytic strategy in turn helps to achieve an abstraction of 'the user' away from specific individuals to a set of functional objects and processes amenable to precise computational description (Robinson, 1990), such as provided by the GOMS model.

The second element that HCI has taken from cognitive psychology is the application of the experimental method to investigating interaction with computers. The assumption is made that examining users' actions in a laboratory setting, where they are given carefully selected and controlled tasks to undertake, can illuminate how people interact with computers in other settings. There are a number of difficulties with this assumption.

First, the experimental method fits most comfortably with an analytical approach which emphasises causality and the measurement of variables (for example, the times taken to complete the basic 'operators' of the GOMS model). But it is not clear that this language of 'variables' and 'causality' is particularly relevant or appropriate to dealing with human action. Second, one of the benefits of the experimental method is that it allows randomised trials from a population and strict statistical controls: an experiment may be repeated a number of times with different subjects using well known statistical designs and the results examined for statistically significant differences. However, these statistical methods depend crucially on the experimenter being able to define and sample from a relevant population.

Unfortunately, because no attention is paid to the context of actual interaction of people with computers, the parameters of the relevant population remain uninvestigated and the samples on which the experiments are carried out are usually drawn from artificial or special populations (typically, college students).

The experimental method, through its focus on the statistical analysis of the results, does accommodate individual variation. However, individual variation (in the sense of variation in biological capabilities) is not the only, nor is it likely to be the main, source of variation between users. A much more important source of variation between users is differences in individuals' social positions. In other words, differences in users' interactions with systems are not, for the most part, the result of individual psychological and physical differences but social structured differences; and these differences are not merely nuisance differences, to be summarised using a mean and variance, as cognitive psychology is prone to do, but as we shall see are susceptible to (sociological) explanation.

The third element that HCI has taken from cognitive psychology is a model of the individual that is framed in terms of a particular computational metaphor that sees human action as resulting from people's internal representations of 'plans'. The notion of a plan being used here is derived from research in artificial intelligence. The actor is assumed to have some goal or 'end' in mind. The problem is to find a sequence of basic actions that, starting from the current state, results in the achievement of the goal, meanwhile satisfying certain conditions dictated by the environment. The assumption is that actors construct such plans before and during action. An analytical explanation of an action can then be phrased in terms of the plan of which it was a component. According to this view, interaction, reduced to its essentials, consists of one actor making a plan to satisfy a goal (to communicate some fact to another person) and executing this plan by carrying out actions (by uttering one or more 'speech acts'). The other party to the interaction determines the meaning of the utterance by inferring from the speech acts the speaker's plan, and thus discovers the speaker's goal (Allen, 1983). For example, person A might formulate a plan to sweeten her tea (the goal) and carry it out by asking 'Would you pass the sugar?' The recipient of the request would interpret this utterance by recognising it as part of A's plan that had the goal of sweetening tea. However, this kind of plan recognition is much more difficult than may at first appear (Gilbert, 1987). This is because there is no simple one-to-one relationship between actions and plans. Most goals can be achieved in a number of different ways, so that there are many possible action sequences that could be used, and any specific item of behaviour can be used to contribute to the satisfaction of many different goals. Consequently, it is not clear how any particular plan can be reliably inferred from any behavioural sequence.

While the planning model can be criticised on these rather technical grounds, there have also been much more radical critiques (for example, Winograd and Flores, 1986, and Suchman, 1987). Suchman argues that although people in ordinary conversation do talk about their own and others' plans and intentions, it is not the case that such talk warrants the existence of plans 'in people's heads' that drive their actions. Rather, plans are 'resources for people's practical deliberations about action' (1987: 49). Following Mead (1934), she suggests that human activity is of two kinds: first, 'situated action', which is essentially ad hoc improvisation, and second, representations of action in the form of plans and retrospective accounts of action. There is no necessary causal relationship between these two.[2]

SOCIOLOGICAL PERSPECTIVES ON HUMAN-COMPUTER INTERACTION

The previous section has suggested some of the limitations of confining attention to an approach that focuses solely on individual cognitive abilities. Sociological concerns and perspectives are also relevant. Over the last ten years, the value of looking not only at individuals but also at the social context in which they act has been increasingly recognised. For example, in work to characterise the technological requirements of users for computer support, sociological methods have been used. In contrast to the experimental protocols which are common in the study of HCI, some researchers are now advocating the use of participant observation of users in natural settings, or the use of 'ethnography' (Whyte, 1955; Lofland, 1971; Hammersley and Atkinson, 1983; Fielding, 1992). This is particularly the case for research on the design of office systems and systems for the work place (for example, Greatbatch *et al.*, 1993; Hughes *et al.*, 1993; Murray, 1993). The benefit of ethnographic methods is that they are effective in describing how people interact in ordinary life, in their normal contexts. One of the general results of such research has been to emphasise that users of computer systems do not work in isolation from others but engage in complex interactions with fellow workers that have a profound effect on their use of the computer.

Sociology has also been used to inform the design of computer systems. One example, relevant to the concerns of this book, is the work by Frohlich and Luff (1990) on an interface for the 'Advice System'. This was a demonstration system intended to show how computers could be used to give welfare rights advice directly to members of the general public. It had to be usable by people who might have very little or no experience of using computers and therefore considerable attention was paid to designing the user interface. Speech technology was out of the question at the time because of the complexity of the information that the system was required to obtain from the user, so a text-based interface was adopted in which questions and answers appeared on the computer screen in a scrolling strip as though transcribed from a spoken dialogue. The system was designed to answer a wide range of user questions on benefits within an open-ended dialogue. Users constructed questions about their entitlements or statements about their circumstances by first choosing the topic of their intended utterance from a series of menus on screen and then choosing the wording of the utterance from a series of phrase menus. The computer processed the question or statement, asking questions of its own to establish facts about the user until it could give appropriate advice.

In order to manage the dialogue with the user, some dialogue control policies had to be built into the system. These policies were particularly important because both user and system could ask questions of the other and make statements. For example, if the user asks a question and then asks an additional question before the first one has been answered, which question should be answered first? Policies were also required to deal with difficulties in the exchange. For example, users were able to respond with 'Don't know' to system questions and could contradict previous answers. Furthermore, some policy was required to control the overall sequence of the dialogue, starting with a question from the user and ending with the final answer from the system.

To develop a dialogue control policy, Frohlich and Luff turned to a branch of sociology known as conversation analysis, or CA (introductions to CA may be found in Chapter 4, and Wooffitt, 1990). CA aims to identify and describe the communicative and interpretative strategies which people use in conversation. Observing that some of the dialogue control problems that the design of the Advice System was required to solve seemed to have analogues in human–human conversation, Frohlich and Luff drew on the findings of conversation analysts about the structure and organisation of turn-taking and question answering in ordinary conversation. For example, Sacks, Schegloff and Jefferson (1974) have described the turn-taking system that appears to be used in everyday conversation. Sacks *et al.*'s description of the principles of this system was used by Frohlich and Luff as a guide in the design of a set of rules to determine when the Advice System handed control over to the user in its dialogue.

Similarly, conversation analysts have developed ideas about the linkages of questions to answers in terms of units known as adjacency pairs (for example, Schegloff and Sacks, 1973). These ideas were also transformed into rules that determined the order in which the user's questions were answered. Frohlich and Luff concluded that conversation analysis was a 'valuable resource for design in a context where good design can mean the difference between a useful and useless system' (1990: 218).

However, there have been some criticisms of attempts to use the findings from conversation analytic studies in the design of interactive systems. For example, Button and Sharrock (1995) have pointed out that the argument outlined by Sacks, Schegloff and Jefferson (1974) focused only on the underlying turn allocation procedures used in interaction, and that it is important to keep in mind that these procedures will always be instantiated in the specifics of the design of particular utterances. Consequently, they warn against an over-emphasis upon relying on an abstract formulation of the turn-taking system and its rules as a design resource in the design of interactive computer tools.

Indeed, Button (1990) and Button and Sharrock (1995), argue strongly that attempts to use conversation analysis as a resource in designing interactive computer systems are misplaced if such use encourages designers to make strong claims to have built 'conversing computers'.[3] The basis of Button and Sharrock's argument is that it is impossible to develop formalised versions of the competencies people use in conversational activity; and that it is precisely these unprogrammable competencies that constitute what it is to be 'conversing'. We will return to these issues in the concluding chapter.

The critical point recognised by Frohlich and Luff's design, and the reason why conversation analysis is relevant to the design of human–computer interfaces, is that the way people interact with other people, as well as with computer systems, is not based on prior plans which the user then works through in a mechanical fashion, but is rather an opportunistic activity in which the users (or speakers) adapt their action to the contingencies of the moment. Schegloff (1989a) states the point forcibly.

> What occurs in interaction is not merely the serial externalization by several participants into some joint arena of batches of talk, hatched in private intentions (or even in socialized ones), and filled out with the docile artifacts of 'language' (as in some versions of speech act theory, discourse analysis and the like). Such a view treats the mind or brain as the scene of all the action, and the space of interaction as structureless medium, or at least a medium whose structure is beside the point with respect to what is transmitted through it, much as the composition of telephone cable is beside the point for the conversations transmitted through it. (Emphasis in original)

These contingencies include, indeed mainly are, the actions of the other parties in the dialogue. The interaction is constructed jointly by all the parties and can only be understood by adopting a perspective that recognises this. A coherent dialogue can be seen as an instance of emergent social order and therefore needs to be treated as a social construction. For example, the turn-taking procedures that Luff and Frohlich drew on in the design of the Advice System's dialogue control policy are a socially organised set of practices that have consequences for the character of the occasion in which they are used. Different turn-taking procedures occur in different contexts, and the use of different turn exchange procedures help to define those contexts (see, for example, Atkinson and Drew, 1979, and Drew, 1985, where turn-taking in courtroom settings is examined). Similarly, the organisation of interaction in terms of adjacency pairs involves interactional considerations. For example, interactionally relevant implications may be drawn by participants when speakers fail to answer or put off answering what may be understood to be questions by virtue of the adjacency pair organisation of the dialogue. These are issues that will be explored in more detail in later chapters in this book.

THE 'CHICKEN AND EGG' PROBLEM

In this introductory chapter we have argued that a sociological approach, in particular one that adopts the methodological and epistemological perspective of conversation analysis, is likely to be fruitful and revealing when applied to human–computer interaction. And we have noted some attempts to utilise the insights from conversation analysis to inform the design of a screen-based interactive computer tool. However, it is in the design and evaluation of speech-based interfaces that CA might be most useful.

In the past few years there have been considerable efforts to try to model ordinary human verbal interaction with computational tools; and almost certainly, in the next decade, there will be much more research on the development of speech-based systems. However, the absence of advanced speech systems means that system designers face a methodological dilemma. Conventionally, it is felt that to produce systems that are 'user friendly' they must be designed to be sensitive to the communicative competencies which human users will bring to bear in their exchanges with intelligent speech systems (Boguraev, 1985; Lehnert and Ringle, 1982). This requirement, however, entails a 'chicken and egg' type of problem: how can system designers know how people will react to computers prior to the development of an experimental system, and how can an experimental system be developed prior to an understanding of users' behaviour and requirements? That is, in advance of an actual system being built and operational, there is little knowledge about the way people will interact with it to inform the design of the system so that it facilitates easy use by a human.

Simulation experiments provide a way into this otherwise closed circle. Simulation experiments involve a person pretending to be an intelligent computer. Human subjects are then led to believe that they will be interacting with an actual computer (either through screen-based exchanges, or through telephone mediated verbal exchanges) when in fact they are connected to the experimental agent, suitably disguised, who is pretending to be the computer. The ways that the subjects behave towards the system can then provide system designers with insights as to the kinds of capabilities which will be needed in the actual system if it is to be easy to use, and informative for future human users.

This 'chicken and egg' dilemma confronted the researchers working on the SUNDIAL project at the University of Surrey. This book is an account of how we attempted to resolve this dilemma by devising our own simulation experiment, and an explanation of the role of conversation analysis in that solution.

OVERVIEW OF THE BOOK

In Chapter 2 we provide a general account of the kinds of problems faced by system designers of speech-based systems, and we also discuss some of the ways that they have tried to anticipate user requirements. First, designers have drawn on their own native intuition about language use; and they have resorted to the collection of large amounts of data on the use of everyday language. We argue that these approaches are flawed, and instead introduce the use of simulation methodology, and discuss its application as part of the wider SUNDIAL project. In Chapter 3 we discuss the design of our simulation study and the collection of a comparative set of data of human–human interaction: calls to a flight information service. We present some preliminary observations on the results of the simulation experiment.

Chapter 4 is an introductory account of conversation analysis. Instead of trying to review the major findings from this extensive literature, we illustrate properties of conversational interaction which have been revealed through CA research. This is done by reference to data collected as part of the SUNDIAL project.

Chapters 5 to 8 are empirical studies of the data generated from the simulation study and a comparable set of data of human–human interactions. Chapter 5 examines the ways in which calls to a flight information service are produced, and then compares them to the opening sequences in the calls to the simulated computer system. Chapter 6 provides a comparative analysis of turn-taking, the organisation of overlap and the closing sequences in the two data corpora. Chapters 7 and 8 examine repair: strategies by which speakers can identify and address trouble or problems in verbal interaction. Chapter 7 identifies some conceptual issues in conversation analytic studies of repair, and these are introduced by reference to data from human–human interaction. Chapter 8 focuses on some ways in which subjects in the simulation study effected repair in their exchanges with the 'system'.

In the concluding chapter we discuss some broader issues concerning the application of conversation analysis to human–computer interaction, and the data generated from simulation studies.

2

INSPIRATION, OBSERVATION AND THE WIZARD OF OZ

At the end of Chapter 1 we raised a problem faced by system designers: anticipating how people will react to computer tools with speech-based interfaces. In this chapter, we describe three different solutions to this problem. We call these Design by Inspiration, Design by Observation and Design by Simulation. Later we will discuss attempts to elicit likely human behaviour with computers through simulation studies. But first let us consider some of the kinds of difficulties these three solutions are designed to address.

The more easily people can use a speech-based interface, the better it will have been designed. Intuitively, then, it seems reasonable to assume that the first task that has to be accomplished is to establish the kinds of plans and goals that people want to pursue with the system, for example, to find out a bank balance, or to discover the arrival time of an aeroplane. With these plans to hand, the system designer can then construct a computer system to mesh with those aspects of the users' behaviour which result from their pursuit of these goals or plans.

In the previous chapter, however, we raised some problems with this approach. Dialogue emerges through the interplay of the participants. Each participant only has the ability to influence the direction of the dialogue on a turn-by-turn basis. Neither can plan a course for the whole dialogue *a priori* and impose it on the other. There is also evidence that human behaviour is not determined by, nor necessarily follows, a set of plans. For example, Suchman's (1987) study of the ways in which people use office photocopiers suggests that the planning model of human behaviour and interaction does not sufficiently take account of the situated nature of human action: people's actions are produced on a moment-by-moment basis, and reflect their interpretation of their immediate circumstances, and the relevance of those circumstances for their actions.

What we need to do then, is not so much try to generate the plans which inform people's talk, but to monitor instead the regularities which occur in dialogue. Consider a conversation in which one speaker begins by producing the utterance 'Hello'. The other speaker is most likely to respond with some reciprocal greeting. Similarly if someone asks a question, the next appropriate turn should be an answer, or an account why an answer is not forthcoming. These kinds of regularities in dialogue will be discussed in more detail in Chapter 4, and in the empirical studies reported in Chapters 5 to 8. But for our present purposes we need only note that dialogues are not like monologues which can be meticulously planned in advance. They are emergent phenomena, arising out of the co-operative interaction of two agents. Their structure is oriented to normative conventions about appropriate courses of behaviour in particular circumstances, but it is not rule-governed. Our task is to capture enough knowledge to inform the design of a technological artifact that will be able to take its place as an agent co-operating with a human in the creation of a unique entity: a spoken dialogue.

When speakers participate in dialogue they are not just producing random linguistic noise. Rather they are co-operating in the negotiation of meaning, or of social relationships. In order to achieve anything of substance in conversation it is necessary both to behave in a fashion which is co-operative and to assume that one's conversational partner is doing likewise. In his seminal work on conversational implicature, Grice (1975) offered a first approximation to the co-operative principle assumed by participants in talk. The Co-operative Principle can be stated thus: make your contribution such as is required, at the stage at which it occurs, by the accepted purpose or direction of the talk exchange in which you are engaged. This principle is further expounded in a set of conversational maxims which can be taken both as a standard for behaviour and as a key in interpreting the behaviour of others: the Maxim of Quality (try to make your contribution one which is true); the Maxim of Quantity (make your contribution as informative as is required for the current purposes of the exchange); the Maxim of Relevance (make your contributions relevant); and the Maxim of Manner (avoid obscurity and ambiguity, and be brief and orderly).

If dialogue is orderly enough to allow for the construction of positive and negative predictions about what could happen next in a dialogue, then how is it ordered? Researchers working in the framework of discourse analysis[1] have assumed that the structure of discourses including dialogues can be described by means of a grammar analogous to the grammars which are used to describe sentences (van Dijk, 1977; Hinds, 1979). Other researchers working in the framework of conversation analysis have argued that the structure of local exchanges in dialogue is described by normative rules which may be instanced or flouted. For example, speakers may instance the 'rule' that a question should be followed with an answer by producing one; alternatively, they may flout this convention by refusing to answer, or by changing the subject. But a decision to flout the rule does not lead to ill-formed dialogue, or a breakdown of conversation. Rather, the fact that a rule has been flouted is itself informative and may warrant certain inferences: that the person did not hear the question, that they are withholding their talk because of some unsettled interpersonal disagreement or conflict, and so on. What is important is that in each case the kinds of inferences which may be drawn from the absence of an answer may inform the subsequent course of action by the person who produced the question (Heritage, 1984).[2] In this view of dialogue, the 'rules' or conventions of interaction are cultural conventions that furnish a set of inferential resources, rather than a set of deterministic prescriptions that must be followed.[3]

Our task in designing a speech-based computer system is not to produce an implementation which accurately reflects human cognitive mechanisms, but it must, however, be capable of displaying behaviour broadly compatible with human expectations as dialogues unfold dynamically.

The rest of this chapter examines three different sources of data and corresponding methodologies which may help us to discover and specify more explicitly the requirements which a speech-based computer system must satisfy.

DESIGN BY INSPIRATION

One of the most remarkable aspects of language is its reflexivity: we are able to use language to talk about language. Humans are authorities on language and, conveniently, have the capacity to articulate that knowledge by means of language. Perhaps the best place to look for data on spoken dialogue is from our own expert intuition.

This view is prevalent in the discipline of theoretical linguistics. The most famous statement of the doctrine of the primacy of native speaker intuition was offered by Noam Chomsky.

> Linguistic theory is concerned with an ideal speaker–hearer in a completely homogeneous speech-community, who knows its language perfectly and is unaffected by such grammatically irrelevant conditions as memory limitations, distractions, shifts of attention and interest, and errors (random or characteristic) in applying his knowledge of the language in actual performance.
>
> (Chomsky, 1965: 3)

There is, then, an approach to system design which takes as its point of departure the importance of native speakers' intuitions about their own competence; and as system designers are themselves native speakers, it is conventionally their own intuitions which have been explored in the pursuit of design recommendations.

In particular, system designers use their own 'lay' expertise as conversationalists to work out the forms that a dialogue could take, given a specific task domain. For example, analysis of the flight information task domain would identify that there are a fixed number of flight objects in the domain. Each of these has a number of parameters associated with it (flight number, departure place, arrival place, scheduled departure and arrival times, actual departure and arrival times, and so on). Any of these parameters can be queried by the user. The basic structure of a successful information exchange therefore involves the user providing the system with a parameter list sufficient to identify the relevant object and with some indication of which parameter(s) is (are) being queried. Once the task has been specified, the human (therefore expert) dialogue designer is able to design an interface on the basis of pure thought. This involves asking questions like 'How could an arrival time query be structured if only the flight number is known?' The subsequent design is informed by the designer's educated guesses.

To indicate some of the kinds of problems generated by this method of dialogue system design, let us consider how it would be applied in designing a telephone banking service. First, a high-level goal is fixed. The goal may be to provide interactive spoken language access to a database; customers' accounts, for example. Next, the domain is analysed in detail to establish its parameters, and the routes by which tasks within it can be accomplished. The next step is to make the leap from an understanding of tasks to a specification of the ways in which they can be realised linguistically.

At each stage in each possible dialogue, the designer attempts to answer the question 'What could happen next?'. This can be answered at multiple levels. An acceptable answer for a given point in some dialogue could be 'The user will ask for an account balance'. However, this simplistic answer is merely an abstraction which can in fact tell us little about the way in which such a request could be realised in actual instances of talk. That is, an account balance query could be realised in many different ways:

a How much is in my account?
b What is my present balance?
c Can you give me a balance, please?
d What have I got at the moment?

Each branching point in a dialogue offers very large amounts of variability. If the question 'What could happen next?' is answered at the level of abstract task-oriented speech acts, there are likely to be several possible next moves with non-negligible probability. This modest branching is complicated by the fact that there are potentially very many different ways of linguistically realising each distinct abstract move type. In turn, each of these linguistic realisations may be acoustically realised in many different ways. The whole solution space cannot be explored by means of pure thought, although carefully chosen sub-parts of it may be designed quite effectively on the basis of a designer's intuitions.

Reliance on systems designers' native competence and expertise in ordinary language use has tended to reflect their own theoretical interests and prejudices. But more telling, perhaps, is the fact that systems designed in this manner tend to perform poorly when used by ordinary people. And when capabilities are found to be lacking in finished systems, designers can only offer the defence that it is hard to think of everything in advance.

In fact, it may be more than hard, it may be impossible. Work in conversation analysis has stressed that many of the skills which speakers use to engage in dialogue are tacitly known: that is, they are not available to conscious introspection.

The tradition of relying on intuitions in theoretical linguistics is based in linguistic *competence*, a term used by Chomsky (1965) to refer to knowledge of language. But when designing a practical dialogue system it is necessary to design for *performance*, or use of language. And while native speakers may possess reliable knowledge about linguistic competence, there is no evidence to suggest that people have accurate intuitions about language use. For example, our linguistic competence tells us that certain sequences of words do not belong to the English language: for example, the sequence 'she eh she'. But, contrary to our intuitions and expectations, such sequences *do* occur in everyday language.

```
(1) (From Schegloff, 1979: 264)

A: Well I don't think she-
   eh she doesn't uh usually come in on Friday does she
```

In this case, the sequence 'she eh she' is produced when the speaker produces a self-correcting restart to an utterance. But there are many other kinds of discursive acts which lead us to question the value of emphasising competence in the analysis of language use. Consider the following data extracts:

```
(a) The school school book store doesn't carry anything
    anymore.
(b) I was- I was just thinking today all day riding on the
    trains that I would go into the ci- I would go into the city,
    but I don't know.
(c) She teaches she teaches a course at City College in
    needlecrafts.
```

All of these examples come from Schegloff's (1979) study of a phenomenon he identifies as 'recycled turn beginnings'. In each case there is a short sequence in which a word or phrase is repeated: 'school school', 'I was I was' and 'she teaches she teaches'. Intuitively, we may assume that such instances are the product of some mistake or speech error. However, Schegloff's analysis shows that these recyclings are not random, nor errors of pronunciation. Rather, speakers produce recycled turn beginnings when a spate of someone else's talk has overlapped with their own talk. The recycled component of the turn (the repeated word or phrase) invariably occurs just at the point at which the overlapping talk has stopped. So, these apparently ungrammatical features of language use do actually exhibit orderly properties.

But it is important to note that the basis for this orderliness is not to be found at the level of language competence, but in language performance: in particular, the performance of language in specific interactional circumstances.

Consider also the case of non-lexical items in speech, such as 'mm hm', 'uh huh', 'oh' and so on. If asked, most speakers would suggest either that these items have random distribution, or that they are inserted when the speaker cannot think what to say next. In fact, research has shown that these items are used in a highly ordered way. For example, Jefferson (1984) analyses conversational materials to reveal the way in which speakers use 'mm hm' as a minimal token of encouragement to propose that a current speaker should continue talking. Similarly, Schegloff (1981) examines the way in which non-lexical items such as 'uh huh' can be regarded as interactional achievements. Finally, Heritage (1984) has shown that the particle, 'oh' is used systematically as a 'news receipt' item. These kinds of features of language use may have significant implications for system design; yet they would not come to light simply through introspection of a native speaker's linguistic competence.

These objections may seem rather petty since anyone is almost certainly capable of inventing a flight information dialogue. However, it is our experience that invented dialogues are immediately distinguishable from 'the real thing'. In inventing a dialogue it is comparatively easy to concern oneself with issues of information exchange and sentence structure. It is much harder, however, to anticipate the subtle interpersonal matters which are addressed in interaction; and it is even more difficult to try to anticipate the ways in which such issues may be negotiated in the fine detail of utterance design.

In reality, most dialogue systems developed to date have side-stepped these problems by producing systems which do not allow human users to take any initiative in the dialogue. (For exceptions, see Frohlich and Luff, 1990 and Smith, 1991.) So, whereas in natural conversation participants co-operate and collaborate in the unfolding of the talk, dialogues involving designed systems tend to require the user to follow a strictly pre-determined dialogue plan. In these menu-based systems, standard conversational conventions are set aside and the system conveys to the user a non-negotiable rule of interaction, namely 'I ask the questions; you answer them'. In designing such a system, all that is required of the designer is to come up with some way – any way – of performing each task in the application domain. This approach could be called 'Design by dictat', as there is no need whatsoever for the designer to look beyond his or her intuitions about how best to structure dialogues in order to develop a working system. There is, of course, no guarantee that the chosen design will be ergonomically optimal.

Once the decision has been taken to renounce unnatural system-led, menu-based dialogue (as in the case of the SUNDIAL project), the use of intuitions alone must be called into question for at least three reasons.

First, the range of possibilities is too large for designers to anticipate. For any non-trivial task there are simply too many alternatives for each possible turn in the exchange. There is a strong possibility that any attempt to build a dialogue system with comprehensive facilities will therefore be riddled with gaps in coverage; and, as we have already mentioned, the only defence the designer could offer would be 'I didn't think of those'. Second, as we have seen, intuitions about performance are unreliable. Third, we may have no intuitions to go on anyway: we have no experience of how people will react when confronted with a speech-based computer interface. It may be the case that they will react very much as they react to any conversational partner; but this is just a guess which may turn out to be mistaken. Indeed, as a very considerable part of human–human talk is taken up with interpersonal concerns, it is legitimate to ask whether or not the word 'conversation' makes any sense at all in the context of human–computer dialogue, so intimately entwined are our notions of conversation and social interaction (Button, 1990). It is hard to know where to begin speculating about how people might react when faced with a non-human dialogue partner.

DESIGN BY OBSERVATION

Within sociological and sociolinguistic studies of natural language use, there has been emphasis upon the collection of corpora of verbal interaction in a variety of mundane and institutional contexts. Until recently, though, there has been a dearth of discussion of data in the natural language processing literature. This is now beginning to be addressed through a growing interest in the collection of corpora which are used to define the coverage of grammars and parsers.

For example, the Linguistic Data Consortium established in the USA with government funding aims to collect and distribute large quantities of computer-readable text. This is just one of a number of initiatives around the world to collect really large corpora (counted in millions of words) from which to extract information about aspects of language use. While it is true that much of the data takes the form of edited texts such as novels, some significant corpora of spontaneous spoken language do exist; for example: the London-Lund Corpus (Svartvik and Quirk, 1980), and the more recent British National Corpus, part of which was collected by attaching tape recorders to subjects for twenty-four hour periods. For surveys of the field of 'corpus linguistics' see Meijs (1986), Garside *et al.* (1987).

Do corpora of spoken language have a role to play in the process of designing spoken dialogue systems? The answer to this question must be 'yes'. Many of the objections to using native speakers' intuitions as the basis for system design are addressed by observational data. One of the problems with intuitions was that the space of possibilities in spoken dialogue is too large: there are just too many different possibilities to allow the designer to explore them by pure thought. What a corpus of dialogues offers is concrete evidence to give the system designer leverage on the problem.

All speech recognisers are bounded by the limitations of the current technology. Suppose that some speech recognition system is only capable of operating in real time if it has a lexicon of 100 words or less. The most reasonable way to decide which words to include in the lexicon (assuming that the user is not explicitly restricted by means of a menu) would be to select the 100 most frequently occurring words in the chosen domain of discourse. While most people could make fairly good guesses at the two or three most frequently occurring words, no-one could discriminate reliably between the 100th and the 101st words on the basis of intuitions alone. For this, an empirical study of word frequency is required (for example, Johansson and Hofland, 1989).

What is true in the case of lexical selection is also true for higher levels of the system. At a given point in a human–computer dialogue, a co-operative user could say almost anything. The only reasonable way to design a practical dialogue system would be to equip it to deal with the most likely cases, and provide it with a battery of general purpose recovery strategies to enable it to repair understanding failures and proceed in orderly fashion with the dialogue. The task of deciding which cases to manage specifically and which to leave to general failure repair mechanisms is, perhaps, even more difficult than that of selecting which words to include in the recognition vocabulary. By observing human–human dialogues in the chosen application domain it is possible to base these difficult design decisions on a solid foundation of empirical fact, rather than on conjecture.

So far, all that we have done is to argue for the proposition that some empirical data is better than none. But it is important to consider just how reliable human–human dialogues can be as data sources for dialogue system design.

It is necessary at this point to consider exactly what is meant when we refer to a language such as English. Are we referring to a single communicative code shared by all speakers of the language? Linguists claim that each speaker possesses a unique *idiolect*; that is, a particular version of their language which is unique to them. However, broad generalisations across speakers can be made, so it is reasonable to speak of regional dialects such as the Yorkshire, Ozark and Jamaican dialects of English, and social dialects such as 'Standard' ('BBC') English.

Most languages have a 'Standard' dialect which serves as the basis for Natural Language Processing (NLP) systems, sometimes to the exclusion of a significant number of speakers of the language. However, it should not be thought that (ignoring minor ideolectal differences between speakers) dialects are constant across all situations of use. On the contrary, each dialect encompasses a rich variety of different *registers*. A register is a variety of the language which is selected according to the context of use. So, for example, one might greet an old friend, an angry employer and a complete stranger in very different ways.

Although it is certainly better to rely on empirical analyses of human–human interactions than to rely on intuitions alone, there are, however, drawbacks with this approach. It should not be overlooked that human–human interactions are not uniform across all social situations. An assumption which informs much sociolinguistic research is that human–human relations are to some degree hierarchically organised. This is most easily seen where the hierarchy is institutionalised, for example in an organisation's management structure. In such a structure it is possible to be subordinate, equal or superior to each other member of the organisation. Relative positions on the hierarchy play an important part in determining the register used. For example, a discussion of grievances with one's colleagues at work is unlikely to share many similarities with a discussion of the same topic with one's boss. In each situation a speaker either uses a register appropriate to that situation or uses a register which is considered to be marked.

Halliday identifies three dimensions on which an act of communication may be located: field, mode and tenor (Halliday, 1978: 33). Field is concerned with the purpose and subject of the communication; mode refers to the means by which the communication takes place; and tenor is dependent on the relations between the participants. An earlier model proposed by Hymes (1972) identified thirteen separate variables which determined a speaker's choice of lexical item (in addition to 'dialect' which is invariant for each individual). These variables included a number rooted in the relationship between dialogue participants, for example, 'power' and 'solidarity'. Our object here is not to argue for or against any such model. Rather, we are interested in the phenomenon of register variability which led to the development of these models. If we accept that we each tailor the form of our dialogues to fit the people we are addressing, then we must also accept the possibility that we might do the same when talking with a computer and that the register for talking to computers might differ from all known human–human registers in important ways. Thus human–human interactions could provide misleading data on which to base the design of human–computer dialogues.

These issues raise intriguing questions: for example, what kind of hierarchical relationship will people construct when relating to a computer? Until the answers to questions like this are known, the utility of human–human dialogues (with or without intuition-guided modifications) will remain unknown. According to von Hahn (1986), the problem is that 'we have no well-developed linguistics of natural-language [person]-machine communication'. We might extend this remark to register that neither do we have any understanding of the social and interactional bases of human computer interaction.

Hence, the computer dialogue designer is caught in the vicious circle which we discussed in the previous chapter: it is necessary to know the characteristics of dialogues between people and computers in order to be able to build a human–computer dialogue system, but it is impossible to know what such dialogues will be like until a system has been built.

DESIGN BY SIMULATION

In this section we present one way of breaking into the vicious circle by simulating the future computer speech system in order to collect a corpus which can be used as a basis for the design of the system. The simulation method adopted – known as the 'Wizard of Oz' technique – sheds light on what human–computer speech dialogues would look like if only the systems which are currently at the planning stage were in fact implemented and running.

The Wizard of Oz (WOZ) simulation technique involves a human (usually known as the *wizard* or *accomplice*) playing the role of the computer in a simulated human–computer interaction. It is not known who coined the term, although its etymology is obvious. In the children's novel *The Wizard of Oz* (Baum, 1900), the 'great and terrible' Wizard turns out to be no more than a device operated by a man hiding behind a screen. For this reason it is also known as the PNAMBIC ('*P*ay *N*o *A*ttention to the *M*an *B*eh*I*nd the *C*urtain') technique. Again, the source of this name is unknown, though it has been attributed to J. Bernstein (Newell *et al.*, 1987).

For the simulation to be most effective, it is necessary for the experimental subject to believe that she is interacting with a computer. If there really are significant differences in the registers appropriate for human–human information exchanges and human–computer information exchanges, they are most likely to be reflected in the simulation corpus when the subject genuinely believes that she is conversing with a computer. Although many different types of computer system could be simulated using a WOZ methodology, what primarily interests us here is a simulation of a system that takes spoken natural language input, processes it in some principled way, and generates spoken natural language responses.

WOZ simulations are not a panacea: they are only useful if certain preconditions are met. We shall consider three of these.

The simulation must be possible

The first basic condition is that the future computer system can be imitated realistically given human limitations. For example, if it is known that the future computer system will need to undertake substantial database manipulation as part of its function and the database has not yet been implemented, there is little point in setting up a WOZ simulation. This does not imply that WOZ simulations are only appropriate for simulating interfaces to existing applications. They may also be used to simulate the applications themselves if these fall within human capabilities. For example, humans are currently rather better at visual object discrimination than computers. There is no reason in principle why a single wizard should not simulate both the interface to an object recogniser and the recogniser itself if both tasks are humanly possible.

The future system must be specifiable

A second, less obvious pre-condition is that it must be possible to formulate a fairly detailed specification of the future system prior to running the experiments. This is necessary in order to ensure that the wizard correctly simulates the intended system.

This specification often needs to be more precise and more detailed than would normally be necessary just to build the computer system. For example, in a speech simulation the wizard ideally needs to make recognition errors at the same rate and in the same way as the future system. However, while descriptions of speech understanding systems often specify error rates, they rarely indicate what kinds of errors are made in sufficient detail for the errors to be simulated. A number of systems do supply error information in the form of confusion matrices and probabilities of lexical or phonetic items being inserted or deleted, but it seems unlikely that these could constitute an adequate specification for a human wizard's real-time recognition errors. In fact, one of the aims of using the WOZ technique may be to help devise such a specification. The way round this apparent paradox – that the design of the simulation requires a specification but the content of the specification depends on the results of the simulation – will be discussed later when we consider WOZ methodology.

The simulation must be convincing

A third condition for the usefulness of the WOZ methodology is that the task is such that the illusion that the wizard is a computer can be convincingly maintained. In systems which communicate using text on terminals, only minimal precautions have to be taken, since the only evidence of the 'computer' the subject sees is the output of characters on a screen (but even here, there may be value in buffering the output so that it appears a line at a time, rather than at the speed of the wizard's typing). In speech output systems, it is necessary to ensure that the wizard's speech is disguised to sound as though it was computer generated. Similar problems arise in controlling the content of the wizard's output, which must use only knowledge likely to be available to a computer. The degree of attention which has to be paid to these issues is related to the likely gullibility of the subjects.

In this book we are concerned with those WOZ simulations that simulate speech input/output systems. We shall call these spoken WOZ simulations. (See Fraser and Gilbert, 1991, for a review of findings from WOZ simulation studies which use, for example, typed text, or in which only the subject speaks.) In this section we shall review the findings of three spoken WOZ simulation studies: the experiments of Guyomard and Siroux, Morel, and Richards and Underwood.[4] We shall show how the design of our own WOZ simulation study was informed by and developed from the methodological strategies used in these earlier studies.

Guyomard and Siroux conducted spoken WOZ simulations based on a dial-up Yellow Pages information system (1986a; 1986b; 1987; 1988). Since no such service existed at the time of their experiment, they were not able to analyse human–human interactions in order to generate a preliminary specification of lexicon, grammar or dialogue. Consequently they decided to conduct the research in two phases; in the first phase they concentrated on gathering data which they then used as a basis for a more constrained second phase.

In order to set upper and lower performance limits, phase one was divided so that experiments were conducted either with a highly directed dialogue (formalised by a finite state automaton) or with a completely unrestricted dialogue. This was done

> in order to find the constraints that won't be respected by the majority of users and the dialogue functions that are used spontaneously by the typical user. A judicious compromise can then lead to an acceptable dialogue both from the user's point of view as well as from the point of view of the state of the art in automatic speech recognition and dialogue management.
>
> (Guyomard and Siroux, 1987: 2)

Guyomard and Siroux used fifteen subjects in each experimental phase. In the first phase, it was found that directed dialogue was not viable for occasional users. For example, subjects did not produce appropriate answers to yes/no questions. The majority of utterances in the unrestricted dialogues included hesitations, false starts, re-starts, or self-corrections. However, they were able to collect a vocabulary of 353 words.

In the second phase of the experiment, 70 conversations were collected. The proposed methodologies arising from phase one for dealing with co-operation, follow-on dialogues, implicit utterances, and phatic management were found to be largely satisfactory. Initial requests were found to be concise and subsequent requests could be classed as 'slidings' (modifications to the previous request), 'mutations' (introduction of a subject not raised in the preceding dialogue) and 'reproductions' (re-presentations in some form of the preceding request). Once again, a lot of what Guyomard and Siroux term 'speech problems' (failure to end words, hesitations, and so on) were observed. From this second experimental phase a vocabulary of 324 words was collected.

From their experiments, Guyomard and Siroux identified two problems in person–machine interaction. First, they found that it was very difficult to make useful predictions of user input. The authors note that 'the predictive power of a dialogue is an inverse function of the degree of freedom envisaged for the user' (1987: 5). Second, they found that the management of hesitations was extremely difficult.

In many respects, Guyomard and Siroux's approach to patterns of verbal behaviour, which they termed 'speech problems', echoes the Chomskyian distinction between performance and competence. Like Chomsky, they seem to view these apparently ungrammatical features of talk as a form of verbal pollution which contaminates the production of otherwise well formed grammatical sentences. Consequently, they are regarded as an 'interfering' variable, and therefore a problem which has to be managed and resolved. However, we take issue with this view.

As conversation analytic studies have shown, seemingly ungrammatical features of talk may not be simply random errors in the speech stream, but exhibit orderly properties. But that orderliness is not to be found in their conformity to the rules of grammar; rather, the basis of their use derives from their function as resources in social interaction. But, of course, unless the subjects' talk was examined as a series of actions through which they pursued specific interactional tasks, the orderly features of 'hesitations', 'false starts' and 'self-corrections' would never be recognised. These observations have important practical implications. As false starts, self-corrections and non-lexical items, such as 'uh huh', are a fundamental part of human speech, it is imperative that system designers should try to build systems which can actually attend to these features of language use. But this can only be done by developing a greater awareness of the interactional contexts in which they are embedded. Consequently, it is necessary to examine data generated from WOZ studies to focus on and describe the actions and sequences of actions which are constituted through the subjects' exchanges with the system. And this in turn implies the need for an empirical approach to the analysis of language use which is informed more by sociology than traditional linguistics.

These observations are relevant also to Morel's studies. She conducted a three-phase spoken WOZ experiment modelling a telephone train timetable information service (1986; 1987; Delomier *et al.*, 1989; the latter paper also reports a WOZ simulation of a student information service). In the first phase the subject communicated with a human operator. In the second and third phases the subject was given the impression that she was communicating with a computer. In the third phase the subject was forced to re-phrase some utterances.

In the first phase, no constraints were applied. In the second and third phases, a number of constraints were imposed on the output of the wizard:

no ellipsis, no anaphora, no co-operation phrases, no confirmatory questions, no resumption of 'already given information' (it is not clear what Morel means by this), and a strict adherence to simple declarative sentences. In the third phase, the wizard was also constrained as to what 'system understanding' could be simulated: the wizard was not supposed to understand utterances which contained ellipsis or anaphora, or utterances which were complex sentences. In these cases the subject was asked to rephrase the request.

Morel compares her examples of speech to a human with those to a computer. Utterances to a computer are more 'concise and precise' than those to a human. The vocabulary used in talk to a (simulated) computer is more technical and less varied than in human–human interaction, and there are fewer questions or anaphoric phrases. The speaker in phases two and three produced very few resumptions, no justifications, and no questions seeking confirmation, all of which were evident in phase one.

On the basis of her studies, Morel identified what she termed three paradoxes in the human–computer communication. The first paradox is that the length of the speaker's and the simulated computer's utterances are inversely proportional. So, when the simulated computer produced very long sentences, the subject produced very short sentences. The second paradox concerned occasions in which the system requested that the subject rephrase his or her question. In these cases, the subjects did not seem to realise what exactly had been misunderstood, and, in their subsequent reformulations of their question, they exhibit what Morel calls more 'natural' dialogue.

> He [the subject/speaker] also substitutes a prepositional phrase for a relative clause. One may notice that in front of a human operator, relative clauses are frequently produced by the speakers and that systematically they use in front of the simulated computer prepositional phrases instead of relative clauses . . . When there is a constraint of re-phrasing . . . the speaker uses a more spontaneous language, as if he interpreted it as a kind of natural dialogue. It is remarkable too that the speakers never realise that they must give the precise reference of an anaphoric phrase.
>
> (1986: 5–6)

Finally, the third paradox concerns the relative degree of trust in the pronouncements of the simulated computer and a human operator. According to Morel, most of the speakers *said* that they were confident that the computer had provided the correct information. So it would seem from these comments that the subjects were fairly confident in the abilities of the simulated system. However, when they were later discussing the experiment with a human operator of the train timetable service, the subjects tended to ask for confirmation that the information they had been given by the computer was in fact correct, which would suggest some uncertainty as to the reliability of the system.

This may be less of a paradox than it might at first seem. What Morel has observed here is a discrepancy between people's accounts of their behaviour and their actual behaviour. Within the social sciences there is little evidence to suggest that there is a symmetry between what people do and what they say they do. But this is not to imply that people are being dishonest. Rather, the assumption that there could or should be a symmetry between actions or beliefs, and accounts of those actions and beliefs, reflects the influence of a view of the nature of language use which is deep rooted in the social sciences. (This assumption also pervades most areas of scientific research in which people's accounts are used as a resource for the analytic study of those events or states of affairs to which those accounts refer.) This view treats language largely as a passive vehicle for the transmission of information about the world. Research which is informed by this assumption characteristically treats people's accounts of their actions and beliefs as essentially 'standing in' for those actions or beliefs. However, there is a range of compelling philosophical and sociological arguments which suggest that language is not a neutral passive medium. Studies in conversation analysis in sociology, and discourse analysis in social psychology, have emphasised that it is a dynamic medium through which people perform social actions. Consequently, accounts of our behaviour (or, for that matter, any other state of affairs in the world) may be informed primarily by the speaker's tacit understanding of the interactional and interpersonal contingencies relevant to the circumstances in which the account is made. On the basis of these arguments, we should not expect a symmetry between accounts of action and the actions so described (Gilbert and Mulkay, 1983; 1984; Potter and Wetherell, 1987; Wooffitt, 1992). This in turn urges that those involved in the development of interactive systems should pay greater attention to the description and analysis of people's actual verbal behaviour, rather than relying upon subsequent accounts of that behaviour. Consequently, in devising the protocol for the Surrey WOZ simulation, it was decided not to interview subjects to try to discover their opinions on the usefulness of the system, its drawbacks, and so on, but to rely instead on the detailed analysis of the subjects' actual exchanges with the simulated system.[5]

Richards and Underwood conducted two spoken WOZ experiments modelling a telephone train timetable information service (1984a; 1984b). All subjects were told that the service was provided by a computer. In the first experiment (1984a) the subjects also talked to a human expert. In fact the 'human expert' and the 'wizard' were one and the same person answering queries in a uniform fashion. This accomplice did not know for any experiment whether he was being presented to the subject as a human or as a computer with a synthetic-sounding voice.

Richards and Underwood found that when the subjects believed that they were addressing a human operator they spoke at a normal pace and used a fairly extensive vocabulary, including the kind of ambiguous pronouns that occur in everyday speech. When they thought they were talking to a computer, however, the subjects' speech patterns changed. They spoke more slowly, employed a restricted vocabulary, tended to use less ambiguous pronouns, and generally asked questions in a more direct manner. Richards and Underwood concluded that the differing speech patterns were actually fortuitous in that they would facilitate a future system's ability to understand human speech.

The second experiment (Richards and Underwood, 1984b) focused solely on subjects' responses to the wizard's output. In particular, they wanted to discover the effects of the wizard's degree of explicitness and politeness on subjects' utterances. There were four experimental conditions: *explicit and polite* ('Hello. This is British Telecom's train timetable service. Would you please tell me where you wish to travel from, where to, and the day and approximate time that you wish to travel'); *explicit and non-polite* ('British Telecom's train timetable service. State where travelling from, where to, and the day and approximate time of travel'); *inexplicit and polite* ('Hello. This is British Telecom's train timetable service. Can I help you?') and *inexplicit and non-polite* ('British Telecom's train timetable service. State your request').

Richards and Underwood examined the order in which subjects provided items of information relevant to their request:
They report that:

> Though significantly less pronounced in conditions 3 and 4, the trend towards providing information in a particular order (place of departure, place of arrival, day, and finally approximate time of travel) was nevertheless reliably found in subjects in all experimental conditions . . . The probability of each item of information occurring in a particular position within the user's initial question was around 0.9 for positions 1 and 2, and 0.6 for conditions 3 and 4.
>
> (1984b: 35)

Another observation concerned the number of turns required to complete the request. It was found that subjects most commonly gave all four pieces of information in one go. In almost all other cases three pieces of information were given and the fourth had to be prompted. However, the tendency for all four pieces to be given at once was significantly greater in the explicit conditions.

The explicit, non-polite condition drew the most concise requests. A significant learning effect was noted for all conditions, with requests getting more concise over time. However, it is interesting to note that the age of the subjects was the most important factor in determining the conciseness with which people expressed themselves. Subjects in the highest age group (50–60 years) were, according to Richards and Underwood, particularly verbose.

The range of vocabulary used by subjects did not seem to depend upon explicitness or politeness, but the polite, inexplicit condition did elicit a wider vocabulary across all speakers (about 150 words as opposed to about 100 words in other conditions).

In concluding, Richards and Underwood note that:

> Any reduction in 'politeness' on the part of the system, though it may lead to a useful degree of conciseness in the dialogue, must not be at the expense of creating negative reactions to the system as a whole.
>
> (1984b: 36)

Richards and Underwood's studies are important because they point to some of the differences between the ways in which humans talk to other humans and the ways in which humans talk to (simulated) computers. Recall that in their first study Richards and Underwood told their subjects that they were talking either to an experimental computer system or a human agent. But the same experimental accomplice played both the part of the agent and the part of the simulated system. Of course this allowed Richards and Underwood to hold one variable constant (the actual utterances of the simulated system/agent); any differences in the subjects' speech could then more reliably be linked to their belief that they were talking to a computer, rather than to a human. Their data, then, were gathered in somewhat artificial circumstances in which experimental variables were controlled to allow precision in the way that the effect of these variables on the subjects' verbal behaviour could be assessed and measured.

However, there is a sense in which this comparative approach could be extended. The next step in the development of a comparative research methodology would be to attempt to incorporate naturally occurring data. For example, consider a situation in which a researcher is interested in trying to build a computer-based version of a public information service which people can contact over the telephone. It would be useful to have recordings of people actually using this service. One of the benefits would be that any subsequent simulation experiment could be closely modelled on the kinds of tasks the service agents are asked to perform; and of course it would be possible to assess more accurately the kinds of verbal behaviour exhibited by the users of the system, who are of course the potential users of the eventual computerised version of the information service. The ways in which subjects in any subsequent WOZ study talked to the simulated system could be compared to ways that ordinary people spoke to the operator of the information service on which the simulated system was modelled. This would allow the comparison of naturally occurring data with materials generated in the more formal and constrained setting of an experimental simulation study.

Our discussion of the studies by Guyomard and Siroux, Morel and Richards and Underwood has provided important suggestions as to how we may refine future simulation studies, and has indicated the range of empirical issues which need to be addressed in the analysis of the data generated from them. The specific methodological issues will be addressed more formally in our next chapter, in which we discuss the WOZ methodology employed as part of the SUNDIAL project; and the empirical issues will be developed in Chapter 4, when we discuss the use of a conversation analytic approach for the analysis of human (simulated) computer interaction. But for the rest of this chapter we wish to discuss some of the more practical details involved in staging a WOZ simulation study.

VARIETIES OF SPOKEN WOZ EXPERIMENTS

In this section we consider some variables in spoken WOZ simulations. By 'variables' we simply mean things which can vary. We make no distinction here between control variables which are set by the experimenter, response variables which are measured by the experimenter, and confounding factors, in which the experimenter has no interest or over which he or she has no control. For example, in simulations of a telephone train timetable enquiry service, the caller's level of familiarity with telephone information services might be a confounding factor, producing significant differences between speakers. However, in an experiment which divides users into 'experienced' and 'novice' classes, this would be a control variable rather than a confounding factor.

We shall restrict our discussion here to a straightforward listing of some of the variables in spoken WOZ simulations. For the purposes of our presentation, the variables can be divided into those relating to the scope of the simulation, the task, the subject, the wizard and the communication channel.

Scope variables

In a WOZ simulation a variety of different components of the future system can be simulated. For example, a wizard can sit between a subject and a database, simulating the interface alone. Alternatively, components of an existing interface can be used while the wizard simulates only one part of it, e.g. a dialogue manager. A wizard may simulate the application instead of or as well as the interface. It is therefore tempting to classify WOZ experiments according to the scope of their simulation. This would involve classification on the basis of checklist questions such as 'Is the interface simulated?' and 'Is the application simulated?' However, it is not easy to see how any classificatory scheme could involve more detailed criteria than these since different systems are not identically modularised and, in principle, any module in a system may be simulated (if this is humanly possible).

Task variables

WOZ simulations can vary in the basic tasks they accomplish. There are many possible applications but only a very limited number of basic tasks. These include database querying and updating, modality translation (i.e. the kind of activity required in 'listening typewriter' tasks) and dialogue management.

Subject variables

Subject recognition variables relate to the subject's ability to recognise the wizard's words. For example, is the acoustic signal intelligible to the subject? The quality of synthesised speech currently available ranges from fairly good to virtually unintelligible. The wizard's speech should therefore display characteristics which locate it either somewhere on this spectrum, or just beyond the best available technology if the system being simulated is expected to include synthesisers currently at the design or development stages. The ability to understand synthetic speech is not constant; rather, it displays learning effects. Thus the ability to decode the acoustic signal is a variable, not just among speakers, but for a given speaker over time.

There is also the issue of lexical recognition: does the subject recognise the words used by the wizard? The important question here relates not to acoustic recognition but rather to whether all of the lexical items used by the wizard are known to the subject. This variable could be expected to interact with the subject's domain expertise. For example, in a flight reservation application, the wizard might refer to an APEX fare. If this word is not in the subject's vocabulary then she may not even know how to segment it (apex, a pex, ape eggs . . .). The subject's unfamiliarity with items of the wizard's vocabulary is likely, sooner or later, to lead to clarification sub-dialogues which would not otherwise be present.

Subject production variables relate to the speech and language produced by the subject in so far as they have implications for the ability of the wizard to recognise and understand the subject's words. For example, a commercial telephone information service cannot screen callers before they make their calls. A strong non-standard accent would cause problems for all currently available speech recognisers (assuming they have been designed or trained for a spectrum of accents centred around a perceived standard). If the wizard is to simulate a plausible future system then he or she must fail to decode strong accents in some principled way. A further problem is that subjects may manifest different dialects. Non-standard dialect words and – more problematically – non-standard syntactic forms would probably be unintelligible to the sort of computer system which can currently be envisaged.

It is important to take account of the subjects' knowledge and experience, both of the current state of attempts to produce computational models of human speech, and the particular task domains being modelled in the simulation. For example, the way in which the subject interacts with the system, the questions she asks of it, and the way in which she expects to be addressed by it, are likely to be affected by her level of expertise. And Richards and Underwood (1984b) have shown that as subjects gained expertise in using a WOZ system so they learned to frame requests more concisely and simply. It is therefore clear that the amount of system expertise a subject possesses is a significant variable.

Also, what the subject is told about the wizard has an effect on dialogue structure and on the subject's view of the experiment. We have already seen how people use different dialogue strategies according to whether they believe they are talking to a human or a machine (Hauptmann and Rudnicky, 1988). Speech to a computer has been labelled 'formal' (Grosz, 1977), 'baby talk' (Guindon *et al.*, 1986), 'telegraphic' (Guindon *et al.*, 1987), and 'computerese' (Reilly, 1987).

The subject should be led to believe that she is actually using the future technology. This can be expected to yield the best guide to how that technology will be used when it becomes available. There are potentially ethical problems here since a responsible experimenter would not choose to tell an outright lie to the subject. A more appropriate approach would be to tell subjects that the research aims to establish how people converse with computers, and to allow them to draw their own conclusions.

Wizard variables

Wizard variables can also be divided into wizard recognition and production variables but these must be supplemented with extra classes of dialogue model variables and staging variables.

Corresponding to the subject's production variables are a set of wizard recognition variables defining the ranges of acoustic, lexical, syntactic and pragmatic phenomena which the wizard is allowed to recognise. One of the hardest tasks for the wizard is to restrict speech recognition capabilities to what is defined by these variables. We have noted that mechanical filtering can help in typed WOZ simulations, but such aids are not available in most spoken simulations. For the most part, then, the constraints will have to be applied directly by a wizard who knows the role intimately.

A particularly difficult problem is that of trying to mimic a speech recogniser which only manages to recognise the words that it knows on, say, 90 per cent of occasions. In order to be faithful to the technology the wizard would have to introduce a random (or partially random) 10 per cent failure rate even with words which the system is supposed to know about. This is an almost impossible task. The best that can be expected is for the wizard to introduce occasional deliberate recognition errors.

Just like the subject, the wizard has production variables, but with the wizard these are defined by the performance of the existing or projected technologies. Thus the whole gamut of speech generation variables (voice quality, intonation, syntax, and so on) need to be considered. Again, the wizard may be required to introduce principled errors at any of these levels if the simulation is to be faithful to the technology.

One production variable of particular interest is the wizard's response time. The object of a WOZ simulation should be to respond in more or less the same time as it would take the future system to respond and not in the time it would take a human to respond. Obviously, systems are planned to run in 'real time' but the time course of a human–computer dialogue is not yet known. It may be appropriate to allow a wizard to take slightly longer to respond than a human expert. The wizard will in any case require all the time he or she can get to apply conscious constraints to normal recognition and generation capabilities.

The model of the dialogue employed by the wizard is central to the interpretation of utterances and selection of responses to them. The problems of constructing dialogue models are too great and too many to present here. One of the objectives of this volume as a whole is to provide an empirical base for the design of such models. At this stage we simply draw attention to the dangers of constructing a prototype dialogue model in advance of running simulations. Guyomard and Siroux's (1987) two-phase experiment indicates the amount of work required to define a minimally acceptable dialogue manager. In spite of their positive reports, it is to be expected that many simulation–analysis–redesign iterations would be necessary to define a truly impressive dialogue manager. Since most research projects run to a tight schedule, a two-stage simulation is probably the best that most experimenters can hope for.

Staging variables

In this section we consider some practical matters relating to the preparation of the wizards and the tools available to assist them in their work.

First, training the wizard. The wizard requires training in at least three areas: the application domain, the system capabilities being modelled, and the tools available to assist in playing the role. The wizard needs a lot of information at his or her fingertips. A range of tools could be designed to present this information as quickly and easily as possible. For example, a range of paper tools (charts, card indexes) and electronic tools (mouse, menu systems, hypertext) could be used. A wizard's assistant might even be considered necessary.

The simplest means of connecting the subject and the wizard is by telephone or similar two-way electronic communication channel. However, the quality of the channel can be yet another variable: no subject is going to believe that they are talking to a machine if they are unable to distinguish its performance from that of a human speaker. An important part of the subterfuge is the 'de-humanising' of the wizard's voice. One way to do this is to pass the telephone signal through a vocoder to strip it of human intonation and make it sound 'mechanical'. A secondary effect might be to make it roughly as difficult for the subject to understand as it would be to understand a speech synthesiser. This similarity could never be better than approximate. The alternative to degrading the wizard's voice is to place a speech synthesiser between the wizard and the subject. Once again, the usefulness of this strategy depends, in part, on the extent to which the synthesiser approximates to the synthesiser in the projected future system.

It is important to decide whether the communication channel should permit signals to pass in opposite directions at the same time. This is important because it may be desirable to let subject and system talk in overlap and interrupt each other, or necessary to prevent them from doing so. In either case, it is important that the capabilities planned for the future system should be designed into the WOZ simulation to ensure that turn-taking features recorded in the experiments are relevant for the future system.

In this chapter we have explored some of the difficulties encountered in designing a spoken dialogue system. We have particularly noted some of the problems arising from the interactive character of dialogues. In our search for a firm foundation for design we have considered three data sources: intuitions, observations and simulations. Each of these has strengths and limitations; it is likely that the design process could benefit from considering data gleaned from all sources, so long as the distinctive merits and disadvantages of each type are clearly understood.

By comparison with the others, the design by simulation approach is a relatively recent and poorly documented development. However, it presents perhaps the most suitable method to allow us to elicit information which will help the design of interactive computers.

Our discussion of three important WOZ simulation studies was in part motivated by an attempt to derive some principles for the design of our own WOZ study, and to derive some guidelines for the analysis of the data so generated. The next two chapters explain the organisation of the methodology we adopted, and describe in more detail the use of a conversation analytic approach to the examination of the data, thereby showing how these principles and guidelines informed the Surrey WOZ research. To end this chapter, however, we wish to raise a more general issue relevant to the methodology WOZ simulation studies, and to do this we need to remind ourselves of a point made during our discussion of the studies by Richards and Underwood.

In their experiments Richards and Underwood compared two types of data: subjects talking to a human operator, whose voice was not disguised, and subjects talking to the same human operator when the voice was disguised to give an impression of a speaking computer. The design of their studies thus had a comparative dimension. We suggested that a logical next step in the design of WOZ simulation studies would be to compare data from experimental trials with data collected from naturally occurring settings. And in the next chapter we report how a focus of our own methodology was to compare data from experimental trials with data from the 'real world'.

This is an unusual step: hitherto simulation studies have been conducted entirely in laboratory settings, and the only data considered were those which had been produced in the artificial environment of formal experiments. In this sense, previous WOZ simulation studies have had an insular character. Our decision to make extensive use of a set of comparative data in the analytic process allows us to avoid the insularity of previous studies. Furthermore, it ensures that the results from the study of naturally occurring interaction can be enmeshed with analysis of data obtained from the more arid confines of experimental settings. Indeed, we suggest that simultaneous analysis of data from WOZ studies and data from a corpus of relevant, naturally occurring interaction should be an integral part of the WOZ simulation methodology.

3

THE SURREY WOZ SIMULATION PROCEDURE

In this chapter we describe the collection of two corpora of spoken language dialogues. The first corpus consists of a sample of telephone conversations between members of the public and British Airways flight information service agents. We shall refer to it as the British Airways, or BA, corpus. The second corpus was generated via a simulation methodology, and consists of a closely matched set of dialogues between subjects and a simulated computer system supplying British Airways flight information. We shall refer to it as the Wizard of Oz, or WOZ, corpus.

THE BRITISH AIRWAYS CORPUS

The telephone number of the British Airways flight information service is published in a wide variety of places, including telephone directories, airline timetables, travel brochures and personalised itineraries. British Airways provided us with several hours of tape recorded calls to their information service. From this body of material a smaller sample, consisting of 100 telephone calls, was randomly selected.[1]

The calls which make up the corpus were transcribed using the transcription scheme described in Appendix B. In those cases where callers made available personal details, these have been changed in the transcription to preserve the caller's anonymity. In the majority of cases, however, the identity of the callers remained undisclosed, and no personal details were offered or solicited.

In the data extracts we shall identify the member of the public who initiated the telephone call as the caller (C), and we shall refer to the member of the British Airways flight information staff as the agent (A).

The following is one of the shorter, simpler dialogues in the human–human corpus.

(1) [84] T4:SB:F:F[2]

```
1    A:   flight information may I help you?
2         (.3)
3    C:   hello? eh:m (.3) can you tell me: (.) what time
4         ehm (.2) eye ay (.2) two three seven, (.6) from
5         baghdad will land
6    A:   ('kay) hold on
7         (3.7)
8         confirmed fourteen ↓fifty.
9    C:   okay then thank you
10   A:   thank you b'bye
11   C:   bye
```

In this exchange the caller's request was satisfactorily dealt with in a straightforward way. Extract (2), however, provides an example of one of the longer, more problematic dialogues in the BA corpus.

(2) [73] T4:SA:M:F

```
1    C:   (       ) if you can help me
2    A:   [british airways]
3    C:   [(              )]  ↑hello
4    A:   hello:
5    C:   can you ↓help me
6    A:   uh ↑huh
7    C:   uhm: can you tell me (.) if you have
8         uhm: a club europe ↓ticket
9    A:   [mm hm
10   C:   [are you able to alternate onto another
11        fli:ght
12        (1.4)
13   A:   er(h) meaning you >wan(a) wu< you want
14        to fly to another air↓line
15   C:   pardon
16   A:   you want to fly to another [↑airline
17   C:                              [(       )
18        say if you were booked on one flight [and
19   A:                                        [mm hm
20   C:   and you wanted to come home earlier (.) would
21        it be possible if you could do that
22        (.7)
23   A:   er:* you'd have to change your reservation
24        cos' that is a confirmed booking
25   C:   oh I see y- so you can't just sort of
26        phone up and say well look I don't want
27        to be on that flight
28        (.)
29   A:   you can phone up yeah I can give you
30        reserva↓tions
31   C:   no it's alright it's just that I'm expecting
```

```
        somebody back from paris today an' I'm (.) ·hh
        I believe they were booked on the three one
        nine but I I (.) I was wondering i(f)- (.)
        if (.) if it was possible that they might
        come home on an earlier fli:ght
A:      well they could possibly because uh (.)
        all you have to do is phone 'em  (.3) tell
        'em (.) over the phone they'll change it
        in the com↑pu[ter
C:                   [mm I mean is there any way
        you c(n)- you could check the pa(ss)enger
        list for me
A:      no we can't do that (it)s against the law
        (.)
C:      [sor↑ry
A:      [its its against the law in (p) (in) and
        against bee ay pol↓icy
C:      oh I see
A:      so we couldn't not really no:
C:      I see there's no way you could tell me
        if that certain person's on the flight [or not
A:                                             [no:
        I'm sorry
C:      (tch) oh alright then
A:      ↑okay
C:      okay sorry
A:      you're welcome [ba' bye
C:                     [bye
```

Out of 100 calls, in 91 cases the agents were female. In total, 52 of the callers were female, 48 were male. In all calls agents and callers spoke English to native-speaker standard.

If we take a *turn* to be (put simply without regard to the problems of simultaneous talk by both speakers) the period from the beginning of one person's utterance to the beginning of the next person's utterance, then the average number of turns per dialogue is 18 (maximum = 62; minimum = 6). The total number of words uttered in the corpus is 12486, with 5966 (48 per cent) of these by the callers. The number of distinct word forms (types) found in the corpus is 1550, with 1004 (65 per cent) of these being used by the callers.

Calls can be classified according to what task the caller explicitly requests of the agent. In most cases, callers were trying to obtain some piece of information. For example, they try to find out (a) the arrival time of a flight, (b) the departure time of a flight, (c) the current status of a flight, (d) the arrival terminal of a flight, (e) the departure terminal of a flight, (f) a flight number, (g) a check-in time, (h) baggage regulations, (i) a telephone number, (j) the duration of a flight, and (k) they even call to leave a message for a passenger. In addition, callers try to use the flight information service inappropriately, for example, to book seats or obtain information about a competitor airline. Under these circumstances, agents respond by providing an alternative telephone number. The following dialogue illustrates one way in which an agent can supply useful information when it is not possible to answer the caller's request directly.

(3) [83] T4:SBF:F

```
A:   flight information may I ↑help you
C:   yes:, ehm ↑I'd like to make an enquiry
     about a pan am ↓flight
A:   ·hh ah we don't handle pan am on this
     number they've got their own enqui↑rie:s
     if I can give you their number
C:   [yes thank you]
A:   [h  h  h  h  h] oh one seven five oh:
     (.5)
C:   seven five oh
A:   nine double five one
C:   seven five oh nine five five one >thank you<
A:   thank you ba' bye
```

Table 3.1 shows the frequencies of tasks in the corpus (only the principal task is counted for each call).

Table 3.1 Principal tasks in the human–human corpus

Task	*Frequency*
Arrival time query	54
Departure time query	9
Current status query	4
Arrival terminal query	2
Departure terminal query	2
Flight number query	1
Check-in time query	1
Baggage regulations query	1
Telephone number query	1
Flight duration query	1
Leave a message	1
Inappropriate task	23

Thus, over half of calls are concerned with obtaining flight arrival times, but almost a quarter of calls are inappropriate for the flight information service and cannot be answered directly. 'Inappropriate tasks' can be classified into the following types (figures in brackets indicate the incidence of each type): arrival time query for another airline (8), attempt to book a seat (5), unspecified query for another airline (3), query about ticket restrictions (2), attempt to confirm a booking (2), offer of information (1), request for information about a passenger (1), and report of lost property (1).

THE WIZARD OF OZ SIMULATION CORPUS

The Wizard of Oz simulation was set up to facilitate the design process by obtaining indicators of how non-expert users will behave when they believe they are talking to a computer rather than a human agent. The availability of the human–human corpus offers the additional possibility of setting up a comparative study of speech to a human and speech to a (simulated) computer.

On the basis of a preliminary analysis of the BA corpus and, in particular, an analysis of the tasks which callers were seeking to accomplish, a collection of scenarios was constructed. A scenario is a script which describes a task; this task may be specified simply and clearly or it may be described in a deliberately complex and confusing fashion. Both alternatives serve useful purposes. Consider extract (4).

```
(4) [20] T1:SB:F:M

A:   flight information can I help you
C:   yes (>wond 'f you could<) >could you tell
     me the: (.) expected arrival time of
     a flight from barcelona (.5) flight bee ay:
     oh four eight one
     (.)
A:   oh four eight one
C:   yeah
     (.7)
A:   hold on
C:   thank you
     (1.7)
C:   (ye)s: it will be landing at terminal one heathrow
     at eleven twenty
C:   eleven twenty thank you very much
     (.3)
A:   bye
C:   bye
```

The basic task in this dialogue can be expressed very simply: the caller is trying to obtain the expected arrival time of flight number BA 481 from Barcelona. A scenario can be constructed on the basis of this dialogue:

Scenario 20

Find out when BA 481 from Barcelona is expected to arrive.

While this scenario is brief and clear, it may, predictably, ensure that the subject's request to the wizard would follow closely the information that has been provided. We can avoid this by embedding the same basic task ('find out the expected arrival time of flight number BA XXX') in a much more complex scenario. For example:

Scenario 3

> Your father is returning from a long vacation in the States and he expects you to meet him at the airport. Unfortunately you have lost the piece of paper with the arrival details: all you can remember is the flight number, BA 296, and that it departs from Chicago and arrives in London today.

It is much more difficult to predict what a subject will say when given this scenario: there is more information which can be employed in the request, and there is also greater scope for varying the structure of the request. For this reason, most of the scenarios designed for eliciting the WOZ corpus were fairly verbose.

To obtain comparable human–human and human–computer corpora it would have been possible to set up a scenario for each dialogue in the human–human corpus and then generate from each scenario a single dialogue in the human–computer corpus. In fact, we chose to do things otherwise so as to address a number of questions which would not have been answered by a pair of exactly parallel corpora. For each scenario we wanted to obtain information about a range of possible ways of proceeding to a solution; this implied that each scenario should be tried more than once and with more than one speaker. For each subject, we wanted to examine how behaviour altered as the subject learned how best to interact with the (simulated) computer; this implied that some subjects should be made to use a given scenario before and after gaining experience of the experimental set-up. In addition, we wanted to check that subjects were not framing their requests simply by using the scenario as a kind of script; this implied that we should present subjects with alternatively worded and ordered versions of the same basic scenario, and monitor whether differences in the superficial presentation of scenario information carried through to discernible differences in the dialogues collected.

With these considerations in mind, we constructed 18 basic scenarios. To these we added 6 more which were alternatively worded versions of some members of the basic set. (The full list of scenarios are presented in Appendix C.)

Ten subjects were obtained, six women and four men. All were volunteers drawn from a student population and were between 18 and 35 years of age. The subjects were placed in a room alone, and were given ten scenarios, an instruction sheet and a pre-experimental questionnaire containing the following questions.

Pre-experimental questionnaire

1 Are you male or female?
2 What is your age?

3 Which of the following best describes your experience of using computers? {none, a little, moderate, quite a lot, expert}
4a Have you ever used a telephone answering machine? {yes/no}
4b If yes, have you found the experience {very enjoyable, fairly enjoyable, OK, fairly unpleasant, very unpleasant}
4c Why?
5 Do you think it is possible to have an intelligent conversation with a computer? {yes/no}

The first two questions were straightforward attempts to elicit information. The remaining questions were designed to predispose subjects to believe that the experiment involved 'intelligent' and 'conversational' computers.

Subjects were told nothing about the purpose of the experiment, about what was going to happen, or about the identity – human or otherwise – of the flight information provider at the other end of the telephone line. They were simply placed in a room, asked to fill out the pre-experimental questionnaire and then read the following instructions.

Instructions to subjects

We are building a computer information system designed to answer queries about British Airways flights.

Your task in this experiment is to enquire about the flights mentioned in each scenario. You have been given ten scenarios. Use one per telephone call, in the order provided.

You can if you wish add more information to each scenario so long as it does not contradict information in the scenario; for example, if you are asked whether the flight arrives at Gatwick or Heathrow and the scenario says nothing about destination airports, then you could answer that it arrives at Gatwick or Heathrow or that you don't know. Of course, you may be told that your information is incorrect!

Carefully read the first scenario. Then pick up the receiver and make your enquiry. When you have finished, put the receiver down and move on to the next scenario. Please ignore the scenario numbers – they are not relevant to the content of the scenarios.

The telephone number is 3002.

Subjects' calls were answered by a wizard whose speech was passed through an acoustic filter (a Roland VP330 vocoder) in order to smooth out normal prosodic variation and make the speech sound synthetic. It was found that slowing the speech rate slightly improved intelligibility and, according to subjects who took part in a pilot study, helped make the speech sound more artificial. Half of the calls were answered by a male wizard and half by a female wizard, although the gender of the wizard was not discernible after filtering. The speech was generally quite difficult – though not impossible – to understand, with special problems being caused by the 'sh' (phonetically [θ]) sound.

At every opportunity, the wizard used exactly the same linguistic forms as those used by the British Airways agents in the human–human dialogues on which the scenarios were based. In order to generate a corpus not too far out of step with foreseeable developments in speech recognition and natural language processing, the wizard asked for utterances of more than about twenty words to be reformulated, asked for some randomly chosen utterances to be repeated, and deliberately misunderstood a small number of utterances, thereby forcing the user to initiate repair sequences. On the whole, however, subjects were allowed to formulate utterances in the ways that they chose. Extracts (5) and (6) illustrate the kind of exchanges generated in the simulation study.

(5) WOZ 4:9:F[3] (W = Wizard, S = Subject)

```
W:   british (.) airways flight information (.3)
     good (.) afternoon
     (1)
S:   ·h can you tell me (.) ehm (.3) which
     terminal I should go to for as british
     airways flight to zurich
     (3.8)
W:   please (.) wait
     (12)
W:   british (.) airways (.) flights (.) to (.)
     zurich (.4) leave from heathrow (.3)
     terminal (.) one
     (1.8)
S:   thank you
     (2.5)
W:   thank you (.) good (.) bye
```

(6) WOZ 2:2:M

```
W: flight (.) information (.3) can (.) I (.) help you
     (.7)
S: ·hh er yes ehm (.) I'd like to fly out (.) er from
     london (.) this afternoon er t- to rome please
     italy ·hh uhm I >wonder< can you tell me
     what sort of flights you have this
     afternoon please
     (1.5)
W: please (.) wait
     (4.8)
W: I (.) can (.) give (.) you (.) times (.2)
```

```
        but (.) not (.) availability
        (12.4)
W: flight (.) bee (.) ay (.) five (.) five six (.3)
        departs (.) for (.) rome (.) at (.) fifteen hundred
        (2.4) flight (.) bee (.) ay six seven two (.2)
        departs (.) for (.) rome (.) at (.) seventeen (.2)
        twenty five
        (11.4)
S: ·hh and can you tell me how long it takes
        to get to rome please hh
        (3)
W: please (.) wait
        (13.6)
W: flight (.) bee (.) ay five five six (.2)
        departing (.) at fifteen hundred (.4)
        arrives (.) at (.) seventeen hundred (1.3)
        flight (.) bee (.) ay (.) six seven two (.4)
        departing (.) at seventeen (.) twenty five (.3)
        arrives (.3) at (.) nineteen (.) twenty (.) five
        (.7)
S: thank you
        (1.8)
W: thank (.) you (.) good (.) bye
```

Although the subjects performed a total of 100 trials only 99 dialogues were recorded, as a technical error occurred during the last trial of Subject 2. Table 3.2 shows the selection and order of scenarios presented to subjects.

Table 3.2 Subject/scenario matrix

Subjects					*Scenarios*					
1	5	12	3	14	1	13	7	18a	1a	7
2	14	26	20	24	5	22	21	35a	14a	
3	23	21	22	14	5	35	3	2a	1a	24
4	12	19	2	1	8	3	18	1a	35a	20
5	14	1	8	3	18	12	23	2b	35a	1
6	22	23	20	7	13	26	21	18a	2a	8
7	24	2	21	12	5	18	20	14a	2b	26
8	13	19	22	7	26	1	8	14a	2b	21
9	18	2	8	35	26	7	19	18a	14a	1
10	2	24	23	20	13	19	35	18a	2a	3

Notice how some subjects were presented with exactly the same scenario twice (e.g. Subject 1, Scenario 7; Subject 5, Scenario 1), and some subjects were presented with alternative versions of the same basic scenario (e.g. Subject 7, Scenarios 2 and 2b; Subject 9, Scenarios 18 and 18b).

After completing ten dialogues, users were asked to fill in a post-experimental questionnaire containing the following questions:

Post-experimental questionnaire

1 Were you able to ask questions the way you wanted to? {yes/no}
2 How understandable was the system's 'voice'? {very easy, fairly easy, OK, fairly hard, very hard}
3 Apart from its 'voice' how easy was it to understand what the system said? {very easy, fairly easy, OK, fairly hard, very hard}
4 Do you think the system understood what you said? {always, mostly, half the time, sometimes, not at all}
5 Were you satisfied with the system's answers to your questions? {always, mostly, half the time, sometimes, not at all}
6 How hard was the system to use? {very easy, fairly easy, OK, fairly hard, very hard}
7 How polite was the system? {very polite, polite, OK, impolite, rude}
8 If you had to describe the system's 'personality' would you say it was: {very friendly, friendly, no personality, unfriendly, very unfriendly?
9a Have you found the experience of using the system: {very enjoyable, fairly enjoyable, OK, fairly unpleasant, very unpleasant?
9b Why?
10 Do you think it is possible to have an intelligent conversation with a computer? {yes/no}

In addition to the written questionnaire, subjects were interviewed informally after the simulations.

QUESTIONNAIRE RESULTS

As we have already indicated, the questionnaires served several different purposes. One of these – fulfilled by the pre-questionnaire – was to predispose subjects to believe that they were talking to a computer. Clearly, subjects' responses were also of interest, although these had to be treated with some caution.[4] We have seen in the previous chapter how difficult it can be to introspect about conversation with sufficient reliability to make design by inspiration a failsafe method. What the questionnaires offer subjects is the opportunity to describe their subjective feelings about using the simulated system.

The first two pre-experimental questions elicited the basic gender and age data reported above. Pre-experimental question 3 asked how much experience of using computers subjects had. The results were evenly split between those who claimed 'a little' and those who claimed 'quite a lot' of computing experience, as summarised in Table 3.3 (level of experience appears on the left of the table; subject numbers are indicated on the right).

All but one of the subjects (Subject 2) claimed to have used a telephone answering machine at some time in the past. We shall consider this further below.

Table 3.3 Experience of using computers

none	
a little	1 4 5 6 9
moderate	
quite a lot	2 3 7 8 10
expert	

All but two of the subjects (5 and 8) believed before taking part in the experiment that 'it is possible to have an intelligent conversation with a computer'. There are, of course, a number of hidden assumptions in the question as posed. It would be possible to retort, for example, that it all depends what is meant by 'intelligent' and 'conversation'. The exact nature of intelligence in the context of computers has been a long-standing and contentious issue in artificial intelligence for some time.[5] And as we noted in Chapter 1, a similar debate has begun more recently about whether or not it makes sense to describe the interaction of a computer with a human as 'conversation'. (See the papers in Luff *et al.*, 1990, especially Button's contribution; and see also Hirst, 1991.) These controversies are of considerable interest to specialists but they are unlikely to form part of a randomly chosen subject's background knowledge. The fact that all subjects answered with a simple 'yes' or 'no', and chose not to make use of the space provided for additional comments suggests that they had no difficulty in interpreting the question. (It is likely that the element of subterfuge necessary in a WOZ simulation was made easier by the images of articulate computers which resonate in science fiction in particular, and popular culture more generally.)

The post-experimental questionnaire asked subjects to reflect upon the dialogues in which they had engaged. Instructions on the questionnaire offered subjects the option of adding extra comments after each question if they wanted to. This option was exercised by several subjects, and the additional comments proved to be quite revealing.

Question 1 asked: 'Were you able to ask questions the way you wanted to?' All subjects answered in the affirmative. This unanimous agreement is most significant since it shows that subjects felt that they were not constrained by the system. All existing speech-based telephone information systems (such as home banking services) lead callers through a series of menus in which they are explicitly forced to segment and order their requests in ways determined by the system. Typically these systems fail if callers deviate from the predefined pattern of behaviour. Given how bad callers can be at following constraining instructions in menu systems and, additionally, given the tedious unnaturalness of menus in all but the most trivial of application domains, a system which places no a *priori* constraints on the user is, in principle, a worthy target to aim for.

As we shall see in a later section, in spite of the fact that callers had a sense of unconstrained flexibility in the way in which they could ask questions, nonetheless they did interact with the simulated computer in a much more constrained fashion than callers to human agents in the human–human corpus. This surely represents the holy grail of system design: a system which forces users to constrain their behaviour, but leaves them feeling completely unconstrained. The differences between speech to a human and speech to what is assumed to be a computer forms the substance of much of the rest of this volume.

As we have indicated, the quality of the vocoded speech which subjects heard was quite low. This is borne out by the answers to question 2 ('How understandable was the system's voice?'), summarised in Table 3.4.

Table 3.4 Intelligibility of system's voice

very easy	
fairly easy	1
OK	4 5 6 7
fairly hard	2 3 8 9
very hard	10

The fact that subjects felt little difficulty in interpreting the content of system utterances is shown by their responses to the question 'Apart from its "voice" how easy was it to understand what the system said?' The responses are summarised in Table 3.5.

Table 3.5 Interpretability of content of system utterances

very easy	1 2 6 7 8
fairly easy	3 4
OK	5 9 10
fairly hard	
very hard	

Subjects evidently were fairly satisfied that they understood what the system was trying to communicate. Question 4 ('Do you think the system understood what you said?') set out to measure subjects' confidence that they were being understood by the system. The results are summarised in Table 3.6.

Table 3.6 System's understanding accuracy

always	2 3 4 5 9
mostly	1 6 7 8 10
half the time	
sometimes	
not at all	

As pointed out earlier, an object of the simulation was not to second-guess the undoubtedly limited capabilities of an as-yet undesigned spoken language system. Rather, the central objective was to find out how subjects would choose to speak with such a system, thus providing a goal to aim for. On a limited number of occasions, subjects were forced to repeat or reformulate utterances, and on other occasions they were deliberately misunderstood.

However, as the subjects' questionnaire responses confirm, in the majority of instances subjects' utterances were correctly understood first time.

Question 5 addressed the satisfaction of subjects with the content of the system's responses to questions ('Were you satisfied with the system's answers to your questions?'). Since the intention of the experimenter was to supply the subject with reasonable – though not necessarily expected – answers to questions, the high degree of satisfaction reflected in Table 3.7 should come as no surprise.

Table 3.7 Satisfaction with system's answers

always	1 3 4 6 9
mostly	2 5 7 8 10
half the time	
sometimes	
not at all	

In response to question 6 ('How hard was the system to use?'), all subjects answered 'very easy' with the exception of subjects 3, 5 and 9 who answered 'fairly easy'. Given these encouraging usability judgements from untrained and inexpert users, it may be concluded that for this task at least, spoken natural language represents an interface medium worthy of further exploration.

Question 8 was designed to elicit perceptions concerning the 'personality' of the system. All subjects agreed that the system had 'no personality'. (One speaker commented that the system seemed 'very impersonal'.) We would expect politeness to be absent in dialogues in which one speaker believes the other to lack any personality at all. A glance at the human–computer corpus reveals, however, that at least one of these assumptions must be wrong, since a significant amount of politeness behaviour is to be found in the corpus. This issue is addressed in many places in later chapters.

The only time when most people are currently forced to talk to a non-human in order to achieve some serious goal, is when a telephone call is answered by an answering machine. Telephone answering machines are, of course, non-interactive: they deliver their general-purpose message and record any caller utterance which is forthcoming. Pre-experimental question 4 was designed to elicit some subjective feelings about using answering machines. Post-experimental question 9, on the other hand, was designed to elicit such feelings about talking with an interactive machine. Here we find that no subject claimed to enjoy using a non-interactive telephone answering machine more than using the simulated interactive system. Additional comments offered by subjects shed light on the perceived differences. There is a striking amount of agreement between the subjects that using a telephone answering machine induces largely negative feelings including frustration and annoyance. A very different set of comments was offered describing the experience of using the simulated interactive system. They are marked not by the frequency of references to negative feelings but rather by the frequency of references to absence of such feelings or presence of positive feelings. The only note of caution is sounded by Subject 5 who is uncertain about the extent of the system's linguistic competence. This contrasts with the comments of Subject 9, who found the system 'easy to use', Subject 2 who was not aware of any constraints, and Subjects 1 and 4 who recognised that it was possible to make a 'mistake' but were unconcerned because they considered their failures to be unobserved. It may be, then, that those people who currently avoid using telephone information services for fear of losing 'face' might find the non-human character of a computer information service sufficiently 'safe' to allow them to call it. A final contrast can be found in Subject 7's 'indifference' to telephone answering machines as compared with his enjoyment in attempting to outsmart the interactive system.

Taken together, these comments leave the impression that while subjects grudgingly appreciate *using* telephone answering machines, they had a much more enjoyable sense of *engaging with* the simulated information system.

The final post-experimental question repeated question 5 from the pre-experimental questionnaire: 'Do you think it is possible to have an intelligent conversation with a computer?' The answers obtained after the simulation were exactly the same as those obtained before, with all subjects answering 'yes' except Subjects 5 and 8. Subject 5's negative answer carried the following hedge: 'Only in this context, where the computer has the information and just gives it to you. It can't express its own opinion.' What this amounts to is an objection of the 'it all depends what you mean by intelligence' variety, as discussed above.

There can be little doubt that all of the subjects believed that they were talking to a computer. The post-experimental questionnaire left space for general comments. This was used by some subjects to enthuse about 'the system' or to suggest ways of improving it (the main suggestion was to improve the voice quality). Here are some comments provided by subjects which tend to reinforce the view that they believed 'the voice' to be produced by a computer.

> It's a good system, works well, etc <u>but</u> if you just had a one off call to make you could be completely put off initially. Some people would hang up I'm sure. (Subject 1)

> It handled all the questions and got around the waffle, and the word 'damn'. (Subject 2)

> As I was talking to a machine I didn't feel nervous. (Subject 4)

> I think a lot of people may be put off if they ring up and hear that. If they are warned by a 'human' voice first saying 'this is a computer system,' it would be better. (Subject 5)

These and other similar comments encourage the belief that the wizard's disguise worked. Nothing which was said in the subsequent informal interviews challenged this conclusion, and much which was said supported it. There can be little doubt that subjects genuinely believed that they were talking to a computer and not to a person.

SOME PRELIMINARY ANALYSIS FROM THE WOZ CORPUS

In this section we report some initial, mostly quantitative, analyses of the human–computer corpus.

Table 3.8 indicates the average number of turns from the human–human and human–(simulated)computer dialogues.

Table 3.8 Average number of turns in the human–human and human–computer corpora

	Human–human	*Human–computer*
No. of turns	18	7

The total number of words uttered in the human–computer corpus was 8103, with 4005 (49 per cent) of these being spoken by subjects. The number of distinct word forms (lexical types) in the corpus was 445, with 399 (90 per cent) of these being used by subjects. These results are compared with those obtained for the human–human corpus in Tables 3.9 and 3.10.

Table 3.9 Number of lexical tokens in the human–human and human–computer corpora

	Human–human	*Human–computer*
Whole corpus	12486	8103
Caller only	5966 (48%)	4005 (49%)

Table 3.10 Number of lexical types in the human–human and human–computer corpora

	Human–human	*Human–computer*
Whole corpus	1550	445
Caller only	1004 (65%)	399 (90%)

To what extent did subjects treat scenarios as scripts, borrowing the structure of their queries from what was written in front of them? This can be answered in two ways. First, if it is found that subjects using the same scenario structure their requests differently, this will show that at least some subjects brought their own creativity to bear in forming requests. Second, if alternative wordings of the same basic scenario fail to have a discernible effect on resulting dialogues, this will show that subjects organised requests according to their own criteria and not according to the structure present in any scenario. Here we sketch a preliminary set of results based on the latter test. Consider Scenario 1 (reproduced here for convenience).

Scenario 1

> Your boss is due to fly back from Germany tomorrow morning and you have to meet him off the plane. His flight number is BA 903 and the flight departs from Frankfurt and arrives at Heathrow airport.

The task specified by the scenario is made up of a number of parameters (underlined above) such as the country of departure, day and time of day, flight number, and so on. These are presented in Scenario 1 in the order:

1 Germany ('G')
2 tomorrow morning ('TM')
3 BA 903 ('BA')
4 Frankfurt ('F')
5 Heathrow ('H')

The order of these parameters is almost completely reversed in Scenario 1a:

1 Frankfurt
2 Heathrow
3 BA 903
4 tomorrow morning
5 Germany

Two of the subjects (one and four) were presented with both Scenario 1 and Scenario 1a. As Table 3.11 shows, both subjects structured their queries fairly consistently in all of the dialogues, and that structure differed from both of the structures found in Scenarios 1 and 1a.

Table 3.11 Parameter order in scenarios and dialogues

Scenario 1	G	TM	BA	F	H
Scenario 1a	F	H	BA	TM	G
Dialogue 1:5 (1)	BA	F	TM	H	
Dialogue 1:9 (1a)	BA	F	H	TM	
Dialogue 4:4 (1)	BA	F	H		
Dialogue 4:8 (1a)	BA	F	TM		

Subjects consistently reorder their queries in a way which appears to have more to do with the structure of the underlying task than with the superficial wording of the scenarios. Queries are structured around the flight number; this should not be surprising, since a flight number uniquely specifies a flight and thus implies most of the other task parameters. Analysis of dialogues from scenarios that do not mention a flight number reveals greater uncertainty on the part of subjects about how best to formulate the query. This manifests itself in a higher incidence of problems in talk and, in some cases, in a tendency for subjects' queries to reflect the parameter order of the scenarios on which they are based. For a discussion of the way in which callers order task parameters in train timetable enquiry dialogues (where trains do not have unique identifiers comparable to flight numbers) see Richards and Underwood (1984b).

In this chapter we have outlined the method and procedure by which two approximately parallel corpora were collected, the first by recording calls to an existing telephone information service, the second by staging a WOZ simulation. In addition we have presented some preliminary – mostly quantitative – analyses of the corpora. Although these first observations have scarcely looked below the surface of the data, it is clear that there are significant differences between the corpora. To cite just one example: subjects managed to accomplish the same kinds of tasks as callers to the human–human corpus while using less than a third of the number of distinct lexical types. A small proportion of the extra types are accounted for by the fact that the corpora were not exactly parallel (so, for example, some place names appear in the human–human corpus which are not found in the human–computer corpus), but these do not explain the scale of the disparity between the corpora.

Data from previous simulation studies have primarily been analysed using quantitative techniques. In this research, however, we are using a more qualitative methodology, conversation analysis, which developed from the sociological study of naturally occurring everyday verbal interaction. Before we go on to discuss our analysis of the corpora, it is necessary to describe some of the principal analytic and methodological features of conversation analysis.

4

CONVERSATION ANALYSIS

In the following chapters we will be examining two related but somewhat different kinds of data. The first kind is the recordings and transcripts of ordinary members of the public calling the British Airways flight information service. The second kind of data consist of recordings and transcripts of people talking through a telephone system to what they believed was a prototype speech-based computer information service. Our examination of these materials will focus on the systematic properties of the ways that speakers verbally interact with each other, or with what they think is a computer. With this goal in mind we are adopting a broadly conversation analytic approach to empirical investigation. There have been other attempts to adopt a conversation analytic approach to inform the development or analysis of interactive systems (for example, see the collection of papers in Luff *et al.*, 1990). However, the use of a conversation analytic approach is still sufficiently novel to require us first to address some methodological issues, in particular, some of the assumptions which underpin empirical work in conversation analysis. Our emphasis upon explaining the principles which inform empirical work means that we will not try to review here the major findings from conversation analysis. In subsequent chapters, however, we do draw upon and discuss the research literature on turn-taking, the organisation of overlap, preference, closing sequences and repair in conversation.

After having established what kind of analytic enterprise conversation analysis offers, the rest of this chapter will discuss a related issue. As conversation analytic studies primarily investigate naturally occurring, everyday *conversational* interaction, it is necessary to consider whether it is an appropriate methodology with which to examine data gathered from the more circumscribed domain of calls to a public information service. It is important also to assess its utility for the examination of data generated from the rather more controlled and artificial setting of an experimental computer simulation study.

CONVERSATION ANALYSIS AND THE TURN-BY-TURN ANALYSIS OF VERBAL INTERACTION

Conversation analysis emerged as a distinctive form of sociological research in the mid-1960s. Pioneered through the work of Harvey Sacks, Gail Jefferson and Emmanuel Schegloff, the goal of conversation analysis is to describe the systematic properties of the ways that participants in a dialogue organise their verbal interaction. It attempts to examine the actions constituted through the design of turns at talk, and describes how turns are produced to co-ordinate with prior turns.[1] Conversation analysis is not unique in this goal: for example, the discourse analytic tradition established by Sinclair and Coulthard (1975) has similar goals. However, conversation analysis has some distinctive methodological characteristics and it is useful to explain them here. To do this, we will examine some aspects of the following exchange, which is part of the BA flight information corpus.

(1) [8] T1:SB:F:M

```
A:   flight inform[ation can I help you,
C:                [ (                  ) jus
     gettin' through tuh (.) airport
     (.)
     >ello,<
A:   ·h good day british
     ↓airways ↑[flight information=
C:             [(>yeh-<)
A:   =can I ↑help you,
C:   are you a real person yeh(t)?
A:   YEs: ↑hello th[ere
C:                 [(ah)hhhh good (.3) er: the bee
     ay five eight four from turin. love.
A:   five eight fou:r hold on please?
     (15)
     er we don't have five eight four sir
     I think you might mean the five seven nine
C:   °eur(gh)° well he did say it might be the
     five (.) eight four when he phone- is that
     coming in from tur[in round about
A:                     [we've got a five seven
     ni:ne from turin whi[ch was scheduled
C:                       [yeah(p)
A:   for ten thirty
     (.)
C:   that's the one
     (.)
A:   it'll be landing hopefully at ten twenty
     five
C:   ten twenty f[ive
A:               [terminal one
```

```
32          (.5)
33    C:    so er:: customs'll be coming through about
34          (.3)
35    A:    well you(r)- you know you [know as well as
36    C:                              [ (     )
37    A:    I do yeh i[(t) could (>gu-<) allow half
38    C:              [okay love
39    A:    an hour at any rate
40    C:    okay dear
41          (.)
42    A:    it may be quicker (.) they may not
43    C:    okay my love
44          (.7)
45    A:    thankyou
46    C:    thankyou
47    A:    bye bye
```

Like many forms of discourse analysis, conversation analysis seeks to describe the way that sequences of turns cohere into orderly patterns of turn exchange. However, whereas discourse analysis tries to explain this coherence in terms of a limited and theoretically derived set of categories of turn types, and the explication of quasi-syntactic rules which are supposed to govern the relationship between these turn types, the goal of conversation analysis is to see how *participants themselves* analyse and 'classify' the kind of business that a turn in dialogue is attending to. That is, in conversation analysis, the goal is not to try to impose an order on the relationship between successive turns: it tries instead to describe how speakers themselves arrive at an interpretation and understanding of how a turn is appropriately placed in a specific sequence of turns. Consequently, the first step in analysis of any sequence is to see how a next speaker interprets the prior turn. Consider lines 1 to 14 of extract (1).

```
1     A:    flight inform [ation can I help you,
2     C:                  [ (              ) jus
3           gettin' through tuh (.) airport
4           (.)
5           >e̲llo.<
6     A:    ·h good day british
7           ↓airways ↑[flight information=
8     C:              [(>yeh-<)
9     A:    =can I ↑help you,
10    C:    are you a real person yeh(t)?
11    A:    YE̲s: ↑hello th [ere
12    C:                   [(ah)hhhh good (.3) er: the bee
13          ay five eight four from turin. love.
14    A:    five eight fou:r hold on please?
```

The opening turns of this sequence are somewhat confusing. It would seem likely from this extract that in previous attempts to get through to a British Airways agent the caller has been redirected to a telephone queue which is serviced by recorded messages. His first recorded utterances in this fragment 'jus gettin' through tuh (.) airport' seem to be spoken to someone other than the agent. He then checks that the line is open, and the agent recycles the routine identification of and introduction to the service. The caller then produces what appears to be a semi-joking query to establish the 'live' credentials of the agent with whom he is now in contact: 'are you a real person yeh(t)?'. The agent confirms that the caller is talking to a human operator, and in lines 12 to 13 the caller produces a receipt token '(ah)hhhh good' thereby acknowledging the agent's prior confirmation.

It is the caller's next utterance on which we will focus. Having produced the acknowledgement token, the next component of the turn is a recital or list of flight details concerning one specific flight. These details are prefaced with a definite article, and could therefore be taken to indicate that the caller is simply making some sort of announcement. The full stops at the end of the words 'turin' and 'love' indicate a downward intonation, resembling a 'stopping' tone of voice. (See Appendix C for a full description of the transcription conventions.)

How does the agent deal with this turn? One observation is that her next turn begins with no gap after the preceding turn. Thus she displays none of the hesitation which might be taken to indicate some kind of ambiguity as to how she should proceed. Nor does she wait to see if the caller is going to say anything else which would specify what exactly he expects the agent to do next. Similarly, the agent does not try to elicit further information from the caller. The agent's next turn is 'five eight fou:r hold on please?'. This is a confirmatory echo of the flight details provided by the caller, and a request for the caller to wait while she locates some information. Thus the design of her turn displays her analysis that the caller's production of a list of flight details means that he wants further information about that flight. Her next action, then, treats the prior turn as if it was an explicit request formulation. That is, despite the absence from the prior turn of any components which would unambiguously indicate the turn's business as 'asking for flight information', the agent treats the caller's 'list of details' as a legitimate enquiry which needs no further elaboration.

The agent's analysis of the caller's prior turn is available to and designed for inspection by the caller. So, the caller can examine the agent's next turn to assess whether or not she has made an appropriate response. In this case, the caller remains silent after the agent indicates that she has taken his prior turn to constitute a request for information. The absence of any attempt to repair or correct her interpretation of the business of the prior turn suggests that on this occasion the agent had made a correct analysis.

There is a sense in which these kinds of observations may seem thoroughly commonplace, and it may be retorted that the fact that agent was able to see the 'purpose' of the caller's list was due entirely to 'habit' or expectations derived from experience of the job. However, in the remaining sections we will show that the agent's interpretation of the caller's prior turn, displayed in her subsequent turn, is informed by her tacit awareness of regular properties of these kinds of conversational sequences. But our present concern is to describe the methodological assumptions which underpin conversation analytic research, and it is this issue to which we return.

An initial inspection of the utterance 'the bee ay five eight four from turin. love.' indicated its ambiguous character as an announcement or as a request. Certain features of its design could be taken to indicate that it is an announcement of some sort, although that information in itself would not facilitate a clear cut analysis of what such an announcement might be doing. As we have seen, however, the agent treated it as a request for flight details. If analysis proceeded on single sentences or utterances, extracted from the circumstances in which and for which they were originally produced, it would be incumbent upon the analyst to derive some form of practical resolution for the ambiguity of this turn. However, one advantage of the method of conversation analysis, and its emphasis upon the importance of next turn positions, is that the analyst is not called upon to make and then warrant ascriptions of 'function', 'type' or 'purpose' to specific turns: the ambiguity or 'puzzle' about a turn is always resolved by participants in the subsequent unfolding of the exchange. Consider the following section from extract (1):

```
28   A:   it'll be landing hopefully at ten twenty
29        five
30   C:   ten twenty f[ive
31   A:               [terminal one
32        (.5)
33   C:   so er:: customs'll be coming through about
34        (.3)
35   A:   well you(r)- you know you [know as well as
36   C:                             [ (      )
37   A:   I do yeh i[(t) could (>gu-<) allow half
38   C:             [okay love
39   A:   an hour at any rate
```

In this sequence the agent has just finished providing the arrival time of the flight about which the caller has inquired. In line 30 the caller then repeats the time of arrival. This repeat could constitute an attempt to query that information, or it could constitute an echoic acknowledgement that this component of the information has been received. The agent begins to provide further information in overlap with the caller's echo of the previous item of information. This indicates that she is treating the caller's repeat as a confirmatory echo, and not as a turn designed to raise the status of the information. And in the subsequent turns, the caller moves to a different but related topic, thereby displaying that the agent's analysis of his previous turn was not misplaced.

If the caller had intended his repeat to be taken as a query about the time of arrival, then his analysis of the agent's next turn would have alerted him to the way that the exchange was going awry, and he would then have been able to repair the misunderstanding which would have been displayed in the agent's turn. (In Chapter 7 we will discuss some of the repair strategies which conversation analysts have examined and see that next turn is a key position in conversation in which speakers can identify that there are problems in the exchange, and in which they may begin to initiate appropriate repair procedures.)

We have emphasised that conversation analysts examine the turn-by-turn unfolding of dialogue because each next turn displays the speaker's analysis and interpretation of the business of the prior turn. At this point, then, it is important to emphasise that this analytic goal does not lead the analyst into speculations about mentalistic concepts such as 'cognitive plans', 'interpretative rules' or 'schemata' through which a participant in a conversation may come to understand a prior turn. Conversation analysts are liberated from having to speculate about how such (hypothetical) constructs inform the way in which an individual comes to make sense of a prior turn in a dialogue because 'understanding' of a prior turn will be embedded in the design of subsequent turns. The analytic goal is to describe the way that displays of understanding are organised in the design of turns, and to explicate how these displays are orchestrated with respect to their sequential and interactional environment.

The methodological import of this approach to empirical research is stressed by Sacks *et al.*

> While understandings of other turns' talk are displays to co-participants, they are available as well to professional analysts who are thereby afforded a proof criterion (and search procedure) for the analysis of what a turns' talk is occupied with. Since it is the parties' understandings of prior turns' talk that is relevant to their construction of next turns, it is *their* understandings that are wanted for analysis. The display of those understandings in the talk of subsequent turns afforded both a resource for the analysis of prior turns and a proof procedure for professional analysis of prior turns – resources that are intrinsic to the data themselves.
>
> (Sacks, Schegloff and Jefferson, 1974: 729) (Original emphasis)

Through the detailed examination of turn design we can also begin to see the kinds of resources, intrinsic to the data, through which speakers make sense of prior turns. Consider extract (2), which comes from an exchange between a mother and her son about a Parent Teachers Association meeting.

```
(2) (From Schegloff, 1988: 442-56)

Mother: Do you know who's going to that meeting?
Russ:   Who.
```

```
Mother: I don't kno:w.
Russ:   Oh::. Prob'ly Missiz McOwen ('n detsa) en prob'ly
        Missiz Cadry and some of the teachers and the coun-
        sellors.
```

In this extract Mother's question 'Do you know who's going to that meeting?' can be interpreted in two ways: as a genuine request for information about who is attending the meeting, or as a pre-announcement that she is about to reveal some news concerning the people who will be attending. In the examination of this exchange, the analyst can identify which of these interpretations Russ makes by looking at his next turn after Mother's question. And in this case, he returns the floor to his mother with a question, thereby displaying that he treats her utterance as a pre-announcement. And Mother's next turn displays that, on this occasion, Russ got it wrong. This extract illustrates an important methodological point. Note that the way that Russ responds to his mother depends upon seeing which of the actions his mother's prior turn is performing: a request or a pre-announcement. The appropriateness of Russ's next turn, and the orderliness of this sequence, is inextricably tied to his tacit reasoning about, his 'coming to see', which of these actions was performed by his mother's prior utterance.

RECIPIENT DESIGN

Conversation analytic studies have shown that turns are built at a very fine level of detail with respect to who the recipient of that turn will be. Consider the caller's utterance in lines 16 to 20 of extract (1).

```
16   A:   er we don't have five eight four sir
17        I think you might mean the five seven nine
18   C:   °eur(gh)° well he did say it might be the
19        five (.) eight four when he phone- is that
20        coming in from tur-in round about
```

In this fragment the agent informs the caller that part of the information which he has provided appears to be incorrect, and she suggests some alternative flight identification details. In the caller's subsequent turn he refers to someone else who gave him that information with the pronoun 'he'. Presumably the caller could have referred to this other person in a variety of ways, but the use of the pronoun 'he' is produced with respect to the recipient of that utterance. That is, it is extremely unlikely that the agent will know who this person is, and therefore the relevance or significance of identifying who the 'he' is would be lost on the agent. Indeed, had the caller identified the 'he' it is intuitively likely that the agent would have assumed that that identification was selected and used precisely because it was relevant to her, and this in turn could have led to all sorts of confusions.

But the issue of recipient design does not merely concern the way that one speaker will refer to an object or state of affairs in the world in a way that takes into account what the recipient is expected to know about that state of affairs. Turns may be designed with respect to some version or formulation of *who* the recipient may be. We say 'with respect to some formulation' for good reason. Any state of affairs in the world can be described in a variety of ways (Schegloff, 1972), and this is true also of people: one person can be described in terms of family position, in terms of occupation, in terms of political affiliation, and so on. So, the construction of a turn may be accomplished with respect to one (or more) of a variety of characteristics relevant to the recipient of that turn.

With this in mind let us consider the caller's production of a list of flight details in lines 12 and 13.

```
12    C:   er: the bee
13         ay five eight four from turin. love.
```

There is a sense in which the agent's interpretation of this utterance as a request for further information turns on her coming to see that it has been designed for her as 'agent-of-a-flight-information-service'. That is, the absence of any lexical items which would unequivocally characterise the utterance as a request, displays the assumption that the recipient will know exactly the purpose of the utterance. '[T]he bee ay five eight four from turin. love.', therefore, is built for a recipient with a specific *occupational identity*: agent of a flight information service. And the agent's coming to see the salience of that design feature informs her (on this occasion correct) analysis that its purpose is to request further flight information.

SEQUENCES OF ACTIONS

Although conversation analytic research can begin with the detailed analysis of the design of single turns, the overriding goal is to examine sequential structures of conversation: that is, to describe the organisation of recurrent patterns of interaction. Perhaps the simplest way to illustrate this is to refer to the concept of the adjacency pair.

It is common to find conversational exchanges which occur as paired actions: greeting–greeting, question–answer, request–acceptance/refusal, and so on.

```
10    C:   are you a real person yeh(t)?
11    A:   YEs: ↑hello there
```

Sacks, (1992, volume one, 3–11) proposed the concept of the adjacency pair to account for the recurrent structural properties of the organisation of paired actions. The properties of the concept were originally described in Schegloff and Sacks (1973); Heritage (1984: 246) provides the following formulation of an adjacency pair:

1 a sequence of two utterances which are
2 adjacent
3 produced by different speakers
4 ordered as a first part and second part
5 typed, so that a first part requires a particular second (or range of second parts)

As Heritage maintain the structural property of paired actions does not entail that the actions are necessarily produced in succession, occuring next to each other. It is not a statement of empirical invariance. Neither is the concept used to capture some empirical generalisation, for example, that in 80 per cent of cases second parts immediately follow first parts. Rather the concept is important in that it underlines the *normative* character of paired actions. That is, the production of a first part proposes that a relevant second part is expectable: a second part is made *conditionally relevant* by the production of a first part (Schegloff, 1972). It is observable that when a speaker fails to produce an appropriate second part, they may produce an utterance which accounts for this failure. Furthermore, by virtue of a common orientation to this relevance, speakers have the basis for inferences about the actions of co-participants. All these features may be illustrated in the following extract.

```
(3) [7] T1:SA:F:M

16   C:   >are you able to tell me (.5)
17        er flight arrival times from
18        zimbabwe oh no you can't i-
19        its at Gatwick
20        (.5)
21   A:   no what's the flight number
22        (.8)
23   C:   urm
24        (.2)
25   A:   WHAt's the fLIght num[ber
26   C:                        [flight number
27        I don't know the flight number
28        it arrives saturday morning
```

In line 21 the agent asks a question. According to the adjacency pair concept, this generates the expectation that an answer should follow. Clearly, the caller has some difficulty with the question insofar as there is a one second pause (although at this stage the basis of the difficulty is not apparent). The agent's subsequent turn exhibits her awareness of the norm that an answer is an appropriate second to a question: she repeats the question. However, this is not merely an echo of the initial formulation; in the second version certain words and syllables are given greater stress. She has not rephrased the question, as she might if she had perceived it to be ambiguous to the caller, or unclear; rather she has reiterated it. Thus the professional analyst – and, more importantly, the caller – is presented with a turn which publicly displays the type of inference the agent drew from the caller's silence; and these are informed by her orientation to structural but normative features of the relationship between paired actions. The caller's subsequent utterance 'I don't know the flight number' provides an account for why he could not answer the question. This displays his awareness of the expectation for appropriate second parts generated upon the provision of first pair parts.

So, next speakers are not required to offer a second part immediately. In between the first and second parts of adjacency pair sequences there may be insertion sequences, often composed of embedded and nested adjacency pairs, during which matters relevant to the first part are dealt with before the second part is produced. Thus one obtains patterns of, for example, questions and answers of the following form:

```
(4) (Taken from Sacks, 1972 lecture 3: 23)

A:      Hello
B:      Is Fred there ?                    Q1
A:      Who is calling ?                   Q2
B:      Is he there ?                      Q3
A:      Yes                                A3
B:      This is Joe Henderson              A2
A:      Just a moment                      A1
```

Because the first part of an adjacency pair sets up the expectation and relevance of a second part, subsequent turns will be heard as being either the second part itself, some preliminary working up to the second part, or some announced failure to provide the second part.

Let us consider the sequence of actions in lines 9 to 17 of extract (1).

```
9     A:   =can I ↑help you,
10    C:   are you a real person yeh(t)?
11    A:   YEs: ↑hello th [ere
12    C:                  [(ah)hhhh good (.3) er: the bee
13         ay five eight four from turin. love.
14    A:   five eight fou:r hold on please?
15         (15)
16         er we don't have five eight four sir
17         I think you might mean the five seven nine
```

While it is true that the turn in line 10 is a question, the turn before that is an offer. So it would appear, initially, that the normative requirement that an offer should be met with acceptance or refusal has not been met. However, the question in line 10 is clearly *preliminary* to a turn which addresses the prior offer: that is, if the recipient is human then the caller can take up the offer component of the agent's introduction to the service. And, having clarified that the current recipient will be able to help him, the caller does go on to produce the announcement or list of flight details, thereby taking up the offer originally formulated in line 9. So, the question–answer sequence in lines 10 and 11 was an insertion sequence bounded by the offer-acceptance/refusal turns in lines 9 and 13/14.

We discussed earlier the kinds of inferential resources through which the agent at this point may have been able to recognise that the caller was actually making a request for flight information by simply reciting a list of relevant flight details. We can now add a further resource. The agent can see that the prior series of turns was an insertion sequence. Thus she has evidence to expect that once that work had been completed, the next turn would be an acceptance or a refusal of the offer of help; and the only circumstances in which such an offer would be refused would be if the caller had actually got through to the wrong airline information service. So the agent has structural interpretative resources from which to infer that the list provided by the speaker constitutes his acceptance and take up of the offer to locate flight information.

LANGUAGE AS A VEHICLE FOR SOCIAL ACTION

So far we have seen that turns at talk can be studied to see how actions they accomplish contribute to the orderly progression of conversation. But it is important to note also that turns can be designed for social actions, and attend to interpersonal, inferential and interactional contingencies that are generated in the course of the exchange. Intuitively, in the course of everyday conversation such interpersonal matters will be particularly relevant to participants. But it is true also that interactional business is addressed in the more circumscribed domain of service calls. Consider the following sequence:

```
12   C:                  -(ah)hhhh good (.3) er: the bee
13        ay five eight four from turin. love.
14   A:   five eight fou:r hold on please?
15        (15)
16   A:   er we don't have five eight four sir
17        I think you might mean the five seven nine
18   C:   °eur(gh)° well he did say it might be the
19        five (.) eight four when he phone- is that
20        coming in from tur-in round about
```

In lines 12 and 13 the caller lists the details of a flight which the agent takes to be an inquiry, and she spends some time checking the details she has been given. However, it transpires that the flight identification details provided by the caller do not identify an aeroplane, and the agent offers the details of a flight which the caller might be referring to. So, basically, the caller has made a mistake. But his next turn is designed to minimise his culpability in this error. His subsequent turn is prefaced by the utterance 'he did say', which reveals that the source of the mistaken flight details was an unspecified other person. The caller then goes on to re-characterise the status of the (now revealed to be erroneous) information which he had been given by stating that this other person said 'it might be the five (.) eight four' (lines 14 and 15), thereby modifying the factual status of the flight details he provided. Modifying the status of the information provided to him allows the caller to perform two delicate interpersonal tasks. First, he does not have to acknowledge explicitly that he was wrong: recharacterising the now incorrect information as only a candidate flight identification at the time it was used minimises the extent of the error. Second, by modulating the factual status of the incorrect information after the agent provides an alternative set of flight details, the caller is able to produce an oblique acceptance of the agent's correction. The issue of the caller's error and the agent's correction does not then become an explicit topic of the exchange.

CONVERSATION ANALYSIS AND WOZ SIMULATIONS

As we mentioned in Chapter 2, materials generated through previous studies of the interactions between humans and WOZ simulations have been examined through the use of primarily quantitative methodological techniques. We have decided to examine our data using a conversation analytic approach, and it is appropriate here to explain why this analytic methodology has been adopted.

Conversation analysis has emerged in the past twenty years as one of the pre-eminent approaches to the study of naturally occurring conversational interaction. Studies have produced a substantial and cumulative body of findings about various dimensions of conversational organisation. These findings provide an invaluable store of information to which we can refer to inform our understanding of human interaction with simulated and, eventually, actual interactive speech interfaces.

More relevant to the present study, however, is recent research on spoken interaction which occurs in various institutional settings. There are now a number of studies which point to the ways that features of the organisation of everyday conversation are modified in specific contexts and settings (Atkinson, 1984a and b; Atkinson and Drew, 1979; Drew and Heritage, 1992; Greatbatch, 1988; Heath, 1984; 1986; Heritage and Greatbatch, 1986). One upshot of these findings is that everyday communicative competencies can be treated as having a foundational or 'bedrock' status in relation to talk which occurs in institutional contexts. Furthermore, this research suggests that there is no deterministic relationship between contexts and language use which takes place within those contexts. Rather, it emphasises that through local modifications of specific conversational practices, participants display their orientation to, and thereby instantiate and reproduce, the institutional dimensions of the settings in which interaction occurs.

With this in mind, we can begin to analyse data generated from simulation studies to explicate which conversational resources, rooted in the domain of everyday verbal interaction, are marshalled in exchanges with computerised artifacts. Furthermore, in the exploration of the ways that communicative resources are so modified to meet the practical contingencies of actual dealings with artifacts, we can start to sketch the organisation and operation of interactional resources through which human–computer interaction, as a series of institutionalised communicative arrangements, is constituted and rendered distinctive from, or similar to, other instances of talk-in-interaction.

5

GETTING STARTED

Opening sequences in the BA and WOZ corpora

With regard to his studies of the organisation of opening sequences in ordinary, everyday telephone conversations, Schegloff remarked that:

> The beginnings of telephone conversations can seem a peculiar object on which to lavish scholarly attention. Being historically shallow products of technological innovation, they may seem parochial when set aside other specific sub-genres of speech as political oratory, for example, whose occurrence and study have greater historical depth and cross-cultural generality, and whose consequences seem self-evidently potentially substantial.
>
> (Schegloff, 1986: 111)

In this chapter we are going to examine the opening sequences in calls to the British Airways flight information service and to the (simulated) computer, focusing in particular on the callers' and subjects' first turns in the dialogues. Thus it is important to explain why opening sequences deserve detailed attention.

The first utterances are clearly crucial for the subsequent dialogue. It is here that the callers describe the information they require. But it is also the first place in the exchange that a misunderstanding or possible difficulty can be detected and exposed. However, our interest in these request formulations is not restricted to, for example, assessing whether one way of making a request seems to be 'more appropriate', or 'easier to understand' than any other. Similarly, we do not view request formulations as the verbalised instantiations of a speaker's 'plans' or 'goals'. Rather our analysis, particularly of the BA material, begins with the assumption that request formulations are produced in a sequence of turns. Consequently, we are interested in the way that request formulations are designed with respect to the sequential organisation that underpins these opening sequences. Similarly, we do not view request formulations as a passive conduit for the caller to make public their particular requirements. Although, of course, they do have the function of describing callers' requirements, we are interested also to see what kinds of interactional work is addressed through them. That is, we approach request formulations as a site of, and a vehicle for, interpersonal action, and our analysis of that feature of their design will be a central theme in later sections of this chapter.

Our analytic interest is not confined solely to the way that callers specify the information they require. We are also interested in the kind of (apparently trivial) items, such as 'hello', 'good morning', 'yes', 'yes please', 'thank you' and 'erm', that tend to occur prior to the actual request. For example, in the following extract the caller prefaces the request formulation with 'yes hello. erm:'.

(1) [4] BA:T1:SA:F:F

A: flight infor↑mation british ↑airways
   good ↑da:y
C: yes hello. erm: bee ay two nine two. h- >urh<
   it >should've< bin scheduled for seven fifteen.
A: hold on a moment,

It may seem strange to examine in detail these components of the very first turns in the exchanges between the users and agents of the BA information service. After all, the 'purpose' of the vast majority of calls is to elicit information about plane arrivals and departures. However, in a data corpus of 100 calls to the British Airways flight information service, in only three instances do the callers move directly to formulate a request for information after the agent's identification and greeting. In all other cases, callers produce items such as 'hello', 'thank you' and variations on non-lexical sounds, such as 'erm', before actually asking for information. The sheer frequency of these items thus belies their apparent unimportance, and thereby warrants examination. More important, however, we wish to show that the occurrence of these items is not merely random, or the product of idiosyncratic behavioural traits, but is underpinned by the same sequential and organisational constraints that more generally inform the opening sequences of these calls.

Before we proceed further there is a methodological point. Later, we will be using elementary statistical analyses to underscore some preliminary observations on the differences between the opening sequences in the respective corpora. Traditionally, conversation analytic studies have not been concerned with the relative frequencies of observed conversational phenomena, as the goal of analysis is to describe the systematic properties of conversational phenomena.[1] However, there have been some notable exceptions to this. In his seminal paper on the openings of telephone conversations, Schegloff (1968) reported that a single case out of a data set of 500 cases did not fit with his analysis, and thus he re-examined his corpus to produce a more comprehensive account. Zimmerman and West (1975) and West and Zimmerman (1985) provided tabular representations of conversational phenomena in their study of gender-based differences in interaction. Finally, Heritage and Greatbatch (1986) have also furnished some statistical analyses in their study of rhetorical devices used in political speeches to generate affiliative audience responses.[2] Following the example of these studies, we will try to establish some rudimentary statistical descriptions of the respective opening sequences.

We begin by examining the BA corpus to provide a more technical description of features of the callers' first turns to the flight information service. We can (loosely) categorise these utterances into two types: response tokens and hesitation items.

RESPONSE TOKENS IN THE BA CORPUS

(2) [BA 14] T1:SB:818 F:F

```
A:   flight infor↑mation can I ↑help you[::
C:                                       [>oh hello<
     (.)
     yes I'm just inquiring about the:
     uhm bee ay flight two two seven,
```

In extract (2) the caller produces 'oh hello' and 'yes' before stating what information she requires. We call these items response tokens simply because, intuitively, they have some relationship to the two components of the agent's initial turn 'flight information can I help you'. In fact, they appear to have been 'triggered off' by the design of the agent's introduction. So, the caller's 'hello' is a response to the agent's service identification, and the caller's 'yes' is a response to the offer 'can I help you'.

In an earlier chapter we introduced the concept of the adjacency pair. Schegloff and Sacks (1973) formulated this concept to account for the empirical observation that conversational interaction occurs largely through sequences of paired actions, such as greeting–greeting, question–answer, offer–acceptance/refusal. We also noted that conversationalists orient to the normative expectation that, upon the provision of a first pair part, the appropriate second is conditionally relevant. This concept accounts for the features of extract (2). '(O)h hello' is the appropriate second pair part to the agent's greeting 'flight information' and 'yes' is the appropriate second pair part to the offer 'can I help you'. Furthermore, we can observe that the order in which the caller produces the second pair parts mirrors the order in which the agent produces the respective first pair parts.

We might conclude, then, that the production of response tokens is simply a consequence of callers' orientation to the conversational convention that one action makes the appropriate second conditionally relevant. However, there are many cases where this explanation does not account for the details of the callers' initial utterance. Consider the following extract.

(3) [13] T1:SB:F:F

A: flight inf(i)mation: british ↑airways good day
↑can I ↓he:lp ↑you
(.)
C: ·h erm: yes I wonder if you could tell me

In her first turn the agent produces three discrete first pair parts: there are two forms of introduction, ('flight inf(i)mation' and 'british ↑airways), one greeting ('good day') and one offer ('↑can I ↓he:lp ↑you'). But the caller does not provide the appropriate second pair parts to all three of the pairs initiated in the agent's turn. Instead, she says 'erm: yes', and thus provides only the second pair part to the offer component of the prior turn. In this case, then, the normative convention that relevant second pair parts should be produced does not seem to hold.

In 85 of the 100 transcribed calls, the agent's opening turn ends with the utterance 'can I help you' or 'good morning'. The appropriate second pair parts to these would be an acceptance, such as 'yes' or 'yeah', and a returned greeting respectively. In only 34 per cent of these calls did callers immediately produce an acceptance item or a returned greeting. A further 24 per cent produce an acceptance or a greeting, but only after providing another response token.

There are also cases in which the callers produce no utterances which are recognisable as appropriate second pair parts.

(4) [81] T4:SB:F:F

A: flight information may I ↑help you?
C: ehm can you tell me if (air) two three four
hs- has it landed ↓yet

(5) [9] T1:SB:F:M

A: ·hh flight information british ↑airways
can I ↑help you:,
C: er- could you jus' tell me: er:
incoming flight from toronto bee ay nine two

In these extracts the agents provide two first pair parts, but in each case the caller produces a hesitation item and then immediately begins to formulate the request.

In the following extract the agent merely identifies the service, and does not produce the 'can I help you' part which usually occurs in these turns. However, the caller says 'yes' as though the offer component had been produced. This is a case, then, of the caller producing a second pair part despite the absence of the relevant first pair part.

(6) [49] T3:SA:F:M

```
A:   british airways ↑flight information
     (.)
C:   yes ur: (>its<) london gat-wick >er gatwick
     o:ne er: ex stockholm bee ay
     seven eight fi:ve
```

There is a similar phenomenon in extract (1), reproduced below; here, the agent produces an identification and a greeting, but no explicit offer. However, the caller produces an acceptance item before she produces the second part of a greeting pair.

(1) [4] T1:SA:F:F

```
A:   flight infor↑mation british ↑airways
     good ↑da:y
C:   yes hello. erm: bee ay two nine two. h- >urh<
     it >should've< bin scheduled for seven fifteen.
A:   hold on a moment,
```

HESITATION ITEMS IN THE BA CORPUS

In this section we describe some features of the 'uhms' and 'erms' which callers produce. It is important to note, though, that we are concerned only with instances of these items that occur before the caller begins to produce a request formulation. Hesitation markers and micro pauses which occur, for example, in the actual request, are not considered here. (The criterion for this distinction is purely pragmatic: we are investigating sequences in which callers co-ordinate their entry to the exchange; clearly, this occurs right at the start of their first turn. By the time a request for information is being made, we can consider the phase of entry co-ordination to be completed.)

Vocalised hesitation markers can occur right at the beginning of the caller's turn, prior to a response token.

(7) [26] T1:SB:F:F

```
A:   flight information can I ↑help you,
C:   er: yes please could you tell me what time
     your flight to rome is this afte[rnoon and if
A:                                   [·hh  (hhYES:)
C:   there are seats available
```

(8) [51] T3:SA:F:F

```
A:   british airways ↑flight information
     can I help you:?
```

C: ·h er yes (>I'm<) can ↑you >tell me if< the
flight from ibetha is it bee eye ay
four five one six i-(s) is arriving
on time,

Hesitation items can occur after response tokens, and prior to the start of the request formulation.

(9) [BA 5] T1:SA:1349 F:F

A: flight infor↑mation can I ↑help you[:,
C: [oh yes
please. >urm< I'm just phoning to inquire, ·h
flights to barcelona.=which terminal do they go
from?

(10) [BA 6] T1:SA:1973 F:M

A: flight infor↑mation may I ↓h:elp ↑you,
C: yes um: two eight two bee plea:se, (.)
um can you tell me if you've got a
confirmed arrival time for that,

Finally, hesitation items can occur in conjunction with short gaps; these pauses in the talk usually last between one tenth and three tenths of a second.

(11) [84] T4:SB:F:F

A: flight information may I help you:?
(.3)
C: hello? eh:m (.3) can you tell me: (.) what time
ehm (.2) eye ay (.2) two three seven, (.6) from
baghdad will land.

(12) [24] T1:SB:F:M

A: flight ↑information ↑may I help you:?
C: er::m (.) yes I'm actually trying to make an
inquiry about (.3) gibraltar airways. (.)
which I think you (.) handle as well

RESPONSE TOKENS AND HESITATION ITEMS IN THE WOZ CORPUS

The first point to make is that both types of turn components occur in the WOZ corpus. Extracts (13) and (14) provide examples of response tokens; extracts (15) and (16) illustrate hesitation items.

(13) WOZ 3:5:M

```
W:   flight (.2) information (.5) can (.) I help (.) you
S:   ·hh yes I'd like to know: when ·hh
     there are flights tomorrow morning
     from gatwick to barcelona
```

(14) WOZ 7:1:F

```
W:   flight (.) information (.4) may I help you
     (.6)
S:   ·hhh y::es I'm trying to get in touch with: (.)
     gibraltar airways? their number doesn't seem
     to be in the phone book. would you have
     their number?
```

(15) WOZ 5:8:F

```
W:   flight (.) information (.4) can (.) I (.)
     help (.2) you
     (.7)
S:   ·hhh uhm (.3) can you tell me what time (.)
     tomorrow's flight from warsaw arrives (.2) please
```

(16) [WOZ 10:7]

```
A:   british (.) airways (.2) flight (.) information
     (.4)  good (.2) afternoon
     (1.7)
C:   ·hhh er I'm flying to zu↑rich:. with br-
     british airways, ·hh is ↑that terminal four?
```

Table 5.1 Incidence of response tokens in the WOZ corpus

	Subjects										
Trial	1(f)	2(m)	3(m)	4(f)	5(f)	6(m)	7(f)	8(m)	9(f)	10(f)	
1	✗	✓	✓	✗	✗	✗	✓	✓	✓	✗	
2	✗	✓	✓	✓	✗	✗	✗	✓	✗	✗	
3	✓	✓	✓	✗	✗	✗	✓	✓	✗	✗	
4	✗	✓	✓	✗	✗	✗	✓	✓	✗	✗	
5	✗	✓	✓	✗	✗	✗	✓	✗	✗	–	
6	✓	✓	✓	✓	✗	✗	✓	✗	✗	✓	
7	✓	✓	✓	✗	✗	✗	✓	✓	✓	✗	
8	✗	✓	✓	✗	✗	✗	✓	✓	✗	✗	
9	✗	✓	✓	✗	✗	✗	✓	✓	✗	✗	
10	✓	–	✓	✗	✗	✗	✓	✓	✗	✗	
✓ =	4	9	10	2	0	0	9	8	2	1	**45**
✗ =	6	0	0	8	10	10	1	2	8	8	**53**

✓ = response token
✗ = no response token

We will begin by considering the incidence of response tokens. In the British Airways corpus, response items occurred in 87 calls out of the total of 100; in the simulation study, they occurred in 45 out of 98 completed calls.

These figures reveal some interesting differences. To explicate these, we will focus on the design of callers' turns after they have heard an introductory message that ends with the wizard offering overt offer 'can/may I help you'. The first point to make is that, in the simulation data, 46 per cent of the wizard's introductory remarks that end with overt offers receive the appropriate second pair part, such as an overt acceptance. (Examples of these are illustrated in extracts 13 and 14.) In most cases the overt acceptance appears as the first item in the subject's turn. In some cases, however, the acceptance was delayed by the inclusion of hesitation items.

(17) WOZ 2:1:M

W: flight information (.3) can (.) I (.) help (.)
you
(.7)
S: ·hh er yes ehm can you tell me (.) what time
er flight be ay two two seven ·h uh arrives
in atlanta please

'Deferred' acceptances of this kind account for 7 per cent of the total number. Table 5.2 indicates the incidence of appropriate second pair parts, and gives this number as a percentage of the total possible number of second pair parts. (In this table there is no separate provision for immediate and deferred second pair parts.)

Table 5.2 Incidence of second pair parts: explicit acceptances

Subject	*Second pair part*	*No second pair part*
1(f)	3 (43%)	4 (57%)
2(m)	8 (100%)	0 (0%)
3(m)	7 (67.5%)	1 (12.5%)
4(f)	0 (0%)	5 (100%)
5(f)	0 (0%)	6 (100%)
6(m)	0 (0%)	10 (100%)
7(f)	9 (90%)	1 (10%)
8(m)	6 (75%)	2 (25%)
9(f)	1 (12.5%)	7 (87.5%)
10(f)	1 (14 %)	6 (86%)
Totals	**35 (45.5%)**	**42 (54.5%)**

The incidence of explicit acceptances showed a distinct positive or negative skew in the trials of nine out of ten subjects: in these cases, subjects either produced response tokens in 80 per cent or more of the trials, or they did not produce response tokens in 80 per cent or more of the trials. In one case there is a 100 per cent incidence of second pair parts (subject 2), and in three cases there is a 100 per cent lack of overt acceptances (subjects 4, 5 and 6). Therefore, this table reveals that subjects tend either to produce second pair parts, or they do not. The only exception to this is subject 1: in the seven possible cases where a second pair part could be produced, this subject produces three appropriate seconds and produces no appropriate second in the remainder.

Table 5.2 also reveals a gender bias in the distribution of response tokens. There were five cases cases in which response tokens were not produced in 80 per cent or more of the trials; of these five subjects, four were female. And there were four cases in which response tokens were produced in 80 per cent or more of the trials; of these four subjects, three were male.

In the BA corpus, hesitation items appeared in 35 calls out of 100; in the 98 calls to the WOZ simulated system, they occurred in 35 calls.

Table 5.3 Incidence of hesitation items in the WOZ corpus

	Subjects										
Trial	1(f)	2(m)	3(m)	4(f)	5(f)	6(m)	7(f)	8(m)	9(f)	10(f)	
1	✗	✓	✗	✓	✓	✓	✗	✓	✓	✗	
2	✗	✓	✗	✓	✓	✓	✗	✓	✗	✗	
3	✗	✓	✓	✗	✗	✓	✗	✓	✗	✗	
4	✗	✓	✗	✗	✗	✗	✗	✓	✗	✗	
5	✗	✓	✗	✗	✗	✗	✗	✓	✗	–	
6	✗	✓	✓	✗	✗	✗	✗	✓	✗	✗	
7	✗	✓	✓	✗	✓	✗	✗	✗	✗	✓	
8	✗	✓	✗	✗	✓	✗	✗	✓	✗	✓	
9	✓	✓	✗	✗	✗	✗	✗	✓	✗	✗	
10	✗	–	✓	✗	✗	✗	✗	✓	✗	✓	
✓ =	1	9	4	2	4	3	0	9	1	3	**35**
✗ =	9	0	6	8	6	7	10	1	9	6	**63**

✓ = hesitation item
✗ = no hesitation item

There is also a slight gender bias in the distribution of hesitation items. There are just two subjects who exhibited hesitation items in 80 per cent or more of their trials, and both of these are male. There are four subjects who do not display hesitation items in 80 per cent or more of the trials, all of whom are female. If we widen the boundary mark to include subjects who did not use hesitation items in 60 per cent or more of their trials, this number increases to eight, six of whom are female.

REQUEST FORMULATIONS IN THE BA CORPUS

There are two types of request formulation: simple and non-simple. The ascription of the terms 'simple' or 'non-simple' is not premised on analytic observations, nor on vernacular or 'lay' categorisation: it does not, for example, refer to the apparent ease (or lack of it) with which the agent can attend to the request. It refers merely to systematic patterns in the ways the requests have been produced. Let us consider recurrent features of simple request formulations.

In the following exchanges the callers systematically formulate their requests to reveal the flight identification details and other flight parameters, such as the place of departure and time of expected arrival. For example:

```
(18) [40] T3:SA:F:F

1    A:   british airways flight information
2         can I help you
3         (.)
4    C:   hello can I check on british airways
5         six three one from athens please
6         (.3)
7    A:   yes I'll just check for you hold o:[n
8    C:                                      [thank you
```

```
(19) [4] T1:SA:F:F

1    A:   flight infor↑mation british ↑airways
          good ↑da:y
2    C:   yes hello erm: bee ay two nine two. h- >urh<
3         it >should've< been scheduled for seven fifteen.
4    A:   hold on a moment
5    C:   thank you
```

```
(20) [11] T1:SB:F:F

1    A:   flight information can I help you
2    C:   yes could you tell me the arrival ti-
3         the expected arrival time of british airways
4         two five eight from caracas please
5    A:   yes certainly can you hold the
6         line please
```

In all of these cases callers identify the flight in which they are interested by giving the code of the airline, 'bee ay' or 'british airways', and the flight number. This can be used in conjunction with other flight identification details. For example, in extract (18) the caller uses the flight's place of departure:

```
4    C:   hello can I check on british airways
5         six three one from athens please
```

Alternatively, in extract (19) the caller cites the arrival time of the flight:

```
2    C:   yes hello erm: bee ay two nine two. h- >urh<
3         it >should've< been scheduled for seven fifteen
```

In each case the one consistent feature of these ultimately successful calls is the use of the BA flight number.

It is also noticeable that in those calls where other flight parameters are used to identify the flight, the flight identification details are introduced first. So in extract (18) 'british airways six three one' comes before 'from athens please', and in (19) 'bee ay two nine two' comes before the caller states that 'it should've been scheduled for seven fifteen'. Similarly, in extract (20) the caller mentions 'british airways two five eight' before 'from caracas'. The fact that this ordering occurs so regularly suggests that this is recognised by callers as the most expedient way to proceed. Additionally, and related to the previous point, it may be that this is a 'conventional' way to formulate requests. (See also Richards and Underwood, 1984a; 1984b.)

The majority of the request formulations in the BA corpus are designed to indicate early in the production of the turn what kind of service the caller actually requires. So, for example in extract (20) above, the caller's request formulation indicates what he wants to know ('the arrival time') before stating the relevant details of the actual flight about which he is inquiring ('british airways two five eight from caracas'). There are cases, however, which deviate from this format and these we have termed non-simple request formulations. For example, in the following extract the caller provides the flight details before specifying what information he requires.

(21) [19] T1:SB:F:M

A: flight information may I help you
british airways here
(.3)
C: oh good morning ·h your bee ay two
three eight from orlando could you
tell me what time it landed
A: yes certainly can you hold the line a
moment

REQUEST FORMULATIONS IN THE WOZ CORPUS

Simple and non-simple formulating requests identified in the discussion of the BA data account for 95 per cent of the request formulations in the WOZ corpus. First, simple formulations:

(22) WOZ 3:2:M

A: flight (.) information (.4) good (.) morning
(.7) british (.) airways (.4) can (.) I
help (.) you
(.3)
C: yes I'd like to know when flight two five eight
from carcas (·hh) caracas comes in

(23) WOZ 5:2:F

A: good (.) morning (.4) british (.)
airways (.) flight (.) information
(1)
C: ·hhh em (.) can you tell me what time the
bee (.) ay nine (.) oh (.) three from
frankfurt arrives at heathrow airport please

In the following non-simple case the subject provides some relevant information prior to specifying her request.

(24) WOZ 10:10:F

A: flight information
(3.5)
C: er:m (.3) I'd like some information
on flight number bee ay two nine six (.3)
er it departs from chica:go and ('t)
arrive in london today
·h er:m I would like
to know the exact arrival time please

SEQUENTIAL CONSIDERATIONS

Our observations so far have indicated that before callers begin to formulate their actual requests for information, their turns exhibit periods of minor dysfluency; this manifests not only in the occurrence of hesitation items, but also in the frequent misalignment between response tokens and the appropriate first pair parts in the agent's prior turn. To explain this it is necessary to examine some of the organisational principles which inform the openings to telephone calls generally. To do so we need to refer in detail to Schegloff's (1968) study. We will then describe how these principles underpin the sequences of events that we have observed in the openings to calls to the British Airways flight information service.

From his study of the beginnings to over 500 telephone conversations, Schegloff initially formulated a 'distribution rule' which stated that the called party spoke first. This rule seemed to explain all his data except for one example in which, after the phone had been answered and the called party had not said anything, the caller spoke first. To account for this 'discrepancy' Schegloff rejected the notion of a distribution rule and formulated an alternative explanation which accounted for all the data. The latter analysis was informed by the properties of adjacency pairs, and by the properties of summons–answer pairs in particular.

Schegloff argued that the ringing of the telephone acts as the first part of a summons–answer adjacency pair. It constitutes the caller's first (albeit non-vocal) contribution to the conversation. As such, it establishes certain obligations upon the summoned party; for example, that they should answer the summons. (This accounts for the one deviant case in Schegloff's data corpus in which the caller spoke first. The call had been received, in that someone had picked up the telephone and the line was clearly open. The caller's subsequent turn was thus an attempt to solicit the normatively prescribed 'answer' that the called party should have produced as a second pair part to the summons initiated by the ringing of the telephone.)

Summons–answer sequences have three main properties. First, they are non-terminal exchanges; that is, no single summons–answer sequence by itself constitutes a complete conversation. Second, answers to summonses 'borrow' some of the properties of questions (Schegloff, 1972: 375). That is, a summons will often be met with a response such as 'what?' or 'yes?'. This feature of answers to summonses is quite explicit in the British Airways agent's utterances which contain a 'can/may I help you?' component. Although this 'offering' character of the agents' utterance is less easy to discern in the simple self-identifications 'flight information', or 'British Airways flight information good morning', it is reasonable to argue that it is there nonetheless. That is, this is what the agent is there to do as an occupation – to provide information. The offer to provide such information is therefore implicit in the fact of them being there to answer the telephone call in the first place.

Third, and most crucially, answers to summonses project further turns. So, the 'yes?' or 'what do you want?' character of such answers establishes that in the immediately next turn the summoner can raise the reason for the summons. That is, insofar as the agents' utterances 'borrow' the properties of questions, these are not only the second parts of summons–answer adjacency pairs, but also the first parts of question–answer pairs.

These properties inform the opening exchanges of calls to the British Airways flight information system in the following way. First, the occurrence of a summons to the agent makes an answer the appropriate next turn.[3] The answer completes the first summons–answer sequence in this exchange. This is not a terminal sequence, however: the execution of the summons–answer sequence makes provision for the caller to speak. (In an interaction not conducted on the telephone, where the summons was accomplished through some vocalised item, there would be provision for the caller to speak again, but as the first summons was done through the telephone, the caller's next 'turn' will in fact be the first spoken turn in the exchange.) This is reinforced by virtue of the construction of the answer component of the sequence: the second section of the answer is also a question, and thereby establishes the relevance of a question and answer adjacency pair. This also projects a relevant next which is also another turn by the caller. And, given that the business at hand is to obtain flight information, then the appropriate next turn would be a request for flight information.

However, the second part of the agent's identification utterance – the answer to the summons – can itself constitute the first part of a greeting–greeting pair, the first part of a question–answer pair, and the first part of an offer–acceptance/refusal pair. There is, therefore, a sequential ambiguity constituted by the dual character of the agent's first turn in the exchange, in that it not only projects a place in which the caller can immediately raise the reason for the call, but also projects the relevance of one or more appropriate second pair parts. The agent's turn thus constitutes both the go-ahead for the caller to turn to the business at hand and also the grounds for deferring that move. And it is this sequential ambiguity which may underpin the minor dysfluencies manifested in the occurrence of misaligned response tokens and hesitation items. So, for example, hesitation items placed prior to the response tokens may be indicative of the caller's procedural dilemma.

Extracts (25) and (26) illustrate the momentary indecisiveness marked by hesitation items.

```
(25) [89] T4:SB:F:M

A:   flight information may I ↑help you:?
     (.3)
C:   e(h)r: morning (.) c-could you tell me >the-<
     if ehm (.3) aerofl(oat) (.4) flight
     has come.
```

```
(26) [85] T4:SB:F:F

A:   flight information may I help you:,
C:   °*er:m° good morning I just wanted to kno:w
     is the inward flight ee kay (.5) f(uh)
     fifteen I think on time (.) to dubai? (.5) this
     afternoon at two o'clock?
```

However, hesitation items which appear after response tokens, and prior to the formulation of specific requests, exhibit the caller's sensitivity to a marginally different procedural issue: they mark an orientation to 'addressing the business at hand' – namely, asking for flight information.

```
(27) [83] T4:SB:F:F

A:   flight information may I ↑help you:?
C:   yes:, ehm ↑I'd like to make an enquiry
     about a pan am ↓fli:ght.
```

```
(28) [12] T1:SB:F:F

A:   flight information british airways good
     ↓day can I help y[ou.
C:                    [good morning to you er:::
```

I have a flight booked by bee ay london
heathrow airport next friday

In the following cases there is some confusion at the start of the call, and in each case the agent makes an attempt to establish that the line is open and that there is someone at the end of it. The caller's subsequent confirmation that they are there displays their understanding that the agent's prior turn was designed to test the line. However, having participated in securing confirmation that the line is open, the callers furnish hesitation items prior to formulating a request. It is in these circumstances that the character of these items as orienting to 'proceeding to business at hand' is particularly evident.

(29) [46] T3:SA:F:M

A: british airways ↑flight information?
can I help you?
(1.3)
A: hel↑lo:
C: >hello?<
A: can I help you at al[l sir?
C: [oh yes (.) erm: I've (got
a note) here to sort of find out about ehm:
(1)
a flight from gatwick (.) (ker) to
los angeles eleven o'clock tomorrow
morning bee ay two eight fi:ve

(30) [93] T4:SB:F:F

A: flight information may I help you:, hhh
(.8)
A: (e)<u>lloo</u>: hh
( ) (4.5)
A: (e)L:ow::?
C: hello,
A: can I help you,
C: ye:ah °um° can you tell me the flight uhm
one two nine from i<u>n:</u>dia (.5)

So far we have observed some features of the sequential organisation which underpins the openings to calls to the BA service and in the subjects' trials in the WOZ experiment. In the next two sections we will focus more on the ways in which callers to the BA service actually design their request formulations. In these formulations callers obviously specify the information they require. But in addition to that we want to demonstrate that request formulations can be built to address other kinds of pragmatic or interactional work. Subsequently, we will examine a strategy of request formulation through which callers obliquely address the possibility that part of their request may be in some way inappropriate given the service they are contacting. For example, calling a British Airways information service about flights operated by a competitor airline is inappropriate because the BA agent might not have access to that information, and because there is an impropriety (almost cheekiness) about asking one airline to provide details of a competitor's services.[4] But first we will describe how callers can design their request formulations to display their sensitivity to the normative convention that in calls to an information service, request formulations *should* be produced in the caller's first turn in the exchange.

REQUEST FORMULATIONS ARE NORMATIVELY PRESCRIBED

We have noted that the BA agent's first turn projects a slot in which it is not only appropriate for the caller to request flight information, but in which such a turn is made conditionally relevant. This observation can inform our understanding of those cases in which callers use their first proper turns in the exchange to do something other than formulate a request. In the following extract the caller's first turn does not provide a request for information, nor a recognisable prelude to a request.

```
(31) [8] T1:SB:F:M

A:   fligh[t information can I help you]
C:        [(                           )] just
     gettin through tuh (.) airport
     (.)
C:   >ello,<
A:   good day british
     ↓airways ↑[flight information=
C:             [(>yeh-<)
A:   =can I ↑help you
C:   are you a real person yeh(t)
A:   YEs: ↑hello th[ere
C:                 [(ah)hhhh good (.3) er: the bee
     ay five eight four from turin. love
```

In the initial stages of this call the caller overlaps with the agent's identification and offer of a service. This overlap may not actually result from the caller talking to the agent while she is talking to him; the caller's 'just getting through to (.) airport' (lines 2 and 3) suggests that he is talking to someone with him at the time. This is further corroborated by his 'hello' which acts to test if the line of communication is open. After this the agent provides another identification (although, interestingly, a longer version than the one she originally produced.) Having 'restarted' the conversation in this way, it might be expected that the caller would move to a request for information; however, this does not occur. Instead he produces yet another question. This is designed, we suspect half-jokingly, to assess whether he has got through to a real human agent or has been diverted again to the recorded message occasionally used by British Airways. Thus, in a slot in which a request formulation is conditionally relevant, the caller produces a question addressing a different issue.

In the introduction to some of the methodological principles that inform conversation analysis, we examined this data extract to show how the question 'are you a real person' was the beginning of a question–answer sequence inserted within the overarching offer–acceptance/refusal adjacency pair. Insertion sequences can be heard, and are conventionally treated as, dealing with business that is in some way preliminary to the business addressed in the turns in which the insertion sequence is nested. And so here, the caller's attempt to clarify that he is talking to a human is clearly designed to discover whether or not there is any point in producing a request formulation: recorded messages simply provide information that the lines to the human operators are all occupied. In this sense, however, not only does the question 'are you a human' attain the character of a turn-which-is-preliminary-to-some-overriding-business, but can also be hearable as an account for the absence of a conditionally relevant request formulation. The underlying organisation of this sequence ensures that the question 'are you human?' is hearable not only as 'working up to' other business, but displays why that other business has been (momentarily) deferred.

A similar accounting procedure occurs in the following data. Here the slot in which the caller could legitimately move to a formulation of a question is used to secure confirmation that the call has got through to the appropriate airport. Thus, it establishes that the request would be an appropriate one to make, thereby providing a warrant for its production.

(32) [98]:T4:SB:F:F

A: flight information may I help you
C: is that heathrow
A: ·hh this- this is heathrow ye:[s:
C: [yes I'm
enquiring about olympic airways fli:ght
two six oh:

The following extract provides an interesting variation on this theme.

(33) [29] T2:SA:F:F

A: flight information good afternoon
(.)
C: oh hello (.) erm I've been asked to
erm (.3) warn someone and I'm not

```
         quite sure where to start but three
         passengers on a british airways flight
         to er (.) new york will be cutting it a
         little bit fine this evening uhm but they
         should be there within sort of (1) couple of
         minutes of uhr:m (.7) check in time
         (.)
    A:   [(          )
    C:   [so who do I speak to about that
```

In the first turn here the caller does not ask a question, but is attempting to find out from the agent the appropriate airline representative to whom she should relay the information that some passengers will be late arriving for the flight check-in time. There are two interesting observations about the way in which the caller designs her initial utterance 'I've been asked to erm (.) warn someone' (lines 3 and 4).

First, the caller prefaces this description with the phrase 'I've been asked . . .', which portrays her forthcoming utterances as having been occasioned by someone else's request, thereby providing the basis for the inference that these are remarks that would not be made as a matter of routine. Second, the urgency of her message is embellished by the use of the word 'warn', thus characterising this information as being more important than, for example, mere informing. Embroidering the purpose of the call in this way provides the warrant for providing this information in this turn instead of formulating a request, and, at the same time, accounts for the absence of a request for flight information.

In each case, then, where the caller has not produced a request for information, or an utterance which could be taken as a request for information, the utterance which is produced stands as an account for that absence. This suggests that there may be a mild normative constraint informing the production of request formulations, or utterances which could be seen as such, in this turn in the exchange. It is not merely the case that callers' first turns are places in which appropriate questions can be asked, but they are slots in which appropriate questions should be asked.

PROBLEM WORK DONE THROUGH REQUEST FORMULATIONS

There are many calls to the British Airways flight information service in which it turns out that the agent is not able to deal with the caller's request. This is primarily due to the caller asking for something which is not within the brief of the BA agent: for example, callers may ask about flight reservations, or they may request information about a specific flight which is not operated by British Airways (see Table 3.1). For information such as this, the callers have to ring another service number. We will refer to calls such as these as problematic calls. We want to show that callers can orient to the possibility that their request may be problematic, and can formulate their requests in the light of this possibility. That is, we want to show that the status of a call as problematic does not merely revolve around the agent's identification of the call as being problematic, but that it is a concern which may influence the way that callers ask for information in their very first turn in the exchange with the agent.

Request formulations may be designed in such a way that callers do not produce all the relevant aspects of the flight about which they are inquiring: that is, they do not produce the triple 'airline-flight number-date' sequence in its entirety. Instead, only a select few of the flight details are produced. In the following call, for example, the caller produces an initial request which includes only one aspect of the relevant information about the particular flight.

(34) [42] T3:SA:F:F

```
A:   british airways flight information
     can I help yo[u:
C:                [yes ur:m: (.) flight, (.3)
     from geneva to gatwick,
     (.5)
A:   geneva to gatwick do you have a flight
     number ma[dam
C:            [yes seven five nine >no ah(m) so-
     (.) seven (.) three (.) seven
A:   seven three seven just a moment please
     I'll check for you
```

A first observation is that the caller does not cite the flight number or any airline identification details. Instead, she asks merely about a flight between two destinations. However, there is evidence to suggest that the caller's request is initially designed to make use of the flight details: after the turn initial items she begins 'flight' and then pauses. Had she decided at the outset to ask about a flight between Geneva and Gatwick the syntactically appropriate construction would be *a* flight. Similarly, the pause after 'flight' suggests that what comes after is not a designed extension of the utterance beginning 'flight', but a change of direction in the way the request was being constructed. Thus, we have an *in situ* instance of the caller vacillating between options available to her by which to design her request.

Second, in her subsequent turn (line 8) it transpires that the caller does have the flight details omitted in the request formulation: she is able to produce these after the agent's request for them. One simple explanation for the absence of these details in the initial formulation is that the caller had forgotten them. The fact that the caller can produce them upon request, however, implies that the caller knew them all along and had not suddenly remembered them at that stage in the exchange. Furthermore, the caller's turn produces an example of a terminal onset (Jefferson, 1983) in which the beginning of the next turn collides with the anticipated terminal sound of the prior's utterance. Whatever else it may be doing, the agent's request about whether or not the caller has the remaining flight details minimally proposes the possibility that she may not. Hitching on to the last sound of the agent's request in this manner displays not only that she recognises what the agent is asking of her, but also that the doubt which informs that request is misplaced. The overlapping utterance in which the caller provides the remaining details proposes that she had not forgotten them, but that she just wasn't using them in her initial formulation. This implies that these were being withheld. There is a sense, then, in which the provision of these remaining flight details is in some part conditional upon the agent's response to the information the caller *had* provided.

The third aspect of the caller's request is the slight upward or 'continuing' intonation at the end of 'flight' as marked by the comma. This mild intonation shift gives the utterance 'geneva to gatwick' an 'inquisitive' character, as opposed to a fully developed question.

To summarise: the caller uses only a small amount of the relevant information to which she has access; she appears to display some hesitancy in the initial construction of her turn in that she embarks on a syntactically different utterance from the one she eventually completes; and the entire utterance is marked by a mildly questioning intonation. Why should the caller produce this type of utterance in this way?

Note that the caller does not describe the flight simply as coming from Geneva; nor is it reported as coming 'to London', or 'to England', or 'to the UK', or however else the destination may be described. Rather, the caller's request focuses precisely on 'flight (.3) from geneva to *gatwick*'. However, the service the caller is using is based at Heathrow airport, not Gatwick airport. This could be the basis of concern for the caller: that she is not ringing the right place to find information about flights arriving at Gatwick. The caller may anticipate that the agent can not deal with her request because the location of the service and the destination of the flight are not the same. Thus, presenting only this information could be a way of 'flagging' an aspect of her inquiry which the agent may not be able to deal with.

Clearly, this is a speculative account; however, the agent's next turn provides a 'proof procedure' by which this analysis can be assessed (Sacks, Schegloff and Jefferson, 1974: 729). And the design of the agent's next turn does indeed suggest that she has recognised that the caller's formulation was designed to premonitor a possible problem.

```
A:   geneva to gatwick do you have a flight
     number ma[dam
C:            [yes seven five nine >no ah(m) so-
     (.) seven (.) three (.) seven
```

So, the agent provides a confirmatory echo of this information and begins a request for the details by which she can further identify the flight, thereby confirming that the details so far presented pose no difficulty for her. At this point the caller overlaps (almost enthusiastically) to deliver the necessary flight details.

In the following two cases there is further evidence that callers may be using their first turn proper in the exchange as a slot in which to premonitor anticipated trouble.

(35) [20] T1:SB:F:M

A: flight information can I help you
C: yes (>wond 'f you could<) >could you tell
me the: (.3) expected arrival time of
a flight from barcelona.
(.8)
C: flight bee ay:
oh four eight one
(.)
A: oh four eight one
C: yeah
(.7)
A: hold on
C: thank you

In (30) the first part of the caller's request reveals that the flight in which he is interested comes from Barcelona. The essential flight information details are delayed until after the gap of nearly one second. Thus, unlike standard requests, the flight identification details are not produced as the first items of information to allow the agent to deal with the request. Indeed, the information 'a flight from barcelona' does not provide the agent with sufficient information to begin to find the arrival time. It is only after the gap that he goes on to produce the relevant details (indicating that these were being withheld at the time that he described the flight in terms of the place of departure).

The silence in line 5 is treated by the agent as the caller's silence: that is, the agent does not say anything. Nor does she produce any sounds of hesitation, which would display that she recognises that she should say something, but that she doesn't quite know what. Her silence displays a state of 'passive recipiency' (Jefferson, 1984). Clearly, there would be no point in waiting for the caller to produce other information if there was a problem with the details he had already offered. The absence of any talk by the agent therefore displays to the caller that she has nothing to say, and indicates she is still waiting for him to say something else. Thus, the caller can analyse the agent's silence as furnishing an oblique indication that the information already provided does not provide a problem for the agent. It is after this that he provides the rest of the flight identification details.

In the next extract we can see an interesting variation of the use of the modified request format. As in the previous two cases, the information presented early in the request is not a problem for the agent. However, information which is produced after the agent's confirmation of the first item does turn out to be problematic.

(36) [2] T1:SA:F:F

```
A:   ·hh flight information can I ↑help you:.=
C:   =oh good ↓morni:ng ·hh >ah wond'd?< I'm
     jus:t checking on a pla:ne that's due in
     tomorro:w [·h
A:             [y(h)es[:
C:                    [from wa:r:sa:w=
A:   =↑Yes:=
C:   =at half past ni:ne. on: (.) terminal ↓two
     I think. (.3) °I'm jus' checking.°
     (1.3)
A:   ·h >Well< that sou:nds li:ke (th't) you're talking
     about polish air↓li[:n es]: .
C:                      [>yes<]
     (.)
A:   ah (w'll) >yu've<=↑actually wro(t)-
     rung the wrong ↑number-in future you need
     tuh dial seven five ni:ne? (.7) one ↑eight (.5)
     one ei:ght.
```

The potentially problematic issue here is that the flight being inquired about arrives the day after the call. The enthusiastic response from the agent indicates that this is clearly no problem. Equally, the fact that the flight is coming from Warsaw also receives a clear display that this does not present any problem. It is only when the caller announces that the flight is arriving at Terminal Two that the agent becomes aware that the flight is run by Polish Airlines. (British Airways do have regular flights from Warsaw; however, only Polish Airlines flights arrive at Terminal Two. It is this information, then, which indicates that the flight is not within the agent's brief.)

In most calls the callers present the most relevant details of the flight right at the start of the request, and these tend to occur in a routinised order. In these somewhat modified formulations, callers do not use the most salient flight identification details. Moreover, by virtue of the fact that these details are delivered without any problem later in the call it would appear that the callers do not present these details, and thereby identify the flight for the agent, at the *first* opportunity in the call to do so. Instead, they are withheld. The organisation of these requests focuses instead on those aspects of the flight which could be problematic for the agent: that is, they may be features of the flight which mean that it is outside the brief of the agent, given the institutional and organisational constraints under which the agents are working. The way that agents treat this organisation suggests that they interpret these request formulations as having been designed to flag potentially problematic facets of the particular flight, and they subsequently produce turns which either confirm that the details flagged in the prior turn are not problematic, or they provide tokens of encouragement/anticipation. The agents *themselves* treat this type of request organisation as one that allows the caller to draw attention to a possible problem.

Finally in this section, we can make some comparative remarks about data from the WOZ simulation, particularly those trials in which the subjects used the following scenario to formulate their request.

Scenario 22

> You've got to meet your great uncle who is flying in on Hungarian Airlines' 6.10 flight. Nobody seems to be answering the phones at Hungarian Airlines. In desperation you call the world's favourite airline, British Airways. After all, your girlfriend/boyfriend works for them. But will they tell you about another airline? You're not optimistic . . .

This scenario was worded so that the subjects were led to believe that the information they required could not be provided by the simulated 'system'. The last sentence, especially, hints strongly that there might be a slight impropriety about asking the information service associated with one airline about the details of flights carried by a competitor. Recall that it was precisely this kind of impropriety which seemed to underscore the way in which callers to the British Airways service designed their initial request formulations to 'flag' those features of the request which may be outside the scope of the agents' brief. But, given that they seemed to believe that they were talking to a computerised representative of the BA service, would subjects in the WOZ experiment address this impropriety? And if so, would this pragmatic work be done in their first turns in the exchange?

There is evidence that the subject's request formulations did indeed reflect their sensitivity to the slight delicacy of asking a system designed to provide information about British Airways flights about Hungarian Airline. This is most starkly illustrated in the following extract in which the subject's request has an almost apologetic tone in that he explicitly raises the fact that he is not calling about British Airways flights.

```
(37) WOZ 6:1:M

A:   flight information good day can I help you
     (1.5)
C:   erm (.3) I'm ringing (.) not about british
     airways I'm afraid I'm trying to get (.5) some
```

```
            information about hungarian airlines
            (4.5)
      A:    please wait
```

When he actually produces a request the subject does not make use of all the flight details he has; like the cases from the BA corpus, the substantive request focuses on only that part of the information which, according to the scenario, might be potentially problematic.

Scenario 22 was used four times in the WOZ study. In all of the subsequent trials, the subjects' request formulations oriented to the sensitive issue of asking British Airways about a Hungarian Airlines flight. In the next case, for example, the subject's request formulation has two interesting design features. For example, it is produced to assess whether in fact he can obtain information about Hungarian Airlines from this source. His sensitivity to the delicate nature of this request is exhibited in the way in which he recycles the information from the scenario that Hungarian Airlines' telephone number is not being answered. And in this sense the request formulation also provides an *account* as to why this information is being requested from what might turn out to be an inappropriate source.

(38) WOZ 8:3:M (Simplified transcription)

```
      W:    flight information good day
            can I help yo[u
      S:                 [(mm)
            (1)
      S:    er yes I'm ringing about h urh a flight
            from hungarian airlines (.5) but no one seems
            to be answering the ↑phone (bu-) at
            hungarian airlines (.3) can you help me?
```

'DOING' NON-PROBLEMATIC REQUESTS

There is a temptation to view the organisation of request formulations as being determined simply by the demands of the service. So, in requests to a flight information service, it seems reasonable to assume that callers identify the flight in which they are interested because they realise that the agent has to know these things before the request can be dealt with. Clearly it is the case that agents of a service do need to know certain items of information to be able to address the topic of the request. The examination of these data, however, has suggested that request formulations can display features which are not solely answerable to the demands of the service, but which seem to display the caller's orientation to the broader organisation of talk-in-interaction. We have seen how routine features of requests may be exploited by callers to address specifically interactional tasks; for example, designing request formulations to expose a potential source of trouble at the earliest possible place in the exchange, and thereby inviting the agent to acknowledge and deal with it.

In this final section we will pursue this theme further by examining one extract in detail. The relevant exchange comes from extract (34).

(39) [60] T3:SB:F:M

A:	flight inform↑ation can I ↑help y↑ou
C:	oh yeah can you tell me i(f) you got
	any:er: (.) space left on kay tee five nine
	five (.) to malaga on sun↓day.
A:	I ca:n't I'm afraid. you would have to
	go to a local travel agent to actually book
	a s:ea:t
	(.)
C:	they don't (.) really want to ↑know ↓any ↑more
	(.)
	(ch)huhH hahh they said it was too late in the
	day to (.3) check
	(.9)
A:	i-(y)- SOrry you've ↑chAi:n(d) you want to
	change your reser↑va↓tion

Ostensibly, the caller makes a request about seat availability on a specific flight. However, the agent advises him that seat *booking* has to be obtained through a travel agent. The caller's response to this information is interesting in that it reveals that he has already done this. While there is considerable inferential work done in this description, two points are relevant for discussion. First, it reveals that the caller initially had the presence of mind to contact a travel agent with a view to securing a booking, thereby undermining the implication, available from the agent's suggestion, that he may not have realised the appropriate procedure for booking seats on aeroplanes. Second, he provides two separate descriptions of the travel agents' failure to provide him with that service. The first, 'they don't (.) really want to know any more' characterises the travel agents as, at best, uninterested in his request, at worse, positively dismissive. The second, 'they said it was too late in the day to (.3) check' portrays the travel agents as having an excuse for their unwillingness to assist. In this, it downplays the sense of grievance registered by the prior characterisations.

These two descriptions are produced after the BA agent has advised him where to go to book a seat. However, this was not the service he asked for: his initial request was about space on a particular flight. The agent has therefore inferred from his request what he really wanted. In this, then, there is a sense of having been 'caught out': his request for space was seen to be a veiled inquiry about, or pre-request to, a request about booking. The caller's extreme characterisations of the travel agents' unhelpfulness provides the inference that he had no one else to turn to, and thereby portrays the impropriety of his request to the flight information service as 'a last resort'.

Callers' requests can be designed to focus on that aspect of their request which might be problematic. One feature of such formulations was that the problematic details were raised at the first opportunity in the request. This contrasted with routine formulations in which the flight details were invariably produced early in the turn. In extract 39, we have a case of a request formulation with the flight details included; in this, it is built like the types of requests which routinely turn out to be unproblematic. The caller does not design the utterance to reveal any potential problems. However, after being told that he should go to a travel agent to book a seat, he reveals that he has already done this; in which case it is clear that he did not assume that the first place to go to was the flight information service. Thus, although he may not have known for certain that the BA flight information service could not assist him on bookings, the fact that his first choice was a travel agent indicates that he may have suspected that flight information was not the appropriate service for this request.

It has been suggested that callers may design their request formulations to display potential problems. Given this, perhaps the most interesting aspect of this extract is that the caller formulates his request in a way which suggests he is innocent of any possible trouble, despite the fact that his subsequent revelations about his experience with the travel agents provide strong grounds to assume that he may have been aware that he was not asking the right people about booking seats. This implies that request formulations may be designed not simply to elicit information, but to portray the request as a certain type of request; for example, as one which the caller thinks will be unproblematic, and which is therefore appropriate for the service being contacted.

Many of the phenomena examined in this chapter, for example, the use of response tokens and hesitation items, would appear, on first inspection, to be largely trivial aspects of conversation which therefore merit little direct study. Detailed examination of these utterances, however, suggests that these phenomena may indeed have an orderliness which may not be immediately available from a cursory inspection of occasions of their occurrence. These analytic observations are relevant to, and provide an empirical illustration for, some of the points we made in Chapter 2. For example, we noted that system designers have occasionally relied on their own intuitions about human verbal behaviour to anticipate the ways in which people will behave with interactive computer systems. But the empirical points we have made in this chapter furnish a strong argument that the level of detail and order at which language is used by people can best be revealed through systematic inspection of the specific particulars of naturally occurring activities. Equally, the researcher should eschew making pre-analytic decisions concerning the relative significance of specific phenomena. Prior to any empirical investigation it is difficult to assess the interactional or inferential significance of any particular verbal behaviour.

Many of these phenomena have the sense of being 'conventional' practices; that is, things that people do out of custom and habit, rather than being motivated by 'live' interactional concerns which are relevant on a turn-by-turn basis. While this may be true, in no way does it render them insignificant, either for sociological attention, or indeed for those who wish to develop computer technology to understand and produce speech. It may be more useful to view events such as the ones examined here as representing the sedimentation of interactional practices into culturally prescribed forms of behaviour. As such, their contemporary significance is in the way they institutionalise, and give shape to, those everyday practical communicative competences and interactional concerns which computer technology is being employed to model.

6

TURN-TAKING, OVERLAPS AND CLOSINGS

In this chapter we are concerned with three fundamental features of conversational organisation: turn-taking, overlapping talk and the methods by which telephone dialogues can be concluded. An understanding of these conversational phenomena is clearly relevant to designers of interactive systems: for example, it is of paramount importance to produce a system that can recognise the end of a user's turn; and it is equally crucial to have an understanding of the kinds of circumstances in which human users might talk in overlap with any future system. We will deal with each of these conversational phenomena in the following sections, comparing examples from the BA and WOZ corpora.

But are we wasting our time attending in detail to these conversational phenomena? Intuitively, it may seem that it is relatively simple to formulate a 'common sense' explanation for all three features. So, with regard to turn-taking, it may be claimed that the procedure is achieved simply by one person deciding to stop talking and another person deciding to start. It seems plausible also to consider spates of overlapping talk as minor conversational errors, or as a collision of two parties' talk resulting from one person's attempt to interrupt the talk of another. And ending a conversation seems to be the consequence of people finishing what they have to say, and then saying 'goodbye' to each other.

The secondary aim of this chapter, then, is to address these objections, and to demonstrate that these properties of verbal interaction are not mere happenstance, or the manifestation of dysfluencies in speech, but are the consequence of delicate interpretative work by participants in dialogue; and that through this work, specific interactional projects are pursued and accomplished. We will address these issues by drawing on studies of each phenomenon in ordinary conversational materials.

THE TURN-TAKING SYSTEM FOR CONVERSATION

In this section we introduce the turn-taking system for conversation identified and examined by Sacks, Schegloff and Jefferson in their seminal (1974) paper. We then examine British Airways and Wizard of Oz simulation data to see whether this system has any relevance for our understanding of the exchanges in these corpora.

Sacks and his colleagues began their study of turn-taking to try to explicate the kind of systematic procedures that participants were using to conduct conversational exchanges. They stipulated that any adequate analysis had to be able to account for some 'grossly apparent' empirical facts about conversation. For example:

1 one speaker speaks at a time;
2 speakership changes;
3 the right or obligation to speak is not decided prior to the start of the conversation;
4 more than one speaker can speak at once, but such occasions are brief;
5 speakership change is accomplished with the minimum amount of overlap or gap;
6 the number of turns a speaker will have in a conversation are not fixed at the start of that conversation;
7 the length of a speaker's turn is not fixed at the start of the turn, which suggests that there must be some way of displaying that a turn is ending or, alternatively, continuing.

Sacks *et al.* observed that these features of conversational exchanges are independent of circumstance or context. That is, the import of these aspects of talk is not dependent upon, for example, the relative statuses or social roles of the participants, the topic(s) of the conversation, the physical location of the participants at the time of the exchange, when the exchange occurred, why it occurred, and so on. They argued that any adequate analysis had to describe a system for turn-taking, the legitimacy of which did not rely on, or require reference to, any particulars of the context or setting in which a specific exchange occurred.

The system identified by Sacks *et al.* has two components: a turn construction unit and a set of procedures for turn allocation.

Turns at talk are built out of turn construction units: these are syntactically bounded lexical, clausal, phrasal or sentential units. They are, loosely, the building blocks from which turns are constructed. A property of any turn construction unit is that, at its completion, another speaker may start up. So, at the end of each turn construction unit there occurs a transition relevance place.

The procedures for turn allocation are described in the original Sacks, Schegloff and Jefferson paper as a series of *rules*. Before we describe this component, it is necessary to digress to discuss what they meant by the word 'rule'.

In retrospect, describing the turn allocation procedures in terms of 'rules' has led to some misunderstanding and misinterpretation. Many seem to have taken Sacks *et al.* to be pointing to a set of prefixed and determinant causal conditions which propel speakership change. Certainly, this interpretation has proved enticing, especially to system designers who see Sacks *et al.*'s analysis as providing a handy set of guidelines for the design of interactive speech-based computer systems (see, for example, Finkelstein and Fuks, 1990). However, there are good reasons to be cautious when addressing turn allocation 'rules'.

First, it is clear that Sacks himself used the word 'rule' very loosely. In one of his lectures he made the following methodological point:

> The idea is to take singular sequences of conversation and tear them apart in such a way as to find rules, techniques, procedures, methods, maxims (a collection of terms that more or less relate to each other and that I use somewhat interchangeably) that can be used to generate the orderly features we find in the conversations we examine.
>
> (Sacks, 1984: 413)

Consequently, it may be appropriate to replace the notion of 'rule' with another term, such as 'practice' or 'usage'.

There is, however, another more important point, and it is this: in ordinary conversation, when people effect speaker transfer, that transfer is not causally determined by the application of a set of instructions which somehow govern that behaviour. Rather, speaker transfer is an accomplishment achieved as a consequence of mutually coordinated speaker sensitivity to, or *orientation to*, those procedures or conventions for effecting such change. So, any actual verbal exchange is *interactionally* managed. Furthermore, the procedures for managing turn-taking in any interaction are employed as *resources* for the management of that interaction. Although these points are central to the conversation analytic enterprise, we cannot discuss them in sufficient detail here (see Button's 1990 paper for a more comprehensive discussion[1]), although we hope to illustrate these points as we consider empirical materials in this and the other two sections of this chapter. However, in the light of these issues, and to ensure no further misunderstanding of the argument contained in Sacks *et al.*'s original paper, we will refer to the turn allocation system as a series of options, rather than rules.

The turn allocation procedures for conversation are distributed into two groups: those in which the current speaker selects the next speaker, and those in which the next speaker is self-selected. So, at any turn transition place, the following options are relevant.

1 If the current speaker is producing a turn which is clearly using the option 'current speaker selects next', then, at the appropriate turn transition place, the person so selected has the right to speak, and is obliged to speak. No others have the right or obligation to start speaking.

2 If the current turn is produced so as not to involve a 'current speaker selects next' option, then self-selection may proceed at the first turn transition place. However, although self-selection *may* proceed in such cases, it is not the case that it *has* to.
3 If the turn in production does not display a 'current speaker selects next' technique, then the current speaker may continue unless another party self-selects at a turn transition place.
4 If, at the initial turn transition place, one of the first two options has not been taken up, and the third option has been taken up ('current speaker continues') then this series of options again becomes relevant at the next turn transition place.

This series of options meets the criterion, established by Sacks *et al.* at the outset of their research, that the turn-taking system should be context independent. However, this system is also context sensitive, in that any actual instantiation of these options will be locally managed: that is, on a turn-by-turn basis. This is because these turn-taking options become relevant at the completion of each and every turn construction unit.

The system identified by Sacks *et al.* provides an account for the 'grossly apparent facts' of conversational organisation we listed earlier. For example, let us consider the following three features of conversation. It was noted that it is routinely the case that one party speaks at a time; furthermore, that although there are gaps in the conversation during occasions of speaker transfer, these are very rare; and finally, that although there are instances of more than one party speaking at the same time, these spates of overlapping talk are very brief.

We observed that one option to effect turn transfer is for the current speaker to select the next speaker. Consequently, co-participants have at least one motivating reason for not speaking while someone else is speaking: and that is to monitor the turn in progress to see if they will be selected by the current speaker as the next speaker. In those cases in which the turn in progress has not selected a next speaker, then turn transfer may commence at the first available turn transition place. Potential next speakers must therefore monitor the turn in progress to locate the end of the turn construction unit. Thus there are two respects in which the system provides an account for the observation that only one party tends to speak at any time.

There are several ways in which the system ensures that gaps between turns are minimised. If a current speaker selects next, the person so selected not only has the right to start talking, but is obliged to do so, insofar as she has been allocated a turn in which to speak. So, gaps after turns in which the next speaker has been selected would not be mere neutral lapses in conversation, but will be heard by co-participants as the absence of a specific person's talk. In such instances, the absence of talk is a normatively accountable matter. So, the next speaker is motivated to start talking at the earliest point by virtue of her orientation to commonly held conventions which inform co-participants' understanding and interpretation of another's absence of talk. Similarly, if the next speaker is not selected in the turn in production, then potential next speakers may self-select at the first transition place. If there is more than one possible next speaker, there is a premium in starting to talk as early as possible to ensure possession of the floor. So, the system provides a motivation for potential next speakers to begin talking as close as possible to the completion of the first turn construction unit. Similarly, it is possible that the current speaker may self-select and continue beyond the transition place. So, again, to ensure possession of the floor, the co-participant needs to start talking as early as possible at the next available turn transition place.

Sacks *et al.*'s system also furnishes similar explanations for occasions in which more than one party is speaking, and also the briefness of such spates of overlapping talk. However, as we will be dealing with overlap in a subsequent section, we will not discuss these here.

Having identified features of the turn-taking system through which turn transfer in ordinary conversation is organised, we can now begin to examine data from the British Airways and the WOZ corpora. We will begin by investigating the extent to which the system identified by Sacks *et al.* in ordinary conversation is relevant to calls to the British Airways flight inquiries service.

THE TURN-TAKING SYSTEM IN THE BRITISH AIRWAYS CORPUS

A first point to make is that, as in ordinary conversation, there are very few lengthy gaps in the exchanges. Those lengthy pauses that do occur are usually a result of the agent consulting her computer database to check for information. In the following call there are three points in the exchange when the absence of any talk extends beyond one second (lines 13, 17 and 20) but on each occasion the agent's talk surrounding the silence indicates that she is consulting her terminal.

(1) [16] T1:SB:F:F

```
A:   flight information
     may I help you[:
C:                 [good morning um I was
     wondering if you can tell me what time um:
     (.) iberia flight six one four (.3) from
     valencia scheduled to arrive tomorrow
     please
     (.5)
A:   ah you'll have to check with iberia I'll
     give you their number
```

11 C: er thank you very mu[ch
12 A: [hold on
13 (3.5)
14 A: >in fact where did you say it was coming
15 from
16 C: from valencia
17 (4)
18 A: yes iberia's number uh(p) still searching
19 here we go
20 (2.5)
21 A: oh one
22 C: yeah
23 A: eight nine seven
24 C: eight nine seven
25 (.)
26 A: seven nine
27 C: seven nine
28 (.)
29 A: four one
30 C: four one [thank (you)
31 A: [now did you say it was the
32 eye bee six one four
33 C: er::m six one four yes
34 A: that normally gets in about
35 fifteen fifty fi:[ve
36 C: [fifteen fifty
37 f[ive
38 A: [yeah but do check with the carrier concerned
39 C: okay (.) thank you very much
40 A: 'kay >bye<
41 C: b' bye

Similarly, when both parties start, or end up, talking at the same time, one party soon gives way, thus ensuring that the amount of time spent talking in overlap is actually very brief. As overlap will be discussed in the following section, we provide here only a brief illustration of the extent to which two parties end up talking simultaneously.

(2) [31] T2:SA:F:F

[a]

9 A: yes I'll just try for [you >I'll
10 C: [('kay)
11 A: just check that for yo[u sorry
12 C: [okay

[b]

22 A: it- it's left the stand (.) but ah haven't
23 got it confirmed airborne

```
        at the m[oment
    C:          [oh I see maybe it hasn't
        taken off yet
```

More relevant to our immediate concerns, however, are those instances in which speakers' turns display their orientation to the features of the turn-taking system identified by Sacks *et al.* So, for example, consider the following extract in which the British Airways agent is just informing the caller that the flight about which she is inquiring is arriving ahead of schedule.

(3) [3] T1:SA:F:F

```
A:   -yes it(11) be ↑la:nding: ↓now: (.3) ahEAd
     of ↑schedule=let me just check that for you?
C:   a↑head of ↓schedule, [bee   ay   two   ni]ne six.
A:                        [ahead of schedule] (.)
A:   yeah:(p), ↑hold on
     (1)
A:   it was due at ten: er::
C:   twenty ↓fi:ve.=
A:   =ten twenty five, >yeah hold on
```

What is noticeable here is that in line 21 the agent begins to formulate the scheduled time of arrival. However, the agent appears to be having some difficulty: although she knows the hour, the hesitation item 'er::' clearly indexes her inability to provide the complete scheduled time of arrival. The caller's subsequent turn provides this information, thereby displaying her analysis that the agent was 'having problems' rather than, for example, withholding that information while some other items were recalled on her computer screen. Note that the agent's subsequent turn is latched onto the end of the prior turn. This indicates that while the turn was in production, she was able to anticipate that the end of 'five' presented the first transition relevance place in the caller's on-going turn. Similarly, her subsequent turn echoes the information provided by the caller, thus confirming her prior difficulty and accepting the proffered resolution. But, furthermore, it displays that the agent interpreted 'twenty five' as constituting the entire turn. And insofar as the caller does not continue after 'five', which would have led to a spate of overlapping talk, the agent's analysis seems to have been correct.

The agent's analysis of the prior turn is clearly informed by an understanding that, minimally, the construction of an entire turn may be accomplished through only one turn construction unit. So, grammatical constructions, such as sentential units, are not relevant to the agent's practical resolution of this instance of the problem 'when is it appropriate to start talking'. Of course, we are not claiming that conversationalists never orient to the relevance of units of talk organised at the level of sentences. Indeed, Sacks *et al.* make precisely the point that sentential constructions provide special resources for speakers; for example, turn size can be expanded considerably because of the resources sentences provide to allow development of turns in progress (Sacks *et al.*, 1974:709). However, the point being made here is that not all occasions of turn transfer rest upon hearer/speakers' lay intuitions about grammatical or linguistic rules of sentence construction.

The system identified by Sacks *et al.* ensures that turns are not simply distributed between relevant parties, but that turns are allocated to specific individuals, and that the individuals so selected not only have the right to speak, but are normatively constrained to do so. And the absence of such normatively prescribed action is an accountable matter: that is, an absence to which co-participants' subsequent talk will be directed.

```
(4) [7] T1:SA:F:M

C:    right. (.) thank you very much>are you able
      to tell me (.5) er flight arrival times from
      zimbabwe? oh no you can't i- its its at
      gatwick
      (.5)
A:    no: what's the flight number,
      (.8)
C:    urm
      (.2)
A:    WHAt's the fLIGht num[ber
C:                         [flight number
      I don't know. the flight number it arrives
      saturday morning first thing.
```

In extract (4) the caller has been provided with the first set of information he requested, and he begins to formulate a different question (line 18). Having produced a further question, the caller then formulates a reason why he now anticipates that the agent will not be able to deal with the request: the plane is flying to Gatwick Airport, and not Heathrow. However, the agent can deal with queries about arrivals to Gatwick, and seeks relevant details to allow her to identify the specific flight: 'no: what's the flight number,' (line 23). A silence then follows, broken only by the caller's hesitation item 'urm'. The agent's subsequent turn displays her analysis that the caller is experiencing some kind of trouble with this request. She repeats the request, stressing certain parts and speaking with increased volume. Thus she not only indicates that an answer to her question is still relevant, but she also exhibits her analysis of what the problem was: the caller had not heard what she had said in the prior turn.

Finally in this section, we will discuss another source of evidence that the system identified by Sacks *et al.* in ordinary conversation is relevant to the more circumscribed domain of flight inquiry exchanges.

During a call to the British Airways flight inquiry service there are certain places in which turn transfer, or some other sequence of actions, like a closing sequence, become relevant. For example, after the agent has provided the required information, the caller can either initiate a closing to the exchange, or can make another request, or request some clarification of the information already provided. So, after the provision of the required information, the caller is entitled not only to speak, but to engage in a range of related actions. This means that if the agent wishes to continue speaking after the provision of such information, special measures need to be taken to make clear to the caller that the agent is self-selecting to continue speaking. One technique for this is to rush through at a turn transition place so as to ensure that the caller has no opportunity to self-select.

(5) [39] T2:SA:F:M

A: right that's right it says some sort of
(.5) industrial so: (.) it's (.) and retime
(1)
A: 's but it says here 's actually
a planned retime (.3) urm which will be
nineteen twenty five
(1.3)
A: so it'll be going out at nineteen twenty
five>the BEst thing is to ring up
tomorrow morning and check again
C: th the the same number
A: yes

In extract (5) the agent is providing information about the delay to a flight caused by industrial action in Portugal. Note that the provision of this information ends in lines 97 to 98 when she announces the rescheduled departure time. In the majority of cases, at this point the caller obtains the floor. However, in this example the agent rushes into a new but related spate of talk concerning the best time to ring for further information. This in turn exhibits her awareness of the relevance and likelihood of turn transfer at specific places within her turn.

Callers often mark the receipt of the requested information with items such as 'right', 'okay', and so on. It is a routine phenomenon that turns beginning with such acknowledgement tokens tend to initiate a pre-closing exchange, which then leads to a terminal sequence in which the call is ended (see the section on 'closings' later in this chapter). Indeed, agents can treat the provision of pre-closing items as terminal exchanges, and will respond to them by moving to close the call. If callers have more to say there is an advantage in starting as soon as possible at the turn transition place after the acknowledgement token. For example:

(6) [7] T1:SA:F:M

C: right. (.) thank you very much>are you able
to tell me (.5) er flight arrival times from
zimbabwe?

(7) [38] T2:SA:F:M

A: yes: that's: er scheduled for take off
at twenty two hundred
C: right >and< uh- what time am I
supposed to be at the airport
to check in

(8) [38] T2:SA:F:M

C: a:nd (.) which terminal is that
A: it's the north terminal at gatwick
(.)
C: great>dz- dz-< does the railway
take me to the north terminal

It is noticeable that in extracts (5) to (8) the speakers do not begin to accelerate the speed of their delivery as they approach the last words or sounds of turn construction units. Instead they speed up right at the point where turn transfer becomes relevant, thus providing empirical evidence of an orientation to the likelihood and legitimacy of turn transfer at these places.

TURN-TAKING IN THE WOZ CORPUS

The first point to make is that the WOZ corpus does contain data which seem to indicate that, on some occasions, subjects were able to organise their exchanges in ways that were characteristic of calls to the British Airways flight information service. For example, consider the way that callers were able to anticipate the end of prior turns so as to begin their next turns without any gap between the two. Although rare in the WOZ corpus, the same phenomenon is present.

(9) WOZ 6:1:M (Simplified transcription)

W: would you like hungarian airlines telephone number
S: yes please

(10) WOZ 6:9:M (Simplified transcription)

W: I'm sorry british airways does not have
a flight arriving from warsaw tomorrow evening

```
27          (1)
28    W:    you probably want polish airways
29          flight ell oh two eight one
30          would you like the telephone number
31    S:    yes please
```

In the majority of cases, however, the WOZ simulation exchanges do not display the same level of cohesion and fluency. Let us reconsider what typical WOZ dialogues look like.

(11) WOZ 3:5:M

```
1     W:    flight (.2) information (.5) can (.) I help (.) you
2     S:    ·hh yes I'd like to know: when ·hh
3           there are flights tomorrow morning
4           from gatwick to barcelona
5           (3)
6     W:    please wait
7           (13)
8     W:    there (.) are (.) no (.) flights (.3)
9           from (.) gatwick (.) to (.) barcelona (.)
10          tomorrow (.) morning
11          (.3)
12    S:    ·hhh can you tell me if there are any
13          flights from heathrow to barcelona
14          tomorrow morning then
15          (3.4)
16    W:    please wait
17          (12.5)
18    W:    flight (.3) bee (.2) ay (.3) four (.) seven (.)
19          six (.6) leaves (.) london (.4) heathrow (.4)
20          terminal (.) one (1.2) for (.) barcelona (.5)
21          tomorrow (.3) at (.) nine forty
22          (1.5)
23    S:    okay thank you
24          (2.4)      ((subject replaces receiver))
25    W:    thank (.) you (.3) good (.) bye
```

(12) WOZ 4:9:F

```
1     W:    british (.) airways flight information (.3)
2           good (.) afternoon
3           (1)
4     S:    ·h can you tell me (.) ehm (.3) which
5           terminal I should go to for a british
6           airways flight to zurich
7           (3.8)
8     W:    please (.) wait
9           (12)
10    W:    british (.) airways (.) flights (.) to (.)
11          zurich (.4) leave from heathrow (.3)
```

terminal (.) one
(1.8)
S: thank you
(2.5)
W: thank you (.) good (.) bye

It is clear from extracts (11) and (12) that the simulated computer–human exchanges differ markedly from the British Airways recordings. So, for example, whereas in the human–human corpus turn transfer was achieved with the minimum amount of silence between turns, in the simulation corpus comparatively long lapses pepper the transcript. To a degree, this is a consequence of the wizards deliberately delaying the beginning of their turns to foster the impression of computational processes at work. But more interesting, perhaps, it would seem that there are comparatively lengthy silences between system turns and the subsequent subject turns. Indeed, cursory inspection of extracts (11) and (12) suggests that, in most instances, the subjects waited until they were certain that the system had actually stopped before beginning their own turns. Therefore, it appears that the subjects were not monitoring the production of the system's turns to anticipate the onset of transfer relevance place; or at least not monitoring turns in progress with the same degree of accuracy and sophistication that appears in routine, everyday exchanges. This in turn could be cited as some evidence of the breakdown or even abandonment of the kinds of turn-taking procedures which inform human–human exchanges.

The kinds of turns made by the wizards were quite constrained: they introduced the service and formulated a greeting, provided an acknowledgement of the request, provided the required information, or told the subject that they were unable to provide it, pursued a clarification or repeat of a request, and, where appropriate, offered alternative sources of information. With the exception of the request acknowledgement ('please wait'), the subjects could reasonably produce utterances after each of these kinds of system turn. So, the majority of subjects' turns occurred in one of the following sequential positions: post-greeting, post-request for clarification, post-negative answer, post-offer of an alternative information source and post-provision of the required information.

We examined the trials of subjects 1 to 5, a total of 49 trials (only 9 of subject 2's trials were recorded). In these 49 trials there were 138 separate instances of silences which fell into one of the five conditions listed above. The mean for these silences was 1.28 seconds.

In the majority of trials, the system was able to provide the required information, and in the next turn the subjects initiated a closing sequence to exit from the exchange. The mean length of silence between these two turns is 1.91 seconds, noticeably longer than the 1.28 second average silence in all the conditions. As many of the subjects decided to make a written record of the information they received from the system, it may be the case that these longer silences were a consequence of the subjects' attempts to make a note of the relevant times, flights, and so on, before moving to initiate a closing sequence. If we deduct from the total of 138 silences those which fall between the system's provision of information and the subjects' subsequent closing initiation, we are left with only 78 instances of between-turn silences. The mean length of these gaps is 0.8. We will shortly return to the significance of this average. But there are are still lapses in the WOZ exchanges, a variety of which do not routinely appear in the British Airways data, and these need to be accounted for.

To ensure that the wizards sounded convincing in their role as speaking computers, it was necessary to disguise their voices. As we noted in Chapter 3, this was achieved by filtering the human voice through a vocoder. For various technical reasons, which are not relevant here, this method ensured that the wizard's voice was at times severely distorted. Furthermore, at the end of each turn there was a brief spate of electrical 'white noise'.[2] Thus one unintended consequence of our attempt to create the sound of a talking computer was to ensure that what the wizard said, and when they had finished saying it, was always potentially subject to some confusion.

One option for the subjects would have been to wait for some seconds until they were absolutely sure that the system had finished its turn before they started to talk. However, this strategy would have contravened a common maxim of conversational organisation. Jefferson (1989) suggests that there is standard metric of approximately one second in conversational interaction. Her analysis of instances of silences falling within a 0.8 to 1.2 second boundary reveals that speakers orient to this metric as a 'tolerance interval' (Jefferson, 1989: 170) which marks the acceptable length of absence of talk in conversational interaction. After silences of a duration between approximately 0.8 to 1.2 seconds, speakers can be observed to initiate various kinds of remedial actions to terminate the silence.

The subjects, then, had to negotiate a delicate issue: how were they to know that the system has finished its turn? The 'white noise' distortion of the wizard's voice ensured that the turn in progress could not be monitored accurately to anticipate a place where turn transfer would be relevant. Similarly, the mechanical drag of the distorted voice ensured that even when the system had finished, it was not immediately clear that this was the case. In the light of these constraints, we propose that the presence of silences in the WOZ data in part reflects the subjects' impaired ability to track turns in progress and to judge when turn transfer would become, or had become, relevant. But furthermore, it may be the case that the length of those silences reflects the subjects' concern to ensure that the momentary hesitation after the system's turns did not exceed the conversation tolerance boundary of approximately 1.2 seconds.[3]

These observations suggest that, despite the apparent differences in the turn-taking organisation, the exchanges between the subjects and the wizards in the WOZ simulation can be understood in terms of the turn-taking system, and associated aspects of conversational organisation, described by Sacks *et al.*

OVERLAPPING TALK

Intuitively, the occurrence of overlapping talk might seem to be evidence of a failure of the procedures through which turn transfer is achieved. That is, if two people are talking at the same time, it would seem that the behaviour of at least one party is deviating from the turn-taking options outlined in the previous section. And if we follow this argument, a cursory inspection of any transcript from the British Airways corpus might lead us to think that ordinary conversational exchanges are rife with evidence of the failure of the procedures to ensure orderly turn transfer.

(13) [9] T1:SB:F:M

```
A:   ·hh flight information british ↑airways
     can I ↑help you:,
C:   er- could you jus' tell me: er:
     incoming flight from toronto bee ay nine
     two (.)  when it (er:)  (          )
A:   ·h yess certainly can you hold the line
     please=
C:   =sure
     (.7)
A:   yes the flight was scheduled for seven
     fifty fiv[e
C:            [yeah (.) (sure)
A:   unfortunately delayed as you
     probably kno[w
C:               [yea[h
A:                   [·h (.)  and is expected now
     at ten fifty five=
C:   =ten fifty five that's [(terminal)
A:                          [terminal four (.)
     yes
C:   thank you
A:   terminal four heathro[w
C:                        [yah (.3) thank you
A:   thank you [bye bye
C:             [bye
```

Even in this comparatively short call there are five occasions in which both parties are talking at the same time, and one instance in which the agent's inbreath (usually a sure sign that someone is going to say something) occurs in overlap with the prior talk. In the whole British Airways corpus of 100 calls there are 370 instances of overlapping talk.

Despite the prevalence of cases *of* overlap, only a small percentage of actual talk occurs *in* overlap. For example, Levinson (1983: 296) claims that less than five per cent of speech is delivered in overlap. We are faced, then, with two issues to be addressed: given that the turn-taking options outlined earlier apparently provide for the smooth transfer of speakership from one party to another, why is overlap so common? And, given that overlap is so common, why is it that so little actual speech is actually conducted in overlap?

Both these apparent anomalies are explicable in terms of the system for turn-taking identified by Sacks *et al.* So, first, overlap may arise when a next speaker begins to talk at an appropriate turn transfer place *at the same time* that the current speaker provides a further component to extend that turn beyond that transfer relevance place. For example:

```
(14) [27] T1:SB:F:M

14   A:   yes we've got the bee ay zero five six
15   C:   bee ay zero five six
16   A:   to arrive at oh seven hundred in the morning
17   C:   oh seven hundred and which uh
18        which te[rminal [is it
19   A:           [·hh    [terminal four
```

In line 17 the caller echoes part of the information provided in the prior turn ('oh seven hundred') and then begins to ask a related question concerning the terminal at which the particular flight will arrive. Before this turn is complete, the agent is able to predict that the turn will be the question 'and which terminal?' The agent produces an inbreath shortly after the initial sound of the word 'terminal', and then provides an answer, the beginning of which coincides exactly with the end of the (anticipated) question. The subsequent overlap is the consequence of the caller's addition of a tag component ('is it') on to the end of the question. Overlaps generated by the combination of a next speaker starting at a transfer relevance place and the current speaker adding a further turn component are common.

```
(15) [1] T1:SAF:F (Simplified transcription)

9    C:   I just want to confirm
10        what ti:me it is due in [ (          )
11   A:                           [YEs certainly
12        >hold on<
```

```
(16) [7] T1:SA:F:M

14   A:   terminal four (.7) [heathrow=
15   C:                      [(four)
```

```
16   A:   =airport.
17        (.3)
18   C:   right.
```

(17) [3] T1:SA:F:F

```
127  A:   does he know you,
128  C:   yes he does [he does
129  A:               [right
```

Throughout this chapter we have emphasised that turn-taking is crucially arranged around turn transition *places*. Given that any turn can be indefinitely extended by the addition of further turn construction units, any actual ending is a practical accomplishment, orchestrated locally in the conversation. This entails that, because there is no objectively available end point to a turn, potential next speakers must closely monitor the turn in production to identify which of the potential turn transfer places could be realised as *the* appropriate place to effect speakership change. During spates of overlapping talk, the ability to perform this kind of detailed monitoring of another party's talk-in-progress is likely to be impaired. So, there are practical requirements, intrinsic to the turn-taking system, which provide a motivation for overlapping speakers to seek to restore the 'one speaker at a time' condition as soon as possible, thereby ensuring that the amount of time actually spent talking in overlap is minimised.

OVERLAP TYPES

In this section we will describe some of the organisational features of overlapping talk as reported in Jefferson's (1983) classification of types of overlap. Before we discuss the forms of overlap, however, it is necessary to be clear on two points. First, the following discussion is not intended to provide an exhaustive description of Jefferson's (1983) paper on the characteristics of overlap, but merely to illustrate the kind of detailed order that obtains at this level of interaction. Second, and perhaps more important, Jefferson's formulation of a typology is not motivated by an attempt to produce a definitive taxonomy of overlap. Her analysis of overlap is concerned to explicate the orderly communicative competencies that inform spates of overlapping talk; the use of 'types' is simply a convenient way to order collections of instances which display similar interactional competencies. Furthermore, these types are not exclusive: different orders of conversational organisation can intersect in particular instances.

Jefferson describes three types of overlap: transitional, recognitional and progressional.

Transitional overlap occurs when a next speaker, orienting to the propriety of speakership change at a forthcoming turn transfer place, begins to talk at the same time that the current speaker, in some way, extends the current turn. For example, overlap can result when the current speaker stretches the sound of the last part of the turn construction unit in production. In the following extract, the agent stretches the last syllable of the word 'airlines', and the caller starts to speak at the point at which the syllable 'lines' would have finished had it not been extended.

```
(18) [2] T1:SA:F:F

12   A:   ·h >Well< that sou:nds li:ke (th't) you're talking
13        about polish air↓li[:n es]: .
14   C:                      [>yes<]
```

This type of overlap can also occur when the next speaker anticipates that at the approaching turn transfer relevance place, the current speaker will not continue.

```
(19) [39] T2:SA:F:M

37   A:   you're saying there's a strike le[t me
38   C:                                    [yes
39   A:   just have a look to see
```

In extract (19), the caller produces a 'yes' at the point where the turn construction unit 'you're saying there's a strike' has finished, thereby overlapping with the agent's self-selection to continue speaking to indicate that she is investigating whether there is a strike. And in the following extract, the caller echoes information the agent has just provided. The agent treats the echo as requiring confirmation, and provides this at the point that the caller self-selects to initiate a closing sequence.

```
(20) [43] T3:SA:F:F

10   A:   yes the four three one from amsterdam
11        came in at thirteen oh five madam
12        (1)
13   C:   thirteen oh five l[ovely thank you very
14   A:                     [that's right
15   C:   much indeed for your help
```

Similarly, overlap can result when a next speaker hitches the beginning of the next turn on to the last sound of the word prior to the transition relevance place. This is illustrated in extracts (21) and (22).

(21) [29] T2:SA:F:F (Simplified transcription)

```
A:   the number to (che:ck)
C:   thank you=
A:   =is oh one
     (1)
A:   five six two
     nine two oh six
C:   nine two oh six
     (.7)
C:   should I ask for
     anyone in particu[lar
A:                    [no:
```

(22) [3] T1:SA:F:F

```
A:   (tch) well it seems to be ahead of ↓schedule
     I'll just check that
     would you ho:ld pl[ease,
C:                     [yes please thank you
```

Recognitional overlap occurs when the next speaker's start is designed to display their understanding of some aspect of the turn in production. So, for example, extract (23) comes from the beginning of a call. Immediately after providing a greeting component, the caller talks to someone present with her at the time, requesting some information which she needs in order to formulate a request for the agent. Having formulated this request, she then starts to tell a story which would appear to be an account for why she had to go 'off line' earlier in the call. The agent's enthusiastic 'right' overlaps with this story while it is in progress, thereby displaying her recognition that what the caller is currently reporting is not relevant to the 'business at hand', for which task she already possesses sufficient information.

(23) [3] T1:SA:F:F

```
A:   flight infor↑mation,
     (.)
C:   ·hh oh good morn↓ing flight >i(c)- c-
     can I have that piece of paper david
     please=you took from me, (.) ·hhh
     >°right°< >sorry< >thank you<=·hh
     flight infor↓mation, I'm checkin' on the
     fli:ght bee ay two nine ↓six >I think they
     gave it out but my son walked
     off with [(the contact)]·h h h Show(k-) chicago
A:            [(BR)i:ght) ho]ld on
```

Jefferson identifies two types of recognitional overlap. In the first, the overlapper's talk displays recognition of a specific word.

(24) [26] T1:SB:F:F

```
6     A:    is it heathrow
7           (.3)
8     C:    sorry
9     A:    from heath[row
10    C:              [yes from heathrow
```

In the second type of recognitional overlap, the overlapping talk displays the speaker's understanding of the gist, point or 'thrust' of the turn in progress.

(25) [26] T1:SB:F:F

```
38    A:    now would you like reservations' phone
39          number
40    C:    er::m:: (.) i(k)- i(k)- would you
41          be able to put me through to reservat[ions
42    A:                                         [o:h no
43          we can't
```

(26) [31] T2:SA:F:F

```
32    A:    well i(t)s: iss: (.) scheduled
33          for thirteen thirt[y
34    C:                      [yeah I think it
35          was scheduled to (.) (few) erm (.3)
36          to fly a[t twelve fifty]
37    A:            [earlier       ] yes
```

In extract (25) the caller asks whether the agent can redirect the call to Reservations. The agent intercepts the caller's turn, displaying her understanding of the kind of request being made. And in (26), the agent's turn in line 37 indicates that she has inferred that the business of the caller's turn is to make the point that the flight's current estimated time of departure is later than the scheduled time.

Finally, progressional overlap exhibits the next speaker's orientation to the progression or 'forward momentum' of the exchange.

(27) [7] T1:SA:F:M

```
69    A:    you say it's arriving on the: em:
70    C:    it's arriving early mor[ning
71    A:                           [on the
72          twenty third.
73          (.3)
74    C:    on the twenty third yes.
```

In extract (27) the agent begins to ask the caller to repeat, and thereby confirm, when the flight in question is due to arrive. Before this request is completed the caller starts to answer, stating that part of the day on which the flight will arrive. However, the agent requires a repeat of the *date* of arrival. The earliest point in the turn at which the agent can see that the caller is orienting to 'when in the day' rather than 'what date' is during the caller's production of the word 'morning'. And after the first syllable of 'morning' the agent begins to speak to address the issue of arrival date, thereby moving the trajectory of the exchange towards a specific goal.

We can derive two very important points from Jefferson's sustained analysis of the organisation of overlapping talk. She reveals that overlapping speech is not simply a collision of parties in their attempt to seize the floor, but exhibits a hitherto unimagined and unnoticed degree of orderliness and precision. Furthermore, she shows that the various organisational properties of overlap display the speakers' sensitivity to the turn-taking system identified by Sacks *et al.* So, overlap is not indicative of a breakdown or abandonment of procedures for effecting turn transfer, but actually constitutes evidence that speakers' actions are conducted in terms of that system.

OVERLAP IN THE WOZ SIMULATION DATA

We noted earlier that in the British Airways corpus of 100 calls, there are 370 instances of overlap. By contrast, in the WOZ simulation corpus of 99 calls, there are 3 cases of overlap. These are reproduced in extracts (28) to (30).

(28) WOZ 8:3:M (Simplified transcription)

```
1    W:   flight information good day
2         can I help yo[u
3    S:                [(mm)
4         (1)
5    S:   er yes I'm ringing about h urh a flight
6         from hungarian airlines
```

(29) WOZ 9:7:F (Simplified transcription)

```
1    W:   flight information may I help you
2         (1)
3    S:   [yes
4    W:   [british airways here
5         (1.5)
6    S:   can you tell me whether flight bee ay
7         two three eight from orlando arrived on time
```

(30) WOZ 6:6:M (Simplified transcription)

```
21   W:   the telephone number for reservations is
22        zero one
```

```
        (1.5)
W:      eight nine seven
        (1.5)
W:      four zero
        (1)
S:      [>thank you<]
W:      [do-        ] double zero
        (1)
S:      thank you
        (1)
W:      good bye
```

All three extracts provide relatively straightforward instances of transitional overlap. So, in extract (28) the caller's 'mm' is latched onto the very last sound of the wizard's turn. Similarly, in (29) and (30) the callers start to speak at points where it would seem that the wizard has finished. (It is interesting to note that the wizard in (30) immediately stops the production of the last two digits of the telephone number and waits until the caller's overlapping turn has finished, thereby ensuring that the turn would be produced (in the clear). There is no evidence that the caller grasped the significance of this very human piece of behaviour.)

Why are there so few cases of overlap in the WOZ corpus? One factor is the delay that the wizards left before beginning to speak. These delays ensured that it was extremely unlikely that wizards would begin speaking in overlap with the subject's on-going speech.

There is another consideration. Earlier in this section we examined instances of overlap which indicated clearly that next speakers were able to monitor the on-going turn so as to be able to anticipate with some accuracy when that turn would end. So, the subjects' analysis of turns in production is a crucial feature of successful and smooth turn transfer. However, there are two features of the wizards' speech production which are likely to have impaired the subjects' ability to perform this kind of close analysis. First, the policy to leave large gaps between words in a current turn ensured that the subjects could never really know when a silence at the end of a turn construction unit was an indication of the end of that turn, or whether this was just another lengthy gap in an incomplete turn. Similarly, close order anticipation of turn transfer places requires subjects to be able to make sense of the turn in progress, and here again, the distortion of the wizard's voice would have at least diminished the accuracy of the subjects' understanding. Spates of overlap tend to exhibit, in varying ways, the next speaker's understanding of 'what is going on right now in the conversation': in the WOZ study, the likelihood of the subjects' achieving such a degree of understanding was undermined by the protocol adopted to make a human sound like a computer.

In this section we have looked at the organisation of overlap. We now know it to be an orderly phenomenon, a result of the participants' orientation to the turn-taking system and its components outlined by Sacks *et al.* We know also that overlap is not necessarily interruptive; indeed, many instances of overlap exhibit what may be characterised as the next speaker's *affiliation* with the producer of the turn in progress. For example:

```
(31) [26] T1:SB:F:F

A:   is it heathrow
     (.3)
C:   sorry
A:   from heath[row
C:             [yes from heathrow
```

Indeed, in the British Airways corpus, the vast majority of instances of overlapping talk are not treated by the participants themselves as 'trouble in the exchange', or as a case of impolite or rude behaviour. In the entire corpus there is only one instance of a speaker displaying a sensitivity to the inappropriateness of an overlap.

```
(32) [1] T1:SA:F:F

A:   ·hh good ↑morning british airways flight
     infor↑mation:
C:   ·h umm I wonder if you could help me please=
     could you check flight bee ay nine oh three:,
     it's due in tomorrow ↓morning from frankfurt.
     tuh ↑heath↓ro:w,÷h an'I just want t[o co-
A:                                      [oh tomorrow,
C:   °yes please° (.) I ju[st want to confirm
A:                        [sorry,
C:   what ti:me it is due in [ (          )
A:                           [YEs certainly
```

In this case the agent's 'oh tomorrow,' (line 7) appears to be a spontaneous vocalisation of a 'sudden realisation' of an earlier misunderstanding about the caller's request. This exclamation is interruptive in the sense that it does not occur in the vicinity of a turn transfer place in the on-going turn. And, noticeably, the agent then apologises, exhibiting her understanding of the unwarranted production of the overlapping speech. (It is interesting to note that this apology also appears in overlap, but as it is placed close to a turn transfer place – after the turn construction unit '°yes please°' – *it* is not treated as requiring explication or apology.)

In extract (32) it is clear that the first spate of overlapping speech was a consequence of the agent's actions. However, in the majority of cases, it is unproductive to try to identify which of the parties was responsible for causing a specific overlap. Extract (33) contains an instance of overlap in which the current speaker continues at the turn transfer place, and the next speaker begins to speak precisely at the same point. Both parties are therefore orienting to options provided by the turn allocation component of the turn-taking system.

```
(33) [3] T1:SA:F:F

127  A:   does he know you,
128  C:   yes he does [he does
129  A:               [right
```

In a sense, then, it is not useful to think of the occurrence of overlap as a product of the idiosyncratic behaviour of specific individuals, nor as a consequence of their behaviour in accordance with any social roles or statuses that might be attributed to them. Rather, the occurrence of overlap can be accounted for as a consequence of the very procedures which provide for the possibility of smooth turn transfer. We can therefore view overlap as a procedural and structural commodity: a phenomenon which is intrinsic to, and structurally embedded in, the organised methods to achieve conversational turn-taking. Consequently, it is more productive to consider overlap in terms of its sequential characteristics. Although it is beyond the scope of the present study, it may be more fruitful to begin to try to discover if overlap predominates in specific kinds of action sequences: openings, closings, clarifications, repair, and so on. So, instead of investigating *who* perpetrates overlap, we might explore instead *where* overlap occurs, and study the kinds of interactional tasks which are are mediated in such sequences.

CLOSINGS

Like occurrence of overlapping speech, conversational closings are intrinsically tied to the turn-taking system. Recall that the turn allocation component of the system ensured that, at any turn transition relevance place, a turn may be extended by the current speaker, or another speaker may start to speak. Similarly, turns can be allocated to specific individuals, ensuring that a silence may be heard as the absence of someone's talk, rather than an end to the exchange. So, the issue is, what resources are available to

> organise the simultaneous arrival of the conversationalists at a point when one speaker's completion will not occasion another speaker's talk, and that will not be heard as some speaker's silence.
>
> (Schegloff and Sacks, 1973: 237)

In their study of everyday telephone conversations Schegloff and Sacks (1973) identified a four turn closing sequence composed of two adjacency pairs. After a turn which bounds or closes a prior topic, a speaker may produce a turn composed of a single item such as 'well', 'right' or 'okay'. This indicates that that speaker has no new business to introduce into the exchange, and is therefore passing on the opportunity to speak. If the other party produces a similar turn and displays that they too have no other business, the conversation may enter a closing section, consisting of a pair of terminal turns, at which point transition relevance is suspended. For example:

```
(34) (From Button, 1987: 101-2)

Pam:          hhOh [well than:ks [any way]
Vicky:             [I:'m so   so [rry Pa:]m
              (.)
Pam:          Okay,=        pre-closing 1
Vicky:        =Okay=        pre-closing 2
Pam:          =Bye:         terminal exchange 1
Vicky:        =Bye.         terminal exchange 2
End of call
```

So, in the first paired exchange, the pre-closing sequence, the speakers orchestrate a mutual display of 'nothing further to say', which in turn provides the warrant to initiate the second set of paired turns, thus closing the exchange.

Closing sequences are not necessarily terminal, as previously unmentioned items may be introduced to the conversation in the closing exchanges.[4] However, it is recurrently the case that these new topics will be raised in conjunction with displacement markers, such as 'by the way'. It would seem, therefore, that speakers orient to the four turn closing sequence as a discrete and bounded section of the conversation.

CLOSINGS IN CALLS TO THE BRITISH AIRWAYS FLIGHT INFORMATION SERVICE

In the British Airways corpus there is only a single case in which the caller replaces the telephone handset after receiving the required information.[5] In all other calls, the closing sequences share many properties with the closing procedure for ordinary conversation. Occasions in which this procedure deviates from that found in ordinary conversational interaction can be explained by reference to contingencies relevant to the domain of telephone-based, public information services.

The most common closing sequence in the British Airways corpus consists of two sets of paired utterances. In its purest form, the organisation of these two sets of paired utterances has the following characteristics. After the caller has received the requested information, the closing is initiated by the caller's production of a turn in which the agent is thanked. This component may be prefaced by an acknowledgement token, such as 'right', 'lovely', 'okay', and so on. This turn displays that the caller's requirements have been met, and that he has no further request to make. The agent then reciprocates the acknowledgement. The caller and the agent then move into a terminal component and the exchange is completed with an exchange of 'good bye' or 'bye'.

```
(35) [12] T1:SB:F:F

36   A:   yes no change [twelve fifty arriving
37   C:                 [ ( )
38   A:   fifteen twen[ty
39   C:               [(may) seven two eight
40        (.)
41   A:   bee ay seven two eight
42   C:   thank you so much
43   A:   you're welcome
44        [bye bye
45   C:   [bye
46   ?:   bye
```

```
(36) [89] T4:SB:F:M

25   C:   both arrived h[ave they
26   A:                 [that's right
27   C:   both of them have arrived
28   A:   yes
29   C:   oh thank you very much
30   A:   thank you
31   C:   [ba'bye
32   A:   [ba'bye
```

```
(37) [70] T3:SB:F:F

24   A:   yes this is the right flight it is
25        due in at nine fifty five this ↓evening
26   C:   on kay tee six oh seven
27   A:   that's right
28   C:   oh gosh (.4) alr(h)ight thank you
29   A:   you're welcome
30   C:   thank you good bye
31   A:   ↑ba'bye
```

It is not unusual to find cases in which callers compound both pair parts into one turn.

```
(38) [62] T3:SB:F:M

35   C:   that's lovely thank you [ba 'bye]
36   A:                           [o k a y] Bye
```

```
(39) [71] T3:SB:F:F

15   A:   yeah that's fine ·hh if you contact
16        oh two nine three:
17   C:   yeah
18   A:   six six ↑eight
19   C:   uh huh
20   A:   two double ↓one
21   C:   right thank you b'bye
22   A:   you're welcome ba'bye
```

There is a simple explanation for this. In ordinary conversation the first two turns of the closing sequence allow *both* speakers to display that they have nothing further to say. So, closing cannot commence until each party has warranted such a move. However, in calls to the British Airways service, only one party – the caller – is required to show that he has no further business: that is, the agent is there merely to answer questions, and cannot therefore initiate new topics. So, only the caller has to display that there is no more business to be addressed to warrant the move to a terminal sequence, and thus we find callers moving straight from the first pair parts ('thanks', 'right, thank you') to the second pair parts ('bye').[6]

Although the caller may have registered that the current request has been dealt with satisfactorily, the agent cannot know if a new request is to be formulated, or whether the caller may require some further clarification. Consequently, only the caller can initiate a closing sequence. This has two implications. As agents do not have to display to the caller that they have no further business, when they hear that the caller has initiated the first part of a closing sequence, they can, in their subsequent turn, compound both closing components in one turn; alternatively, they can produce only the second part of the terminal exchange. These are illustrated in extracts (40) and (41) respectively.

```
(40) [33] T2:SA:F:F (Simplified transcription)

14   A:   yes that was the rescheduled time
15   C:   okay thank you
16   A:   thank you  b'bye
```

```
(41) [15] T1:SB:F:F

7    A:   yes: it'll be landing at ten fifty five
8         terminal four (.3) heathrow
9    C:   thank you very much
10   A:   by[e
11   C:     [goodbye
```

In some cases, callers produce an acknowledgement token but then do not immediately proceed to the 'thank you' token that conventionally follows, and which clearly marks a move to a terminal sequence. When this happens, the agents' subsequent behaviour displays their orientation to the convention that only callers can initiate closings, or raise new business in the call. In extract (42) the caller provides what appears to be an acknowledgement token, 'yea(p)' (line 24), but he does not proceed to a thank you component. There is a (comparatively) long silence, after which the agent provides the prompt 'awright' (line 26) thereby providing the caller with the opportunity either to move to a closing or to raise new business. Note that after the prompt the caller 'recycles' the beginning of the closing sequence by producing yet another acknowledgement token.

(42) [18] T1:SB:F:M

```
22   A:   but please don't allow for that that
23        may be corrected very shortly
24   C:   >yea(p)<
25        (1.5)
26   A:   awright
27   C:   okay (.) thank you (.)
28   A:   ba[bay
29   C:     [bye
```

Similarly, in (43) the agent's prompt begins in overlap with the caller's move to initiate a closing.

(43) [32] T2:SA:F:M

```
29   A:   we could have a confirmed
30        time by three
31        (.)
32   C:   by three
33   A:   yes may be
34        (.)
35   C:   okay
36        (.5)
37        [thankyou
38   A:   [(al)right  thank you b'bye
```

The initiation of a closing sequence is taken to be an indication that the caller has been provided with the required information. In those cases in which the agent is in the process of providing further information at the same time that the caller initiates a closing, the agent abandons her attempt to furnish supplementary information and collaborates in the closing. For example:

(44) [44] T3:SA:F:M

```
15   A:   yes this flight's showing a provisional
16        delay at the moment it's not expected to
```

```
      arrive into heathrow now until fifteen twenty
      (.)
C:    fifteen twenty [thank you very much]
A:                   [that's-            ]you're
      welcome (.3) b'bye
```

In this extract the caller initiates a closing shortly after echoing the required information. At the same time the agent starts to speak again: her 'that's' would suggest that she is about to provide supplementary information, or embark on clarificatory work. However, she aborts this turn at the first place that it is possible to see that the caller has initiated a closing, waits until the caller's first closing turn is completed and provides the appropriate closing component. In this the agent displays her orientation to the discrete character of closing sequences, and also the precedence of the caller's initiation of a closing over other business which may be on-going at the time the closing is initiated.[7]

So far we have seen evidence that the agents' conduct is informed by their understanding that the closing sequence takes precedence over other possible business of the exchange. Finally in this section, in the following extract there is an example of a caller's pragmatic work to ensure that the agent is aware that a closing has been initiated.

(45) [43] T3:SA:F:F

```
A:    yes the four three one from amsterdam
      came in at thirteen oh five madam
      (1)
C:    thirteen oh five l[ovely thank you very
A:                      [that's right
C:    much indeed for your help (.) [bye
A:                                  [you're welcome
      °b'bye°
```

The caller begins a closing sequence, again in overlap with a turn in which the agent is still addressing the business in hand (lines 13 and 14). Unlike in the previous extract, the agent does not here display that she registers that a closing has been initiated, for example, she does not abandon the turn in mid-production. Indeed, the utterance produced in overlap in line 14 is 'that's right' which has the character of confirming the caller's echo of the information she has just been given, and which provides no indication that the agent understands that a closing sequence has been initiated. To facilitate the agent's understanding of the business of the turn produced in overlap, the caller builds on and elaborates the 'thank you' component ('thank you very much indeed for your help'), thereby ensuring that the turn is extended beyond the spate of overlapping talk.

CLOSINGS IN THE WOZ CORPUS

The most common form of closing sequence in the WOZ corpus has two turns, and tends to occur directly after wizard has provided the subject with the required information (or provided some alternative source). For example:

(46) WOZ 4:9:F

W: british (.) airways (.) flights (.) to (.)
zurich (.4) leave from heathrow (.3)
terminal (.) one
(1.8)
S: thank you
(2.5)
W: thank you (.) good (.) bye

(47) WOZ 2:2:M

W: flight (.) bee (.) ay five five six (.2)
departing (.) at fifteen hundred (.4)
arrives (.) at (.) seventeen hundred (1.3)
flight (.) bee (.) ay (.) six seven two (.4)
departing (.) at seventeen (.) twenty five (.3)
arrives (.3) at (.) nineteen (.) twenty (.) five
(.7)
S: thank you
(1.8) ((*subject replaces receiver*))
W: thank (.) you (.) good (.) bye

This sequence occurs in 46 out of the 99 trials. The subject provides a 'thank you' component, and the wizard produces a return 'thank you' and a terminal component, compounded in the same turn. In the cases presented here, the subjects do not provide any acknowledgement tokens, such as 'right' and 'okay' in their closing initiation. In fact, there are only 12 cases of closing turns which contain acknowledgement items.

There are very few cases in which subjects provide further input after the wizard's closing turn. In extract 48, for example, the subject actually produces a second closing pair part after the wizard has provided a terminal turn.

(48) WOZ 5:7:F

W: I'm sorry (.4) I (.) do (.) not (.) have (.)
that (.) information (.7) please (.) ring (.)
heathrow (.) flight enquiries
(1.2)
S: ring who
(4)
W: please (.) ring (.) heathrow (.) flight (.)

enquiries
(4.7)
S: thank you
(2.7)
W: thank (.) you (.4) good (.) bye
S: bye

This phenomenon is very rare: in the entire corpus there are only two cases of a caller saying 'bye' *after* the wizard's terminal turn.

In 28 cases, subjects initiated a closing sequence but then replaced the handset without waiting for the system to make any appropriate response. For example:

(49) WOZ 2:4:M

W: zero (.) one (3) seven (.2) five (.2) nine (3.2)
one (.2) eight (.2) one (.2) eight
(1.6)
S: thank you
(3.1) ((*subject replaces receiver*))
W: thank (.) you (.) good (.) bye

(50) WOZ 8:8:M (Simplified transcription)

S: quarter to one in the afternoon (.)
rather than: (.) quarter to one in the ↑morning
(5)
W: yes
(1.3)
S: great (.) thanks b'bye
((*subject replaces receiver*))

Overall, there are 76 cases of subjects initiating closing sequences through the production of first turn pair components. However, in 21 cases, subjects ended the exchange after receiving the required information (or being told that they had to contact an alternative number) by simply replacing the receiver without initiating a closing.[8]

(51) WOZ 2:1:

W: flight (.) bee (.) ay (.) two (.) two (.)
seven (.5) to (.) atlanta (.5)
is scheduled (.) to leave (.3) at (.)
twelve (.) forty (.) five
(9)
((*subject replaces receiver*))
(.4)
W: thank (.) you (.) good (.) bye

(52) WOZ 9:10 (Simplified transcription)

```
W:   good morning british airways flight information
     (2.5)
S:   can you tell me (.3) when flight number
     bee ay nine oh three (.5) departing
     from frankfurt arrives at heathrow tomorrow
     (8.5)
W:   please wait
     (33)
W:   flight bee ay nine oh three from frankfurt
     to london heathrow terminal one arrives at
     twelve noon
     ((subject replaces receiver))
```

This phenomenon was not common in the trials of all the subjects: 17 of the 21 cases came from the trials of just two subjects. We may speculate, then, that this particularly brusque method of exiting an exchange may be an idiosyncratic feature peculiar to specific individuals.

There are some similarities between the closings in the WOZ corpus and the closings in the British Airways corpus. For example, in both corpora only the callers/subjects initiate closing sequences. Similarly, these sequences are initiated by the callers/subjects' production of the first part of a pair of closing turns.

This, however, is where the similarity ends: there are many more differences between the two corpora than there are features in common. So, for example, closings in the British Airways corpus occur through a sequence of two sets of paired turns; but in the WOZ simulations, only one pair of two turns is required. In the WOZ corpus, there are 21 instances in which the subjects exit the exchange simply by replacing the receiver without a closing sequence. In the British Airways corpus, there are no instances of a caller exiting without both parties going through a clear closing sequence. In the WOZ corpus, there are 28 instances of subjects exiting the exchange prior to a terminal turn from the wizard. In the British Airways corpus, however, there was just one instance of this phenomenon. Finally, in the British Airways corpus, closings rarely occurred without the final terminal exchange of 'bye's; but in the WOZ corpus, this component is routinely absent from the closing sequence.

In this chapter we have examined some of the ways in which the organisation of turn-taking, overlap and closing sequences differed between the WOZ simulation experiment and their occurrence in naturally occurring exchanges between members of the public and agents of the British Airways flight information service. We began the chapter by pointing out that these features of conversational interaction are of special relevance to the designers of interactive computer systems; for example, it is of paramount importance to design a system which can differentiate between the end of a user's turn and merely a pause within a turn. The analytic observations we have made have clear relevance for system designers.

The second point we made at the start of the chapter is that it is relatively simple to formulate a 'common sense' explanation for conversational practices such as turn-taking, overlap and closings. For example, we pointed out that one obvious 'lay' explanation for closings to conversational exchanges was that they are merely the consequence of people finishing what they have to say, and then saying 'goodbye' to each other. However, our analyses of data from the BA corpus have tried to demonstrate that these intuitively straightforward conversational events are the product of the participants' interactional work. They do not just happen: rather, they are the consequences of speakers' use of culturally available resources for 'doing' talk. And we saw that to some degree, this was true also of turn-taking and closing sequences in the WOZ simulation data.

7

SOME GENERAL FEATURES OF THE ORGANISATION OF REPAIR

A cursory examination of a transcript of routine conversation will reveal a catalogue of instances in which one or more parties engage in the management of some form of difficulty in the exchange. So ubiquitous are such instances of trouble management that it is uncontentious to conceive of everyday communication as flawed, partial and problematic (Coupland, Wiemann and Giles, 1991). Consequently, it is appropriate to view the resources of trouble management as intrinsic to all conversational interaction and not as a set of discrete strategies that come to be invoked on the occurrence of some specific trouble.

In this and the following chapter we examine some communicative resources for the negotiation of conversational troubles. In this chapter we will describe, first, the general properties of what Schegloff, Jefferson and Sacks (1977) call a repair system. To illustrate the features of this system we will use examples drawn from the British Airways and the WOZ simulation corpora. We then discuss empirical studies of specific repair phenomena in everyday conversation. This allows us to illustrate the range of sequential considerations which are relevant to the design of turns in which repair is executed; furthermore, these studies indicate the delicate interactional sensitivities relevant to repair organisation.

To begin our discussion of the repair system identified by Schegloff, Jefferson and Sacks (1977), it is necessary to raise some terminological and conceptual issues.

ANALYSING 'REPAIR': SOME CONCEPTUAL ISSUES

Consider the range of problems that might interrupt the smooth flow of dialogue: incorrect word selection, slips of the tongue, mis-hearings, misunderstandings, and so on. Schegloff *et al.* (1977), however, did not analyse instances of 'correction', 'clarification', and so on, as discrete forms of conversational trouble, each of which is addressed through a distinctive trouble management strategy. Rather, their analytic emphasis was to identify and describe the general properties of an organisation for repair which allows participants to deal with the whole *range* of trouble sources.[1] It is for this reason that the term 'repair' is preferred to, say, 'correction', or any other term that presupposes a specific kind of trouble source. Furthermore, vernacular terms such as 'correction' imply that there will only be trouble management upon the occurrence of some identifiable trouble. But there are instances of repair in which there is no apparent trouble source.

Let us consider cases in which speakers self-interrupt a word in mid-production. The following extract comes from the British Airways corpus. The caller has requested information about a flight, but has not stated where the flight will arrive. The BA agent then asks which airport the flight will arrive at. In the caller's subsequent turn note that she begins to say 'gatwick', the name of one of the two main London airports, but then interrupts herself and produces the name of the other, 'heathrow'.

```
(1) [5] T1:SA:F:F

6    A:   er heath↑row or gatwi[:ck,
7    C:                        [oh sorry er: from ga(t)-
8         er heathrow.
```

In this case the placement of the word cut-off signals the source of the trouble – the actual word being replaced. So, the speaker's action identifies that the trouble source relevant to this self-interruption is the word 'gatwick'. The repair is initiated in mid-production of the trouble source, and the resolution of the repair is the production of the word 'heathrow'.

In extract (1) it is clear that here the caller engages in an overt self-correction: Gatwick is simply not the airport at which the flight will arrive. However, consider the following extract. In this sequence the agent and the caller are negotiating a message that the caller would like delivered to passengers arriving on a forthcoming flight.

```
(2) [3] T1:SA:F:F

102  A:   >ah< would you
103       ↑like me to uhm (.) quickly try: and take
104       a message t' tell them to wait?
105       (.)
106  C:   ye[s  ( )
107  A:     [what's the passenger's name,
108  C:   ar m- (.3) mister adam. (.) ↓mee
```

As the caller begins to provide the name of the passenger (line 108), she begins a word, 'm-', abruptly terminates this relatively early in its projected course, waits a short time and then says 'mister alan.(.) ↓mee'. From the initial sound it is not possible to make out the word that was cut; but the subsequent production of the word 'mister', beginning with the same 'm' sound as the aborted prior item, suggests that here the speaker has simply had two attempts at getting out the same word. In which case, we see an instance of repair on an item which does not seem to be in any way incorrect.

It may be objected, however, that such a slight 'hitch' in speech production is not so much evidence of self-repair as the manifestation of a slight stutter. But in the following extract there is even stronger evidence that repair can be executed on items which are not, in any logical sense, incorrect.

(3) [59] T3:SB:F:M

```
14   C:   w**-wu-what does that mean in
15        layme(h)n's te(h)rms  [ huhh
16   A:                         [oHh sorry um
17        that's fiftee-(H)hh fourteen forty five
18        is quarter to ↓three.
```

Here, the caller is inquiring about an arrival time, and the agent has reported that the flight is due to arrive at fourteen forty-five, thus using twenty-four hour clock time to provide the relevant information. The caller subsequently pursues a clarification of the arrival time with the utterance 'what does that mean in layme(h)n's te(h)rms'. Before this, however, there are two incomplete attempts to produce the word 'what': the 'croaky' production of the first sound of the word, and then the partial production 'wu-'. Note that each attempt makes some incremental progress to the complete production of the word. This is not a phenomenon peculiar to this extract: Schegloff (1979) provides further examples of speakers making partial gains towards the complete production of a lexical item or phrase. He notes also that such incremental efforts tend to culminate in the third attempt with the successful production of the target item. So, the progressive production of the word 'what' follows an established pattern of incrementally organised self-repair, and consequently we can question whether it is the product of an idiosyncratic speech production difficulty.

These observations constitute some preliminary empirical evidence that repair can be executed on items that do not contain any overt source of trouble for the exchange. But there are also formal arguments which suggest that *any* word, phrase, clause or sentence is potentially subject to repair. Let us consider descriptions of a specific state of affairs (or object, or item, and so on). Any state of affairs can be described or referred to in a variety of ways. Schegloff has illustrated this point with regard to the formulation of location, or 'place'.

> Were I now to formulate where my notes are, it would be correct to say that they are: right in front of me, next to the telephone, on the desk, in my office, in the office, in Room 213, in Lewisohn Hall, on campus, at school, at Columbia, in Morningside Heights, on the upper West

> Side, in Manhattan, in New York City, in New York State, in the North east, on the Eastern seaboard, in the United States, etc. Each of these terms could in some sense be correct... were its relevance provided for.
>
> (Schegloff, 1972: 81)

This descriptive variability ensures that any actual formulation is potentially contestable and subject to repair.

Furthermore, Schegloff's example indicates that any actual replacement of one word for another is not necessarily motivated by a striving for 'precision', or to be 'factually correct'. This is true whether the replacement is produced by the producer of the replaced items, or a co-participant. Rather, the replacement of an item by another may be informed by the speaker's orientation to the specific recipient of a turn (Sacks and Schegloff, 1979), or may be produced with respect to specific interactional tasks (Sacks, 1979). So, repair operations may be motivated not by the speaker's awareness of the correctness of referential or descriptive items, but by specifically interactional considerations.

Additionally, instances of conversational repair may be connected to sequential features of conversational organisation. Schegloff (1979) notes that turns that effect topic shift, or initiate new topics, seem particularly susceptible to repair. He also observes that the repair tends to occur at the word that 'keys in' the new topic being initiated.

(4) (From Schegloff, 1979: 270)

```
B:    That's too bad
A:    hhhh!
      (.5)
B:    (I'unno) ·hh Hey do you see V- (.3) fat ol' Vivian
      anymouh?
```

Here B's 'That's too bad' is 'final comment' on a current topic. As the conversation progresses to A's relationship with Vivian, there is an instance of self-repair.

Exchanges between BA agents and callers are constrained by a limited set of objectives and goals and thus there is a limit on the extent to which the 'topic' of any exchange can vary. However, in the following extract there is a sequence in which a caller who has requested flight information now makes an inquiry about the fare. In the context of a flight inquiries service, this constitutes topical shift. (Indeed, such inquiries cannot be dealt with by flight inquiry agents, and in such cases the caller is referred to the appropriate service.) When the caller does shift the topic from flight inquiry to fare inquiry, the turn in which that is done manifests self-repair.

(5) [34] T2:SA:F:M

```
26   A:   =>no no (.5) first one is: yes the
27        first one is: erm: (.) seven thirty
28        then ten o'clock
29   C:   °uh°
31   A:   nine o'clock and
32        then twelve thirty
33   C:   twelve thirty
34        (.5)
35   A:   [ye:s
36   C:   [eR: so how m- how much is a
37        return fare
38        (.)
39   A:   I'm afraid I can't help you with
40        the fares you need to speak to
41        reservations department
```

So, it would appear that the initiation and execution of some repair sequences may be tied specifically to the sequential environment of topic initial turns. This class of turns is formally characterised by its relationship to immediately preceding talk. And, logically, any utterance could be a topic initiator, in that it marks a topical break with preceding talk. So, any utterance is potentially subject to repair.[2]

SELF- AND OTHER-INITIATION AND EXECUTION OF REPAIR

It is important to make some distinctions before proceeding. First, we should distinguish between the *initiation* of repair (marking something as a source of trouble), and the actual repair itself. Second, there is the distinction between repair initiated by *self* (the speaker who produced the trouble source), and repair initiated by *other*. Extract (6) provides an example of self-initiated self-repair; here the caller corrects himself in line 20, apparently thinking (incorrectly, as it turns out) that the British Airways service at *Heathrow* airport cannot provide information about flights into *Gatwick* airport.

(6) [7] T1:SA:F:M

```
18   C:   right. (.) thank you very much>are you able
19        to tell me (.5) er flight arrival times from
20        zimbabwe? oh no you can't i- its its at
21        gatwick
```

In ordinary conversation there are cases of self-initiated other-repair, but there are no cases of this in either the British Airways corpus or the WOZ corpus.

In extract (7) there is a case of other-initiated self-repair.

```
(7) [5] T1:SA:F:F

6    A:   er heath↑row or gatwi[:ck,
7    C:                        [oh sorry er: from ga(t)-
8         er heathrow.
```

Other-initiated repairs involve Next Turn Repair Initiators (NTRIs). An NTRI may be a 'wh-' question, and display the recipient's lack of understanding about the prior turn, or indicates that the recipient detected a mistake by the speaker.

Finally, we may consider other-initiated other-repair:

```
(8) [36] T2:SA:F:M

9    C:   erm I'm just checking is that (.)
10        right you know (.5) I d- I don't know
11        his flight number and[ I'm not sure
12   A:                        [(whi-)
13   C:   whether he's coming in to channel four
14        eh:
15        (.)
16   A:   terminal four
17   C:   yeah
```

Here the agent initiates and executes repair in one turn with the utterance 'terminal four'. Other-initiated other-repair does three tasks: it assigns the trouble source to the prior turn, thereby exposing it; it locates the source of trouble, and it locates and resolves trouble in one turn. It is the repair type which most explicitly raises the speaker's 'error'.

THE ORGANISATION OF REPAIR

There are now several studies which investigate the organisation of repair in conversation (Schegloff, 1979; 1992; Schegloff *et al.*, 1977). In this section we will summarise only the most basic features of repair organisation. The most salient aspect of this organisation is the sequential positioning of those places in which participants initiate the relevance of repair, or actually execute repair. The first place in which repair occurs is within the same turn construction unit as the trouble source.

```
(9) [17] T1:SB:F:M

1    A:   flight information (.) british airways
2         [good morning can I help you
3    C:   [oh (.) good morning
```

```
4          (.)
5          er can you tell me (.3) er a(b)-
6          anythink about flight bee ay (.) two
7          eight six from san francisco will it
8          be on time
```

```
(10) BA [2] T1:SA:F:F

12    A:   ·h >Well< >yu've< ↑actually wro(t)-
13         rung the wrong ↑number
```

In extract (9) the caller begins what appears to be an initial attempt to produce 'about'. This first attempt is abandoned, but re-attempted after the introduction of 'anythink'. Similarly in (10) the trouble source is an incorrect word ('wrote') which is abandoned mid-way through its production and replaced with the correct item ('rung').

The second structural position for repair occurs immediately at the next transition relevance place after the trouble source.

```
(11)     [7] T1:SA:F:M

18    C:   right. (.) thank you very much>are you able
19         to tell me (.5) er flight arrival times from
20         zimbabwe? oh no you can't i- its its at
21         gatwick
```

In extract (11) the caller has been provided with the first set of information he requested, and he begins to formulate a different question. The repair of this request (which formulates a reason why he now anticipates that the agent will not be able to deal with the request) is produced precisely at that point at which the agent's response would be appropriate: after the completion of the request which his repair now characterises as inappropriate.

Repair can be initiated and executed in the turn following the turn containing the trouble source: that is, in a co-participant's subsequent turn. In the next extract the caller requests information about a flight carried by an airline about which British Airways agents have no information. In her first turn after the request the agent identifies the trouble source and offers the correct telephone number as a repair.

```
(12) [16] T1:SB:F:F

1     A:   flight information
2          may I help you[:
3     C:                 [good morning um I was
4          wondering if you can tell me what time um:
5          (.) iberia flight six one four (.3) from
```

```
        valencia scheduled to arrive tomorrow
        please
        (.5)
    A:  ah you'll have to check with iberia I'll
        give you their number
```

It is notable that in the British Airways corpus agents show a marked tendency to initiate and execute repair in the same turn, invariably the turn after the turn which contains the trouble source. Unlike any corpus drawn from recordings of naturally occurring conversation, there are relatively few instances of other-initiated self-repair: that is, cases in which agents initiate caller's self-repair in the turn after the turn including the trouble initiator. In the light of this observation, it is useful to consider the way that the institutional context of calls to a flight information service may impinge upon and influence the shape of repair.

There is an asymmetry in the relative status of the participants with respect to flight information. Agents are flight information 'experts' and in most cases the callers have little or no knowledge of the services about which they are inquiring. Thus, on those occasions in which an agent recognises that the caller has, for example, formulated a request involving an incorrect flight detail, it is probably the case that the caller simply does not know the correct flight parameter. Thus there is little likelihood that repair initiation by the agent will lead to successful repair execution by the caller.

Agents will, however, initiate the caller's self-repair on those occasions in which the callers have neglected to specify an important aspect of the flight information. For example, in extract (7) the caller does not state the airport at which a flight will arrive, and the agent's 'er heath↑row or gatwi:ck' is designed to initiate the caller's repair.

There are also constraints imposed by the need to provide an efficient and speedy service. The British Airways flight information service receives hundreds of calls every day, and it is not unusual to find that the number of calls at any one time is greater than the number of available operators. In such cases the calls are redirected and put on hold until a connection to an operator becomes available. Such conditions facilitate the agents' attempts to locate and deliver requested information as swiftly as possible. So, in cases where a caller's turn produces a trouble source which the agent recognises, it is simply quicker and therefore more efficient for the agent to identify and address that problem within a single turn.

The final repair position occurs in what is called the third position – speaker's turn after recipient's response (Schegloff, 1992).[3] This can be represented schematically as:

A: T(urn) 1 (Trouble source)
B: T(urn) 2
A: Third position repair

Extracts (13) and (14) contain examples of third position repair from the WOZ corpus. In the first extract, the caller initiates repair by requesting a repeat of an arrival time provided in the prior turn. After the standard turn 'please wait', the agent complies with this request. In the second extract, it is the agent who initiates repair.

(13) WOZ 7:3:F (Simplified transcription)

```
10   W:   flight bee ay two five eight from caracas
11        to london heathrow terminal four arrives at
12        fourteen forty
13        (1.5)
14   S:   w-what was the time again please
15        I didn't catch that
16        (5)
17   W:   please wait
18        (7)
19   W:   flight bee ay two five eight from caracas
20        to london heathrow terminal four arrives at
21        fourteen forty
```

(14) WOZ 1:7:F

```
4    S:   ·h yes I'm enquiring about flight number ·hh bee
5         (.) ay (.) two (.) eight six ·h flying in (.3)
6         later today from san (s) francisco (.4) could you
7         tell me
8         ((subject coughs))
9         'scuse me
10         which airport (.6) i- and terminal (.) it's
11         arriving at (.) and
12         what time
13         (9)
14         ((subject coughs))
15         (2)
16         ((subject coughs))
17         (4)
18    W:   please (.) repeat (.) your (.) request
19         (1.3)
20    S:   ·h I'm enquiring about the (.) the flight
21         (.) ·h bee ay two
22         eight six
```

Overwhelmingly, repair tends to occur in close proximity to the trouble source. Repairs which are significantly delayed would require participants to 'backtrack' to locate and articulate what the trouble was, and thus the organisation of repair would have to be more elaborate. It is therefore an economical organisation.

THE PREFERENCE FOR SELF-REPAIR

Before we begin to consider the preference for self-repair, it is important to make some points concerning the use of the word 'preference'. When conversation analysts refer to preference organisation they are not referring to individual dispositions which can be consciously articulated. Rather, the term is used to mark the important and systematic differences in the ways that specific types of turns are produced (Heritage, 1984: 264–9; Levinson, 1983: 307–8). To explain this, consider the concept of the adjacency pair.

In the discussion of conversation analysis in Chapter 4 we pointed out that many types of conversational exchanges are organised as paired actions: greeting–greeting, invitation–acceptance/refusals, request–grantings/rejections, and so on. As these examples illustrate, the production of a specific first part does not determine the production of a specific kind of second. So, an invitation may be followed by an acceptance or a refusal. However, these two types of second pair parts are not equivalent: there are systematic differences in the ways in which each kind of action is produced. And it is these kinds of production differences which are captured by the term preference. Preferred actions are produced without hesitation, are constructed in short utterances, and tend to be delivered right at the start of the turn, and they are unconditionally produced: for example, there are no qualifications. Dispreferred actions, such as a refusal of an invitation, tend to be produced after some delay, prefaced by objects such as 'well' and may be accompanied by accounts which reveal the speaker's 'mitigating circumstances'.

Some of these distinctive features of preferred and dispreferred turn shapes can be illustrated with reference to data from the British Airways corpus. In all calls there is a recurrent sequence of paired actions: the callers make a request and then the agents either confirm that they can deal with that request (usually by repeating the flight details the caller has provided and indicating that they are scanning their terminals for the information), or they indicate that, for whatever reason, they are not able to deal with that request. In extract (15) we see the agent providing the first kind of response, and this is designed as a preferred turn: it is produced immediately, and is unconditional.

(15) [19] T1:SB:F:F

```
A:   flight information may I help you
     british airways here
     (.3)
C:   oh good morning ·h your bee ay two
     three eight from orlando could you
     tell me what time it landed
A:   yes certainly can you hold the line a
     moment
```

However, in the next two extracts, the agents are unable to deal with the callers' requests, and their subsequent turns have many of the characteristics of dispreferred turns: for example, they are delayed and contain objects such as 'well' and 'er'.

(16) [22] T1:SB:F:M

A: (heng) ·hh flight information good day
can I help you
C: (>oh ah<) hope so (.) ah*- (p-) I wonder if
you can give me some erm flight information
other than british airways
A: what airline do you want sir
C: err w- fran what's the airline
(1.3)
hungarian
(.7)
A: ye:ah marlev ·hh well in fact in- that's
handled on seven five nine one eight one eight

(17) [24] T1:SB:F:M

A: flight ↑information ↑may I help you:?
C: er::m (.) yes I'm actually trying to make an
inquiry about (.) gibraltar airways (.)
which I think you (.) handle as well.
(.5)
A: ·h er not on this number sir it's handled on
seven five nine one eight one eight?

In both these cases the agents provide an account as to why they cannot deal with the requests: by redirecting the callers to an alternative telephone number in each case they indicate that the flight in question is actually operated by an airline other than British Airways.

Having established that 'preference' refers to systematic differences in the design of alternative (but not equivalent) turn types, we can now consider preference in the design of repair sequences in conversational interaction.

There are two kinds of evidence to suggest a preference for self-repair in everyday conversation. There are, first, structural features intrinsic to repair organisation that predispose self-repair. We noted earlier that there are four places in which repair consistently tends to occur: within the same turn; at the next possible turn transition place, in the other speaker's next turn, and in the turn which is placed third from the turn containing the trouble source. Three of these places for repair, then, occur in the turn of the speaker who produced the original trouble source. Equally, the first two of these repair opportunities occur in the turn, or just after the turn, in which the trouble source is located, and thereby facilitate self-repair. The structural organisation of the repair mechanism is skewed towards self-repair.

The second source of evidence comes from the behaviour of participants in conversation: turn designs routinely display orientation to the appropriateness of repair by the producer of the trouble source. For example, in extract (15) the caller incorrectly pronounces a flight's place of departure, articulating the silent 'x' in Bordeaux, and in the subsequent turn the agent produces and emphasises the correct pronunciation. Although the repair is initiated and executed by the agent, she pauses after the production of the trouble source, thus providing an opportunity for the speaker of the trouble source to display recognition of an error and effect self-repair.

```
(18) [66] T3:SB:F:M

1     A:   flight information can ↑help yo[u:?
2     C:                                  [yes could you
3          give me an ee tee ey please on bee ay
4          three six five from bord↓ex
5          (.4)
6     A:   three six five from bord↑eaux (.) ↑yeah
```

Furthermore, other-initiated repairs may be modulated. In everyday conversation, for example, other-initiated repairs may be produced in conjunction with jokes. Uncertainty markers, such as 'I think you mean . . .' may also be employed. This is illustrated in extract (19).

```
(19) [8] T1:SB:F:M

11    A:   YEs: ↑hello th [ere
12    C:                  [(ah)hhhh good (.3) er: the bee
13         ay five eight four from turin. love.
14    A:   five eight fou:r hold on please?
15         (15)
16         er we don't have five eight four sir
17         I think you might mean the five seven nine
```

Here the caller has requested information about a flight but has used a flight number unfamiliar to the BA agent. The agent uses 'I think you might mean' to characterise her proffered alternative as a 'candidate' correct flight number, and not as an explicit correction. Consider also the following extract.

```
(20) [7] T1:SA:F:M

59    A:   the time for you, [·h
60    C:                     [yes
61    A:   i:s: oh one seven five ↑night
62         (.)
63    A:   [seven  five   ni:ne,]          ((smiley voice))
64    C:   [seven five what. (.)] yes
65    A:   one eight one eight,
66    C:   one eight one eight
```

Here the agent makes a clear error, saying 'night' instead of 'nine'. The error is recognised by both parties. The agent begins to repeat the last three digits of the telephone number, and does so in a 'smiley' voice which displays her realisation of the mistake, and also its humorous dimension. At the same time, the caller begins to repeat the same last three numbers, and they both progress towards the repairable item in overlap. However, whereas the agent produces the correct last number, the caller instead ends with the word 'what', thereby initiating the relevance of repair and identifying the trouble source as the word produced after the numbers 'seven' and 'five'. Thus the caller displays that he recognises a problem but produces a turn designed to initiate the agent's self-repair, which is produced in overlap with the agent's actual repair of the trouble source.

So far we have shown how repair strategies display a robust organisation. The interest in explicating organisational or structural properties of repair will be developed in the following chapter. But there are two other features of repair organisation that we wish to consider here. In our investigation of repair strategies employed in the WOZ study we want to explore the sequential properties of repair operation; similarly, we will explore the interactional or interpersonal sensitivities which are displayed in the way that users identify and effect repair. To illustrate our interest in the sequential and interactional features of repair, we will briefly discuss empirical studies of repair in conversation.

SOME SEQUENTIAL PROPERTIES OF REPAIR

It is clear that mechanisms of repair and their organisation are not resources extrinsic to 'normal' conversation, available to be employed only when some difficulty emerges. Rather, they are intrinsic to the flow of routine conversation: they are organically implicated in the trajectory of talk-in-interaction. That is, procedures for effecting repair have implications for the sequential development of the spate of interaction in which the repair occurs.

In one sense it is quite obvious that self-repair has sequential importance, in that such operations can significantly alter the shape of the turn being repaired, thus projecting an appropriate next turn different to that which would have been implicated had the turn shape prior to the repair been allowed to develop. Schegloff (1979) has explored this issue in a paper examining the impact of repair on syntax. He provides examples of the way that self-initiated self-repair can alter the syntactic shape (described vernacularly, not technically) of a sentence. So, repair can subsume the shape of a sentence under another 'frame'.

```
(21) (From Schegloff, 1979: 264)

Cathy:        Shit y- I think y'got the original nickel
```

The sequential impact of self-initiated self-repair is perhaps most apparent in those turns in which the repair transforms a turn which was originally designed to be a question into a turn which constitutes some other form of activity, such as an assertion; or in those turns which were not designed to be questions, but which are transformed into such by the repair procedures.

(22) (From Schegloff, 1979:264)

```
L:   Didju s- you saw that, it's really good.
```

(23) (From Schegloff, 1979:264)

```
A:   Well I don't think she-
     eh she doesn't uh usually come in on Friday does she
```

There is evidence, however, that self-initiated self-repair displays an organised set of sequential and structural properties. It is not infrequent to find parts of turns recycled or repeated. For example:

(24) (From Schegloff, 1987:70)

```
(a):   Um, this is a rug- this is a punched rug.
(b):   I was I was just thinking today
```

Schegloff observed that these partial or complete recyclings and repeats occur regularly at sequentially and structurally important places in conversation: the beginnings of turns. These are important places in conversation because they provide critical resources for the management of turn-taking. To ensure the minimum amount of overlap, and the 'one party at a time' feature of conversation, the organisation of turn-taking requires participants to monitor on-going talk to determine the onset of a turn transition relevance place. Turn initial places are important because they project the shape of a turn and provide clues as to possible completion points. Repair on the beginnings of turns, then, will have an impact on the eventual shape of the turn in production.

A feature of the organisation of conversation is that there is a premium in starting early to assure oneself next turn (Sacks *et al.*, 1974). But there is always the potential problem of a current speaker continuing to talk beyond the turn transition relevance place at which a potential next speaker began to talk. So, the earliest place for a potential next to start speaking is susceptible to overlap. This is particularly problematic because the overlap obscures those parts of next speaker's turn which indicate the shape of the turn that is being started: that is, whether it is a question, an answer, a statement and so on; and such an overlap will also obscure the kind of business the turn is designed to deal with. This is crucial, as it will affect potential other speakers' ability to anticipate the onset of the next available turn transition space.[4] Partial or complete repeats occur regularly where that turn has started in overlap with the prior. Furthermore, the relationship between the recycled turn and the prior turn is not haphazard. The recycles appear precisely at that point where the overlap with the prior turn ends, either by coming to its natural end or by being withdrawn by the speaker.[5]

This repair mechanism gives an advantage to potential next speakers, rather than current speakers, because current speakers have no such opportunity to recycle components of their turns. In short, it is biased for potential next speakers. Schegloff argues that this is a necessary counterbalance to the facilities that current speakers have for extending in an *ad hoc* way their current turn (speeding up, latching on, and so on). Indeed, Schegloff examines some data in which the recycling device is used as a direct counterbalance to a prior speaker's attempt to continue talking by rushing through a potential turn transition relevance place.

REPAIR AND INTERPERSONAL RELATIONS

In an earlier section we noted that the organisation of repair predisposes self-repair in that, for example, three of the four positions in which repair can be executed are available for the producer of the turn containing the repairable item. Equally, we have seen empirical evidence of the preference for self-repair. In part this preference may arise from the kind of delicate interactional sensitivities associated with repair. That is, effecting some forms of conversational repair may be taken as a slight, a 'put down' or might even be cited as evidence of deliberate rudeness. Repair work, then, has potential implications for the co-ordination of the interpersonal relations of the relevant parties.

It is useful to think of the co-ordination of interpersonal relations in conversation as a form of alignment between the respective parties. We use 'alignment' to refer to two features of conversational organisation. First, alignment refers to the practices through which repair is engineered to ensure that the smooth flow of the exchange is not jeopardised by the specific actions whereby trouble sources are identified and negotiated. Second, it refers also to the way that participants achieve and display their mutual understanding of the trajectory of the exchange: that is, how turns are designed to show that the producers of those turns recognise the actions (in this case, repair work) accomplished by the design of co-participants' turns.

We can illustrate both dimensions of alignment by considering cases of repair in which one party corrects another (Jefferson, 1987). Consider the following extracts.

(25) (From Jefferson, 1987:87)

```
Larry:   They're going to drive ba:ck Wednesday.
Norm:    Tomorrow.
Larry:   Tomorrow. Right
```

(26) (From Jefferson, 1987:87)

```
Milly:   . . . and then they said something about Kruschev
         has leukemia so I thought oh it's all a big put on.
Jean:    Breshnev.
Milly:   Breshnev has leukemia. So I don't know what to
         think.
```

These data contain examples of what Jefferson calls exposed correction. She notes that this form of correction has three properties. First, it exhibits the following pattern.

A speaker produces an object (X)
A subsequent speaker produces an alternative object (Y)
Prior speaker also produces the alternative (Y)

So, in extract (25) we find the sequence 'Wednesday', 'Tomorrow', 'Tomorrow'. Second, it is noticeable that, for at least some time, the topic of the conversation prior to the repair is discontinued and the repair work itself becomes the focus for the current interaction. So, again referring to extract (26), Norm has corrected Larry, and this is explicitly recognised by Larry in that he provides a turn in which the correction is accepted. Third, this type of correction addresses what might be termed 'lapses in speakers' competence'. So for example, Norm's turn 'Tomorrow' stands as the correct date for an event which is erroneously described as occurring on 'Wednesday'. This kind of correction, therefore, involves activities such as 'putting right', instructing, complaining and so on. Jefferson calls these activities 'accountings'.

These examples of exposed correction illustrate two features which provide the basis for actual or potential disruption of the conversation: correction itself becomes the activity for which that moment of the conversation is organised, and the prior topic is momentarily discontinued. Equally, as the actual correction challenges aspects of the speaker's competence, the production of exposed correction can be a potentially sensitive issue.

There is a device, however, which allows participants to engage in correction while minimising the likelihood of interpersonal difficulties. Jefferson calls this device *embedded* correction, and it furnishes resources to ensure both conversational and interpersonal alignment.

Jefferson begins analysis of embedded correction by noting some properties of cases in which speakers make consecutive reference to the 'same' object or state of affairs by using alternative items. For example:

(27) (From Jefferson, 1987:93)

Ken: Well-if you're gonna race, the police have said to us.
Roger: That makes it even better. The challenge of running from the cops!
Ken: The cops say if you wanna race, uh go out at four or five in the morning on the freeway . . .

Here, Ken says 'police', Roger says 'cops', and then Ken says 'cops' also. Jefferson notes other examples of this pattern and states that:

> Over and above sheer consecutive reference, then, it appears that when a next speaker produces, not a proterm or a repeat, but an alternative item, correction may be underway.
>
> (Jefferson, 1987: 93)

Although this form of correction follows the 'X', 'Y', 'Y' format identified in exposed correction, there are some important differences, and these bear on the issue of alignment raised earlier. In cases of embedded correction the activity of repair is accomplished in the course of the conversation, and does not lead to repair *per se* becoming the focus for the conversation. This ensures that the smooth trajectory of the exchange is preserved. Furthermore, in cases of exposed correction it was noted that the repair was accompanied by instructings, queryings, and the like, which specifically addressed lapses in competence. But embedded corrections permit of no place for such explicit accountings, and issues concerning the speaker's competence are not raised. Moreover, the corrected party demonstrates that correction has been done and accepted by using the alternative term provided by the correcting party, thus ensuring mutual co-ordination between the respective participants. In this sense, embedded correction is an interactionally sensitive device for executing and displaying correction.

In the next chapter we examine some repair devices which occur in the WOZ data, and we will expand upon some of the themes which we have sketched in this chapter. In particular, we investigate some of the sequential implications of repair strategies, and also focus on the inferential or interactional work which may be addressed through the organisation of these devices.

8

SOME REPAIR STRATEGIES ANALYSED

In the last chapter we used examples taken from the British Airways corpus to illustrate some principles underlying the conversation analytic approach to the study of repair. In this chapter, we focus exclusively on repair strategies used by the subjects in the WOZ simulation study. However, we will be developing themes discussed in the previous chapter: for example, our analysis focuses on the way that turns are designed to exhibit the subject's alignment with what they understand to be the system's difficulty with their request.

To start, we examine cases in which the subjects attempt repair when confronted by long silences in the dialogue with the system.

THE INTERPRETATION AND REPAIR OF SILENCE

In Chapter 2 we noted that in order to foster the impression that the subjects were talking to a computer, the wizards tended to speak with a slow staccato delivery. The wizards also left comparatively lengthy gaps between the end of a subject's prior turn and the beginning of their own turn. To further the impression of a speaking computer, wizards also left short pauses between words within the same utterance. It was felt that the combined effect of these speech delivery patterns would be the impression of computational processes operating to digest the subject's utterances, search data banks for the required information and produce it for the subject. These speech delivery patterns are illustrated in the following extract.

(1) WOZ 3:8:M

```
W:   flight (.2) information (.5) can (.) I help (.) you
     (.5)
S:   yes I'd (.) like to: confirm when ·h the
     flight from warsaw arrives ·h at heathrow
     terminal two tomorrow evening=I think
     it's at nine thirty (.) pee em
     could you confirm that please
```

```
        (4)
W:      please (.) wait
        (22.5)
W:      there (.) are (.) no (.) british (.) airways (.)
        flights (.) from (.2) warsaw
        (1)
W:      please (.) try (.2) poland (.2) airlines
        (1)
S:      thank you
        (2.2)
W:      thank you (.) good (.) bye
```

This extract contains some lengthy pauses. For example, 4 seconds elapse after the subject's request formulation and before the wizard's 'please wait' in line 8. Then there is a 22.5 second silence between that turn and the turn in which the actual request is dealt with. Intuitively, a silence of this length is likely to be the source of some confusion for the subject, even though the system's prior turn has indicated that there would be some delay before its next contribution. In the WOZ corpus there are, indeed, instances of subjects showing confusion about the current state of the exchange during the lengthy silences. This is particularly true when subjects were engaged in the first of their trials, before they had become accustomed to the speech delivery patterns of the system.

(2) WOZ 8:1:M (Simplified transcription)

```
W:      flight information british airways good day
        can I help you
        (2.5)
S:      yes: er:m I'd like to ask about (.)
        flights arriving from cre:te today please
        (3.5)
W:      please wait
        (5)
S:      could you repeat that please
        (4.5)
W:      please wait
        (8.5)
S:      huh hel↑lo (.) flights from cre:te (.)
        arriving at gatwick airport
        (.5)
W:      I'm sorry there are no flights leaving
        crete today
```

After a silence of 8.5 seconds in line 12, the subject produces a turn designed, first, to check that the line is still open, and second, to repeat important parameters of the actual request. Thus it addresses a problem (the system's non-participation) and provides a solution (repeat the request).

There is evidence, however, that much shorter silences can be the source of some difficulties. Jefferson (1989) suggests there is standard metric of approximately one second in conversational interaction. Her analysis of instances of silences falling within a 0.8 to 1.2 second boundary reveals that speakers orient to this critical period as a 'tolerance interval' (Jefferson, 1989: 170) which marks the acceptable length of absence of talk in conversational interaction. After silences of a duration between approximately 0.8 to 1.2 seconds, speakers can be observed to begin talking so as to terminate the silence. This suggests that silences which reach beyond approximately 1.2 seconds are being treated as signs of trouble in the conversation. Furthermore, research has shown that silences in conversation are monitored closely, and that such monitoring is consequential for the inferences that participants may arrive at concerning the significance of co-participants' behaviour.

(3) (From Atkinson and Drew, 1979:52)

Child: Have to cut the:se Mummy
(1.3)
Child: Won't we Mummy

In this instance, after the child asks a question, the mother does not answer and there is an absence of talk for 1.3 seconds. However, the child does not merely repeat the question, but provides a truncated utterance which abbreviates the previously formulated question. The child's subsequent turn is therefore informed by an analysis of the absence of talk as indicating not 'Mummy didn't hear', but 'Mummy heard but didn't answer'. The child's behaviour in this fragment is informed by normative requirements associated with paired action sequences (Schegloff and Sacks, 1973). But for our purposes we need only note that the child addresses a 'trouble' – the absence of the conditionally relevant answer – after a silence which reaches the outer edge of the tolerance boundary.

In the light of this observation, consider the following extract from the WOZ corpus.

(4) WOZ 1:6:F

W: flight (.) information (.4) british (.) airways
(.5)
good day (.7) can I help you
(.6)
S: h yes- (.) I'm enquiring about em the flights
coming from crete ·h there's one due in: (.) to
gatwick (.2) approximately ten o'clock this morning
·h but I've heard (.) there's some problems (.) do
you know if there's any flight delays
(4)
W: please wait
(27)
W: please (.3) repeat (.) the (.) point (.) of

```
        departure
        (1.2)
S:      ·hh well >th-< the- it's flying from crete
        (4.3)
S:      to gatwick
        (1.2)
S:      arriving at gatwick
        (4.3)
W:      I'm (.) sorry (.7) british (.) airways (.5) do not
        have (.) any (.) flights (.5) from (.) crete (.3)
        arriving (.) this (.) morning
```

We will focus on the sequence in lines 16 to 20 which is prompted by the wizard's request for a partial repeat of the initial query.

Note that the subject has been asked to provide specific information concerning only one parameter of the relevant flight, and that she complies with this request. Equally, after the word 'crete' the subject makes no non-lexical sounds ('err', 'erm', and the like) which might indicate that there is more to come; neither is the word 'crete' itself elongated, as it might be if the subject wanted to display that it was not the last thing that she was going to say in that turn. It would appear that at the point where the subject utters the word 'crete' she has completed her turn.

The subject's completion passes the floor to the system. There are a variety of relevant responses which the system could produce here: it could acknowledge that the information has been received, announce that the inquiry is now being dealt with, ask the subject to wait, or pursue some further information to enable it to address the flight request. But there are no responses of any kind, and after 4.3 seconds, the subject begins to speak again, saying first 'to gatwick' and then providing a minor reformulation of this information 'arriving at gatwick'.

In one of his early lectures, Sacks considered the delicate issue of no-one starting to talk when someone has demonstrably completed a turn (Sacks, Winter 1969, lecture 9: 15). He focused on one strategy by which conversationalists can address this problem, namely, to treat the silence not as 'nobody's talking', nor as an absence of the talk of the last person to speak, but as a pause within one person's talk. He states that this can be done by turning whatever is said next into a recognisable continuation of what was said prior to the silence. And this is exactly what 'to gatwick' does: it stands as a continuation of the turn 'it's flying from crete'. However, if it is the case that the turn in line 18 is done as a completion for the turn in line 16, then we can also say that it proposes that the earlier turn was incomplete. 'To gatwick' thus retrospectively 'de-completes' 'well >th-< the- it's flying from crete'.

The silence of 4.3 seconds in line 17 is treated by the subject as a trouble source. By continuing a turn prior to the silence, we can see that the subject is not treating the absence of talk as a consequence of a technical glitch in the lines of communication, or any kind of system failure. Such assumptions would motivate attempts to assess whether the telephone line was still working, or would prompt questions directed to the system which focus explicitly on its continued participation. The production of a continuation is premised on the system's in-principle continued participation in that it portrays the absence of system contribution as a *temporary* non-participation.

Insofar as the subject provides a continuation which furnishes additional details of the relevant flight, she proposes that, in the absence of talk, the system should have made some contribution, but that it could not do anything until she had furnished further information. Thus, the responsibility for the absence of talk is identified as the system's inability to participate. And insofar as the subject does work to remedy this, she demonstrably colludes in (what is now taken to be) the system's 'indication' that the turn 'it's flying from crete' was not complete.

'To gatwick', then, both characterises the nature of, and provides a resolution to, a problem. The source of the problem is portrayed as the insufficient information in the subject's initial turn in this sequence; and the additional information is an attempt to remedy this. Through this pragmatic work, then, the subject can be seen to be aligning herself with what has been inferred as the source of the systems' temporary non-participation.

In his lecture, Sacks mentions some 'virtues' which accrue from the provision of turns which continue turns prior to spates of silence, and we may consider these here. First, some inferential virtues. We have noted already that the design of the continuing turn proposes, broadly, the subject's alignment to, or agreement with, what the system's problem is taken to be. But with regards to specific details of this sequence, there is a more concrete upshot of this strategy, in that it allows the subject to propose that the request had been misheard. That is, the provision of the additional information 'to gatwick' portrays the caller as being in the position of 'coming to realise' that it was the departure *and* arrival place that was required, and thereby establishes her 'current understanding' that her own prior turn had not ended. This in turn corroborates a sense of alignment achieved by the subject, in that it characterises the subject as 'coming to realise' that she has made a mistake. Furthermore, and this is an observation taken from Sacks' lecture, it proposes that the co-participant, or in this case, the system, was correct not to participate at this moment, because the turn in which such talk could have started was not at that point complete: had the system started to contribute to the exchange, it would have been an 'interruption' in the subject's turn.

There are some sequential virtues also. The significant feature of this sequence is that the system did not begin to participate upon the completion of the utterance 'well >th-< the- it's flying from crete'. The provision of a continuation furnishes another opportunity for the system to begin in that it projects a further turn transition relevance place (Sacks *et al.*, 1974). Furthermore, a continuation utterance can be so designed to identify and deal with a trouble source as a feature of the on-going exchange, thereby diminishing the likelihood and necessity of an explicit repair or clarification sequence.[1]

Having established some of the basic properties of this strategy for identifying and addressing a specific trouble source, we can now examine some of its broader organisational features. We will begin by considering some further features of the dialogue in this extract.

(5) WOZ 1:6:F:16-24

```
16   S:   ·hh well >th-< the- it's flying from crete
17        (4.3)
18   S:   to gatwick
19        (1.2)
20   S:   arriving at gatwick
21        (4.3)
22   W:   I'm (.) sorry (.7) british (.) airways (.5) do not
23        have (.) any (.) flights (.5) from (.) crete (.3)
24        arriving (.) this (.) morning
```

Here the utterance 'to gatwick' stands as a continuation for the utterance prior to the 4.3 second silence. However, the utterance 'arriving at gatwick' does not continue the turn 'to gatwick' but merely provides another version of it. So, there is a single continuation. But there are cases in which two continuation turns are produced.

(6) WOZ 1:6:F:33-42

```
33   S:   and do you know if any other companies hhh (.8) w-
34        do have any schesuls (.) scheduled flights flying
35        into gatwick
36        (1.3)
37   S:   this morning
38        (.8)
39   S:   from crete
40        (6)
41   W:   this (.) flight (.2) may be handled (.) by another
42        (.2) carrier
```

In extract (6) 'this morning' continues the turn prior to the 1.3 second silence. Similarly, 'from crete' also stands as a continuation of the same turn. Consider also the next extract.

(7) WOZ 1:7:F:18-32

```
18   W:   please (.) repeat (.) your (.) request
19        (1.3)
20   S:   ·h I'm enquiring about the (.) the flight
21        (.) ·h bee ay two
```

```
        eight six
        (1)
S:      flying in later today (.) ·h from san
        francisco
        (.7)
S:      ·h and I want to know which
        airport (.4) it's arriving at (.3) and
        which terminal (.) ·hh and also what
        time (.3) please h
        (3)
W:      please wait
```

In those cases in which subjects produce two continuations, as in extracts (6) and (7), the length of the silence between the original turn and the first continuation is longer than the silence between the first continuation and the second. The duration of the silences in these extracts are, respectively, in extract (6) 1.3 seconds and 0.8 second, and in extract (7), 1 second and 0.7 second. This has a parallel in sequences in which only one continuation is produced. For example, in extract (4) we noted one continuation, silence, and then another utterance which provided a minor amendment to the substantive content of the prior continuation. But even here, the length of the silence between the initial turn and the minor reformulation is longer than that which appeared between the continuation and the subsequent minor reformulation: 4.3 and 1.2 seconds respectively. It would appear that a robust feature of these sequences is the decline in the length of silences which subjects will allow before providing a first continuation and then a second, or some other turn which, although not a continuation, is in some way connected to the business that the prior turn addresses.

While there are cases of subjects producing a second continuation utterance after a first, there are no examples of a subject then producing a further, third, continuation utterance. In each instance, subjects wait for the system to make some response after the second continuation, even if the silence between the end of the second continuation and the system's next turn far exceeds the 1.2 second tolerance boundary. So, for example, in extract (4), there is a 4.3 second lapse after the second continuation; in extract (6) there is a 6 second silence before the wizard's next turn, and in extract (7) there is a 3 second silence before the wizard's acknowledgement that the request is being dealt with. During the silences the subjects make no attempt to extend further the initial turn. There may be constraints operating to circumscribe the circumstances in which subjects initiate remedial actions through the production of continuation utterances.

Intuitively, one such constraint may be, quite simply, that there are no further parameters, or features of the request, which have not already been mentioned in the two continuation utterances. However, this is only a partial explanation, as subjects can always use a simple politeness token to complete a turn prior to a problematic silence. For example:

(8) WOZ 1:8:F

W: flight (.) information (.4) may I help you
(.8)
S: ·h I'm enquiring about the flight from gatwick
(.) to new york ·hh flying at noon today (.)
it's bee (.) ay (.) one (.) seven (.) three
·hh could you just confirm all the details about
that flight for me
(2.2)
S: please
(1.3)
W: please wait

A more satisfactory explanation emerges if we consider some of the sequential properties of this device. We noted earlier that the initial turn projects a place or slot for the wizard to produce a turn; from the subject's point of view, preferably one in which the system will furnish the requested information. In the absence of such a turn, a continuation utterance projects another, second opportunity for the system to demonstrate its continued participation in the exchange. And a second continuation, therefore, provides a third sequential position in which the wizard can address the subject's (now considerably extended) request. Instead of trying to discover why there are no third continuations, it might be more fruitful to ask why are there no instances of subjects designing turns to project a fourth position in which the system can say something.

In ordinary conversation, there are many occasions in which people produce a list of items or states of affairs: that is, listing is a common conversational practice.

(9) (From Jefferson, 1991:63)

(a)
while you've been talking tuh me,
I mended,
two nightshirts,
a pillowcase?
enna pair'v pants.

(b)
That was a vicious school there-
it was about
forty percent Negro,
'bout twenny percent Japenese,
the rest were rich Jews. heh hah

Studies of conversational listing have revealed that participants orient to lists as being complete upon the provision of the third item. There are several sources of evidence for this. For example, where speakers are clearly having difficulty in locating third parts, co-interactants may volunteer candidate third parts (Jefferson, 1991: 66). Similarly, where an appropriate third part does not come to mind easily, speakers may use utterances such as '... and everything', '... and all that'. '... and things' after the first two items as a way of completing the list in three parts.

(10) (From Jefferson, 1991:66)

And they had a concession
stand like at a fair
where you can buy
coke
and popcorn
and that type of thing

Lists produced in three parts also have a significance in other forms of language use. Atkinson (1984a and b) and Heritage and Greatbatch (1986) found that three part lists are a common organisational resource in political speeches. Making political points in three parts not only allows the speaker to provide a rounded characterisation of a political point, but also provides a cue for members of the audience to orchestrate a collective show of affiliation or appreciation (Heritage and Greatbatch, 1986). Similarly, the persuasive import of three part lists has not been lost on advertising agencies: advertising slogans are saturated with three parted components. It would appear also that there is a deeply embedded cultural significance about the number three: the Christian faith has the Holy Trinity, jokes routinely have three characters or three distinct components, and many fairy tales have three central characters.

With this in mind we can reconsider the phenomenon of two continuations. It was noted that the initial request provides a slot for an appropriate next turn by the system, and that each successive continuation re-cycles this opportunity. The second continuation, then, provides the third opportunity for the system to make some response to the initial, now extended, request formulation. That is, the production of continuation utterances is a series of the subject's actions to facilitate a specific consequence. We may speculate, then, that the absence of any fourth such attempt indicates the subject's orientation to culturally available conventions that behaviour such as 'the production of actions in a series' should be organised in three parts. So, although the speakers are not explicitly producing a list of discrete items, the same normative conventions which operate in list production in ordinary conversation also inform the number of times the speakers provide the system with opportunities to participate in the exchange.

Having established some of the cultural constraints on the number of continuation utterances, let us now consider some of the interactional properties of this strategy. Consider the following extract.

(11) WOZ 1:7:F

W: flight (.) information (.4) british (.) airways
(.6) good day (.3) can I help you
(.4)
S: h yes I'm enquiring about flight number #hh bee
(.) ay (.) two (.) eight six h flying in (.3)
later today from san (s) francisco (.4) could you
tell me
((*subject coughs*))
S: 'scuse me
which airport (.6) i- and terminal (.) it's
arriving at (.) and
what time
(9)
((*subject coughs*))
(2)
((*subject coughs*))
(4)
W: please (.) repeat (.) your (.) request
(1.3)
W: ·h I'm enquiring about the (.) the flight
(.) ·h bee ay two
eight six
(1)
S: flying in later today (.) ·h from san
francisco
(.7)
S: ·h and I want to know which
airport (.4) it's arriving at (.3) and
which terminal (.) ·hh and also what
time (.3) please h
(3)
W: please wait

In this exchange the subject requests information concerning the airport at which the flight in question will arrive, the terminal and the time of arrival. However, the wizard's subsequent turn initiates repair by requesting a repeat. This gives the subject a practical difficulty. Does the system require a repeat of the whole request? Is the system's difficulty focused on a specific component of the request? Do specific parts of the request require reformulation to assist the system?

In the subsequent turn the subject repeats only one component of the flight information. There is no attempt at this point to furnish any more information to enable the system to identify the flight. Neither does the subject state explictly what information is required. In this sense, then, it is a candidate repair: it represents the subject's first 'guess' as to what the difficulty may be. It also projects a slot or next turn in which the system can indicate whether or not it can now proceed with the request. The absence of such an indication is treated by the subject as demonstrating the system's continuing difficulty with some aspect of the request, thereby necessitating the production of another turn. This turn, designed as a continuation of the turn prior to the silence, furnishes one more point of information about the flight. This displays the subject's current understanding that the information provided immediately before was insufficient, and required supplementing and demonstrates the subject's alignment with what she has interpreted to be the reason for the system's continued non-participation. When the silence after the first turn reaches the critical tolerance boundary the subject provides the rest of the information relevant to the specific flight, and finally repeats all that is required from the system. So, in the attempt to resolve the system's apparent difficulty the subject gradually releases potentially relevant information.[2]

We end this section by noting some of the interactional virtues to accrue from the gradual release of relevant information. It ensures that the speaker does not, in the first instance, have to repeat everything that was said when the request was originally formulated. In this, the organisation of the device has economical properties. Similarly, had the subject merely repeated the whole request, there would have been no way of ensuring that the original problem was not recycled in that repeat. The gradual repeat of the original request facilitates the subject's ability to locate what exactly was the source of the system's difficulty in the first place.

REPAIR VIA ALIGNMENT

In our discussion of continuation utterances it became clear that the subject's turns were designed to display their alignment with what they understood to be the source of the system's difficulty. In this section we pursue the issue of alignment more directly. In the following extract the exchange runs into difficulty in lines 12 and 13.

(12) WOZ 7:5:F (Simplified transcription)

```
W:   flight information can I help you
     (1.5)
S:   yes I wanted to get the number:
     the flight number for the british airways
     flight (.) lea:vi:ng to↑morrow from gatwick
     to barcelona. (.3) leave in the morning.
     (5)
W:   please (.)  wait
     (38)
W:   british (.) airways (.4) has (.) no flight(s) (.5)
     from gatwick to (.) barcelona
     (1.3)
S:   er: perhaps it's another airline >would you
     be able to check< (.) if: if there's
     flights from gatwick to barcelona: on
     say any other airline leaving tomorrow morning
```

The subject appears to encounter some kind of difficulty in formulating what to say after the wizard's turn in lines 10 and 11. There is a silence of 1.3 seconds, which is curtailed by the subject's hesitation marker, 'er:'. We propose that the silence in line 12 indicates the subject's procedural difficulty, and that this in turn rests upon an ambiguity as to what next action the system's turn projects for the subject. In this section we will focus on this single extract to examine how the subject deals with this procedural difficulty. Broadly, we are interested in the way that her subsequent turn is designed to address the problem raised by the system while at the same time preserving the on-going flow of the exchange.

In extract (12), while it is clear that the system cannot deal with the request as formulated, it is not entirely obvious what the problem is. It may be the case that British Airways has no services to Barcelona, or it may be that British Airways does carry services to Barcelona, but from Heathrow Airport, and not from Gatwick Airport. This ambiguity is in part a consequence of the technical protocol of the experiment: remember that the wizard's voice is distorted so that the subject has no intonational clues by which to interpret, and perhaps disambiguate, the informational content of the wizard's utterances. But more significantly, the ambiguity impedes the subject's tacit analysis of what kind of next turn is appropriate. If the system's turn was designed to indicate that it could not deal with the request, the subject can either exit from the exchange or ask the system to provide an alternative source for the required information.[3] Alternatively, the system may have been indicating (albeit ambiguously) that the subject had incorrectly formulated a relevant flight, in which case the subject has the option of pursuing the information through a suitably amended request formulation.

The first part of the subject's subsequent turn addresses these kinds of sequential issues. 'Perhaps it's another airline' is informed by the subject's understanding that the flight about which he has inquired is not run by British Airways. Moreover, it displays an acceptance of that problem, and as such, portrays the subject's alignment with what is inferred to be the significance of the system's prior turn. However, the identification of the trouble source does not here become the topic of the exchange: there is no explicit reference to a mistake being made. Instead, the reference to the airline as a problematic parameter is designed as an upshot of the system's prior turn. This facilitates the subject's pursuit of the required information. Furthermore, insofar as she identifies and proposes a solution for the source of the system's apparent difficulty, the subject here is doing a form of 'self-repair'. This in turn indicates her analysis that the system's previous contribution initiated the relevance of, and projected a place for, such repair. We have noted that the subject's turn is designed to take account of what is inferred to have been the import of the system's prior turn, and to pursue the required information. As such, aspects of its design may display an orientation to a potential impropriety: asking an agent of the British Airways flight information service about the flights of another airline is to ask about a competitor. We may note that these improprieties are sensitive issues for those callers to the actual British Airways flight information service who are subsequently informed that the flight about which they are inquiring is carried by another airline. For example:

```
(13) [74] BA:T4:SA:M:F

1    A:   british airways may I ↑help you
2    C:   yes can you tell me please if air ukay three
3         ni:ne↓ty is coming in at fifteen twenty
4         five still
5    A:   I'm sorry we're british airways (we) don't
6         handle air u↓kay (.4) [ (       )
7    C:                         [er: >well it just
8         says in the book< heathrow seven five
9         nine two five two five two five
10   A:   that's british airways heathrow
```

In line 7 the caller begins to explain that he has called this number because it is the one provided in the (phone) book. He thus furnishes an account for calling what has been revealed to be the wrong service. Insofar as it has a defensive character, this account mitigates the impropriety of the caller's error. Accounting practices such as this are regular features in circumstances in which required or projected behaviour does not occur (Heritage, 1988). Some features of the subject's turn in lines 13 to 16 in extract (12) seem to display an orientation to this impropriety.[4]

We note first that the request 'would you be able to check' is produced at a faster rate than the surrounding talk. Remember that the subject's previous utterance 'perhaps it's another airline' has formulated the source of the system's difficulty. Given the nature of this difficulty, it is possible that the system is simply unable to help (and, eventually, this indeed turns out to be the case). So at the point after the system's negative turn, there is a chance that the exchange may be entering a terminal phase prior to the subject's exit. The production of 'would you be able to check' as a spate of accelerated speech may indicate the subject's sensitivity to the potential onset of a terminal phase of the exchange.

The appropriateness of this pursuit, however, is in part warranted by the manner in which the subject has displayed her analysis of the nature of the system's difficulty with the original request. We have observed that 'perhaps it's another airline' formulates the subject's upshot of the system's prior turn. Furthermore, it portrays the subject's acceptance that this indeed is a problem, and thereby constitutes her alignment with the system's difficulty. However, the accomplishment of alignment has the consequence of making the subject's turn hearable as offering a candidate solution for that difficulty. This in turn constitutes the problem not as an 'intractable condition', which implies the closure of the exchange, but as 'just another contingency' in the process of locating the required information.

RECYCLING

This chapter has been concerned with repair, alignment, and the interactional and sequential considerations relevant to repair. In this final section we will develop further remarks on these central issues with respect to one specific kind of trouble. The protocol of the WOZ design ensured that, in some cases, the wizard did not provide the information which the subject had actually requested; and on other occasions, the wizard produced only a part of the required information.

(14) WOZ 7:6:F (Simplified transcription)

W: flight information may I help you
(1.3)
S: yes I've got a ticket er british airways
one seven three (.) er from gatwick
to new ↑york I just want to confirm that
and make sure all the flight details
(.5)
S: are the same
(3.5)
W: please wait
(22)
W: flight bee ay one seven three leaves
from london gatwick to new york at twelve noon
(2.3)
S: a:nd is my seat confirmed on that flight.
please.
(4.5)
W: please wait

In extract (14) the subject's first turn reveals that she has a ticket, that she knows the flight carrier, the flight number, the place of departure and the flight's destination. The actual request is somewhat ambiguous: the referent for 'I just want to confirm *that*' could be the flight details that she has already mentioned. Equally, 'that' could refer to her possession of a ticket, in which case her turn can be understood as seeking seat confirmation. (The subject's turns after the wizard's response seems to indicate that indeed she was trying to obtain confirmation that she had a reserved seat.) The simulated service, however, is not able to provide information on seat reservation. Subsequently, the wizard confirms all the details of the flight, but does not provide seat confirmation. But more important, the wizard does not explain that seat confirmation is outside the scope of the service. So, the subject is faced with a response to her request which provides all the required information but for one component.

Let us consider some of the properties of the subject's next turn, 'a:nd is my seat confirmed on that flight. please.'. This turn displays the subject's recognition that the seat confirmation has not been provided, and insofar as it seeks that information, it effects repair of that difficulty. This repair is initiated in such a way that the omitted request component – seat confirmation – is raised again in the exchange. However, the issue of seat reservation is not re-introduced to the exchange as a reminder, or prompt. Turns which do 'reminding' are premised on the assumption that the first time a turn or conversational item had been produced, it had been heard; it would be pointless trying to remind someone of an item which had not previously been raised. There are ways of repeating specific items which display that the producer assumes that the initial production of the turn had in fact been heard by the recipient. This can be illustrated by reference to an earlier data extract.

```
(15) (From Atkinson and Drew, 1979:52) (Originally
     extract 3)

Child:   Have to cut the:se Mummy
         (1.3)
Child:   Won't we Mummy
```

The child's 'Won't we Mummy' is a truncated version of the original question which displays, and is premised on, the child's understanding that 'Mummy isn't answering', rather than 'Mummy hasn't heard' the original request.

It is noticeable, however, that in extract (14) the speaker does not produce a similarly truncated version of the original request. Equally, the subject does not emphasise specific words or phrases, for example 'a:nd is my seat *confirmed* on that flight?', thereby indicating that the business of the turn is to prompt or remind the recipient. Also, the way in which the information is addressed in lines 15 to 16 is markedly different to the way in which it was addressed in the initial request formulation. So, in the original request the subject implicitly raised the issue of seat reservation as one component of a 'general check on the details of the flight'. But in lines 15 and 16 the formulation 'is my seat confirmed' provides an explicit and personal, or possessive, gloss. The subject's pursuit of seat confirmation is therefore done so that it is not a simple repeat, or a reminder.

A feature of the subject's turn is that it is a question – 'is my seat confirmed on that flight' – which is prefaced by the word 'and'. 'And-prefaced' questions regularly occur in interaction in institutional contexts, such as courtoom cross-examinations and doctor–patient consultations. Sorjonen and Heritage (1991) discuss some properties of and-prefaced questions which occurred in data collected from interactions between health care visitors and women who had recently given birth, and their analysis of these data informs our understanding of the kind of work accomplished by the subject's turn in lines 15 and 16.

Sorjonen and Heritage note that and-prefaced questions occur in a series of question–answer sequences. They observe that such and-prefaced questions routinely receive minimal, one word answers. These answers are preferred responses to the prior questions: that is, answers to and-prefaced questions do not depart from the kind of expectations which informed the design of the questions which elicited them. In this sense, they are answers which are built to display that the recipient has no problem with the prior question. Furthermore, Sorjonen and Heritage observe that after the production of a minimal preferred response, the questioner's next turn will be another and-prefaced enquiry. This next question will exhibit only a minimal acknowledgement of the prior answer (such as 'uh huh' or 'okay'), and move the conversation to a next topic or issue. So, the next and-prefaced question treats the prior answer as sufficient or unproblematic: as not requiring, for example, clarification or confirmation. Each and-prefaced question constitutes a 'forward movement within the trajectory of a larger sequence' (Sorjonen and Heritage 1991: 64).

> Finally, if proceeding to a 'next' question acknowledges the sufficiency of a prior answer, the 'and-prefacing' of that 'next' question . . . does particular work in constituting its relation to the prior question. Specifically it constitutes its status as a 'next' question in a 'line' or 'agenda' of issues or topics. As a socially constructed object, this 'line' is understandable as a pre-existing agenda of questions. As an interactional object it is on-goingly established and sustained with each next and-prefaced enquiry. It is this agenda-based 'nextness' between non-adjacent actions which we regard as the major task of and-prefacing.
>
> (Sorjonen and Heritage, 1991: 64)

In extract 14 the subject pursues the omitted component of the original request via an and-prefaced question. It thereby constitutes that component – seat confirmation – as one item in a pre-established agenda of related issues which the subject is progressively working through. So, this turn conveys the impression that this is the first time that the topic of seat confirmation had been produced in the exchange.

A related point is that there are features of the sequential environment of the turn which indicate that it is designed to appear as though it is 'touched off' by the system's prior turn, 'flight bee ay one seven three leaves from london gatwick to new york at twelve noon'. For example, an enquiry about seat reservation is conditional upon some demonstration that the service has access to related flight information; and the system's provision of such details in lines 12 and 13 clearly meets that condition.[5] The subject's turn thus occupies a slot in which it would be appropriate to pursue, as an additional item, information such as seat reservation.

The subject's turn in lines 15 and 16 is not, therefore, designed to remind the system that a feature of the original request has been overlooked or omitted. Rather, its design treats the issue of seat reservation as if this is the first time that topic has been raised in the exchange. It is an old issue recycled to appear new to the dialogue.

In the following extract there is evidence that the design of a turn (line 19) is amended at a possible turn transition space to change its character from a reminder to produce it as a turn dealing with a topic 'as if for the first time'.

(16) WOZ 1:1:F

```
W:   flight (.) information (.5) can I help you
     (.5)
S:   ·hh I'm kwi- I'm trying to enquire (.6) about a
     flight tomorrow going from hh gatwick to
     barcelona
     (1)
S:   ·hh I wonder if you could tell me (.) ·hh what time
     it's departing from gatwick
     (3.5)
W:   please wait
     (1.2)
S:   Pardon
     (2.3)
S:   could you repeat that please
     (10)
W:   All flights (.3) to barcelona (.5) leave (.) from
     heathrow (.5) terminal (.) one
     (2.5)
S:   And what ti:me (.) would that be. hhh
     (5)
W:   Please wait
```

In this call the subject explicitly requests the time of departure of a flight to Barcelona from Gatwick Airport. However, the system offers a correction, as flights to that destination depart from London's other main airport, Heathrow. It is not clear whether the subject realises that she has been corrected: her next turn is consistent with her pursuit of the time of departure after the correction, and with her not realising that she has been corrected.

The subject's next turn is, initially, 'And what ti:me'. After this there is a micro pause, after which she adds 'would that be. hhh'. It is noticeable that there is a slight elongation of the word 'time' a feature which is consistent with the interpretation that 'And what ti:me' was designed initially to raise the issue of the time of departure as a reminder. Equally, 'and what ti:me' is a truncated version of the original question, which would again indicate that the subject's turn was premised on the system's omission of this component, rather than its failure to understand that this was required also. Furthermore, the position of the pause after the initial part of the turn would suggest that the turn was originally designed as a truncated reminder of the original request. However, the subject subsequently transforms this turn by adding further material at the first turn transition relevance place. The extended component now establishes the turn as having the character of the kind of and-prefaced inquiry through which speakers address items from a pre-established agenda of related issues. This transformation of the character of the turn indicates the subject's orientation to the appropriateness for engineering this kind of repair, not as an explicit reminder, but so that it may be treated as addressing the issue as if it is raised for the first time.

This repair strategy shares many interactional and sequential properties with the other devices and strategies examined in this chapter. Recycling an omitted item as if 'for the first time' furnishes another space in which the system can address that topic or issue. Therefore, the subject initiates a repair sequence. Moreover, the design of the turn would ensure that if repair took place it would be executed by the producer of the trouble source. So, with regard to extract (14), if it transpired that the system *was* able to provide information about seat reservation, and indeed *had* omitted to address this aspect of the original request, the subsequent resolution would be a form of self-repair. Furthermore, the initiation of the relevance of the repair is done implicitly: the repair is facilitated in such a way so that the other's execution of repair would not be recognisable as a self-repair to the producer of the trouble source.

In the next extract the subject's first turn provides the relevant flight details and requests that these be confirmed. The system confirms only one component – the time of departure. Thus, at the point where the system has finished that turn the subject still awaits confirmation of a range of other details concerning the flight. The subject's subsequent turn in line 16 pursues these specific details.

(17) WOZ 1:8:F

```
W:   flight (.) information (.4) may I help you
     (.8)
S:   ·h I'm enquiring about the flight from gatwick
     (.) to new york ·hh flying at noon today (.)
     it's bee (.) ay (.) one (.) seven (.) three
     ·hh could you just confirm all the details about
     that flight for me
     (2.2)
S:   please
     (1.3)
W:   please wait
     (10)
W:   this (.) flight (.2) is (.) scheduled (.)
     to leave (.2) at (.) twelve (.) noon
     (3)
```

S: and from (.) >and what time will it arrive
at new york
(6)
W: please wait
(9)
W: flight (.3) bee (.) ay (.) one (.) seven (.)
three (.4) will (.) arrive (.2) at (.) new
york (.7) at (.2) fifteen (.2) thirty (.)
two (.2) this (.) afternoon
(1)
S: ·h and is that leavi- which (.) terminal (.5)
from gatwick is it leaving from
(7)
W: please (.) repeat (.) your (.) request
(.)
S: ·hh which terminal (.8) >which gatwick
terminal (.2) will (.) the flight leave from
(6)
W: this (.) flight (.) leaves (.) from (.2) gatwick
(.) north (.) terminal
(1)
S: thank you
(1)
W: goodbye

In line 16 the subject starts to inquire about one component with a 'from where'-type question; the subsequent pursuit of the departure terminal (lines 26 and 27) would suggest that the abandoned inquiry was originally pursuing precisely that component. After the self-interruption, the subject asks instead about the time the flight arrives at its destination, and this too is an and-prefaced question. Now consider the sequence in lines 26 to 32. In line 26 the subject appears to pursue the component which was abandoned in line 16. This is also introduced as a 'next question in a series of questions' via an and-preface. However, the wizard makes a request for a repeat. But note that the subsequent repeat is not and-prefaced. This should be no surprise, as there is little point in trying to constitute a repeated item 'as if it is being raised first time round' immediately after the system has acknowledged that a version of the request had been produced in a previous turn.

We have noted that the turn beginning in line 16 was originally designed to address a component which is subsequently raised in a later turn. We can make no remarks about why the subject elects to inquire after the time of arrival having started to inquire about the point of departure. But the appearance in the same turn of the beginning of a pursuit of one component, and then the pursuit of another, suggests that the subject was aware that (at least) two components of the original request were still outstanding. Instead of asking about both items in the same turn, however, she asks about one, and then pursues the other in a separate turn. One important feature of pursuing omitted items via and-prefaced questions is that the initiation of repair, and, if successful, the subsequent execution, is facilitated implicitly. So, characterising a pursuit as an and-prefaced question permits the speaker to portray the business of the turn as 'working progressively through a pre-established agenda of relevant items' rather than 'repair initiation'. With this in mind, we can provide an account for the subject's pursuit of discrete components of the original question in separate turns.

There is a sense in which a turn containing pursuit of more than one item would have the character of a list of requirements: the series of discrete request components that the speaker wanted addressed. The production of a list of requirements after the wizard had failed to deliver all the required information would be, effectively, 'unpacking' what was referred to in the original request as 'all the details'. Such a turn would draw attention to the need for repair, in that the unpacking would constitute the subject's reformulation of part of the initial request. And such reformulation would explicitly display the subject's pursuit of an alternative way of making the request, indicating, at the very least, some trouble resulting from the way that the request had been interpreted in the first instance. However, pursuing these discrete components in separate turns through and-prefaced inquiries allows the subjects to characterise these components as raised 'for the first time', rather than 'raised to initiate repair of a specific trouble' in the exchange.

It is useful to summarise the main features of this device. In those cases in which the wizard's answer apparently fails to address (at least) one component of the actual request, the subject may design the subsequent turn to reintroduce the relevance of that component not as a reminder that the system had overlooked something, but as a new issue, the introduction of which is appropriately positioned after the system's prior turn.

We have seen that subjects display considerable delicacy when addressing and resolving difficulties in their exchanges with the simulated system. This is most evident in the ways that turn design displayed the subjects' alignment with what they have interpreted to be the system's 'understanding' of the exchange. This demonstrated the subjects' sensitivity to, and attempts to avoid, the emergence of circumstances in which it would be necessary to make some form of statement concerning the system's inadequacy. Furthermore, the subjects used devices and strategies which allowed them to address what they perceived to be difficulties in the exchange in such a way that the issue of repair never became an explicit focus for the dialogue: the primary purpose of the exchange – to obtain specific information – was not sidetracked during sequences in which particular troubles were raised and solved. This in turn facilitated the resolution of problems as part of the on-going flow of the exchange.

9

CONVERSATION ANALYSIS, SIMULATION AND SYSTEM DESIGN

The last four chapters have generated a range of empirical observations. We have explored, for example, some normative dimensions of the organisation of calls to public information services; differences in the ways in which exchanges are closed in the human corpus and the WOZ data; and finally we have begun to examine some of the ways in which subjects in the WOZ study dealt with what they interpreted to be problems in the exchange with the system. In this final chapter we want to draw upon some of these results to make some observations about the simulation studies, conversation analysis and human–computer interaction. We will organise our discussion in terms of the three key concerns of this study: wizards, and simulation studies more generally; machines, and the use of CA in the design of speaking computers; and humans, or the importance for HCI of taking account of the kinds of everyday communicative practices people will rely on in their dealings with apparently intelligent artefacts.

WIZARDS: IMPLICATIONS FOR SIMULATION STUDIES

The Surrey WOZ methodology was informed by a critical appreciation of earlier WOZ simulation studies. We began by discussing the work of Guyomard and Siroux (1986a: 1986b; 1987; 1988). We noted that they treated many features of their data as forms of speech problems: so for example hesitations, false starts, and non-lexical items were treated as interfering variables: they were problems which had to be resolved. However, we took issue with this stance: we noted that conversation analytic research has revealed that such features of speech production have orderly properties which are tied to the sequential organisation of interaction. From this we developed two methodological principles which informed the analysis of our own data. First, we rejected the assumption that, prior to analysis, we could identify the relevant and irrelevant or problematic features of the subjects' utterances. Second, we examined their contributions to the exchanges to see how they were designed to address specific interactional contingencies on a turn-by-turn basis. Consequently, our empirical focus was informed more by sociology than traditional linguistics.

A third feature of our methodology was that we did not ask our subjects about their experiences with the WOZ system. There were two reasons for this. First, in the social sciences generally, there is considerable uncertainty about the relationship between people's behaviour and what people say about their behaviour. We noted the significance of this uncertain relationship when we were discussing Morel's (1986; 1987) simulation studies. She asked her subjects about the extent to which they trusted the information provided by the (simulated) system, but then noted that on other occasions they seemed to behave in ways which contradicted their answers. There is empirical evidence, then, that there may not be much to gain by asking subjects about their recollections of their exchanges with the simulated system. But there is a more important point: the kinds of communicative practices we are interested in are informed by largely tacit interpretative procedures. Consequently, it is very doubtful that subjects in a simulation study would be able to articulate analytically useful descriptions of the kinds of interactional skills they were using. For these reasons we decided not to rely on people's accounts of their exchanges with the simulated system, but to analyse the transcripts and recordings of their actual exchanges.

Richards and Underwood's (1984a; 1984b) research was important because it introduced a comparative element: their subjects were told that they were talking either to a human agent or an experimental computer system when in fact the same accomplice played both parts. This procedure ensured that the actual utterances of the simulated system/agent were held constant. However, it must be remembered that to ensure that they were able to control experimental variables, Richards and Underwood collected their data under experimental conditions. We argued that the next stage in the development of a comparative simulation methodology would be the use of naturally occurring data. For this reason we examined a corpus of calls to the British Airways flight information service. This allowed the comparison of naturally occurring data with materials generated in the more formal and constrained setting of an experimental simulation study.

The Surrey WOZ methodology, then, developed from the work of earlier researchers, both in terms of the analytic focus of the empirical analysis of the data, but also in the more general design of the study.

There have been subsequent developments in the design of simulation studies. For example, in the SUNDIAL project, the logical next step was to produce a Bionic Wizard, in which some components of the anticipated computer system are actually introduced into the simulation experiments in conjunction with a human accomplice. For example, a human wizard might simply type in a user's request to a computer which has a dialogue manager in operation, thus allowing a test of the system's ability to retrieve the relevant information. Alternatively, the speech recognition component of a system may be used while the human wizard types the required information which is then sent to the speech generator. (See Wooffitt and MacDermid, 1995, for a discussion of the use of a Bionic Wizard in a simulation study.) It is interesting to note that our use of a simulation methodology parallels an increasing use of computer simulations to study social, historical and psychological processes (see, for example, the collection of papers in Gilbert and Conte, 1995).

The use of a a simulation methodology was particularly useful in the SUNDIAL project. Although the design of the experiment was relatively unsophisticated, both in terms of the system capabilities we were trying to emulate and the technical resources available to effect the simulation, the data that were generated were rich and yielded a significant number of insights about the sophisticated ways in which humans conduct their verbal behaviour when they believe they are talking to an interactive, speech-based computer system.

MACHINES: THE USE OF CONVERSATION ANALYSIS AND THE DESIGN OF INTERACTIVE SYSTEMS

Within recent years there has been a surge of interest in the application of conversation analytic techniques and findings to the design of intelligent computer speech systems. Some conversation analysts, however, have argued strongly that this is a futile task and there is a lively contemporary debate as to whether or not it is reasonable to try to build truly conversational computers. This is just one strand of a wider debate about the claims of the proponents of the strong Artificial Intelligence position (see, for example, McCorduck, 1979; Dreyfus, 1992; Searle, 1984, chapter two; and Winograd and Flores, 1986). In particular, Button (1990) argues that the attempt to apply the insights and findings from conversation analysis is akin to 'going up a blind alley'. Similar arguments are rehearsed in Button and Sharrock (1995).

The debate seems to have been been conducted around 'in principle' issues: for example, there is an argument that the nature of conversational interaction is such that it is in principle pointless trying to model it in computer systems. In this section we want to consider some of the relevant issues in this debate; in particular, we will address the primary argument which is used by Button to show that a computational model of conversation is impractical or impossible. This concerns the rules which people use, and those which computers use. He argues that, whereas computers are programmed such that the rules upon which they operate determine what they do, the rules which people use are embodied in their conversational activities. So, whereas computers are driven by rules, people orient to them, and use them as the basis for inference and practical reasoning as to the moment by moment flow of the conversation. On the basis of this he suggests that it may be perfectly possible to build a speech system which can produce a simulacrum of conversation[1] that is, a routine or set sequence of conversation. However, he claims that a human interacting orally with a computer programmed to produce routine sequences of conversational moves cannot really be 'conversing' with each other. This is because of the intrinsic differences in the ways that people and computers use rules.

While we do not wish to argue with Button's assessment of the nature of rule use in conversational interaction[2], we do wish to question the utility of an argument which seems to prohibit empirical investigation of the issues.

Button's (1990) paper is, essentially, an argument which demarcates 'real' conversation from simulacra of conversation. Such an argument clearly presupposes certain assumptions; in particular, it is premised on the existence of an entity 'real conversation'. We want to examine this assumption, and to do this it is necessary to be clear about an analytic theme central to conversation analytic research.

Conversation analysts study 'talk-in-interaction' and more generally, interaction *per se* (Schegloff, 1987:101). Thus, in addition to 'ordinary conversation' there has been considerable empirical examination of materials derived from a variety of settings in which conversation is anything but 'ordinary': in courtrooms (Atkinson and Drew, 1979), in news interviews (Greatbatch, 1988; Heritage and Greatbatch, 1991), in market pitchers' sales spiels (Pinch and Clark, 1986), in doctor–patient consultations (Heath, 1986), and in therapy sessions (Bergmann, 1992). (See Drew and Heritage, 1992, for a collection of research papers on interaction in institutional settings.) Indeed, the materials on which Harvey Sacks began to develop his analytic interests were not everyday conversations, but calls to a suicide prevention agency.

An overriding ethnomethodological concern which informs these studies is that the institutional character of the talk is seen as the product of the participants' practical activities. It is not viewed as being automatically determined by features of the context extrinsic to the talk itself. For example, in a study of doctor–patient interaction the analyst will not approach the interaction as if it occurs simply as the consequence of the participants' respective roles; instead, the analysis will examine the conversational practices through which the relevance of these 'roles' or 'social identities' is realised in the course of the interaction. The essential point of this analytic approach is that the character of talk at any moment is examined as an accomplishment, achieved through the practical reasoning embodied in members' conversational practices.

This point applies equally not only to interaction in institutional settings, but also to the notion of 'ordinary conversation'. The 'conversational' character of any exchange is an accomplishment, constituted through those members' practices through which that specific character of that talk is achieved. Thus, ordinary conversation – what Button assumes is 'real conversation' – is, on all occasions, produced through, and contingent upon, the use of situated sense-making practices. This perspective echoes the ethnomethodological dictum that any social setting or state of affairs is to be viewed as an accomplishment constituted by and realised through members' practical reasoning. Insofar as Button tries to demarcate what is, and is not conversation, he seems to be forgetting this point. He refers to 'conversation' as though it has a set of properties which are independent of any occasion on which members produce 'ordinary conversation'. Thus, he appears to be reifying something which is essentially an accomplishment.[3]

The basis of Button's distinction between human–human interaction and human–computer interaction is that, in the former case, rules are embodied in interaction. People orient to rules, whereas computers are determined by them. Thus, computers cannot converse because they cannot register or display any sensitivity to procedures for producing intelligible interaction. Therefore, it makes no sense to talk of interaction between humans and computers. There are good reasons, however, for assuming that this position may be simply incorrect, because in the case of human–computer exchanges, there is always one party that does possess the range of sense-making procedures which, according to Button, demarcate human–human interaction from human–computer interaction: the human participant will still be doing the things that humans do when they interact. That is, the full range of culturally available sense-making procedures will be brought to bear on any occasion, even if the other party to the interaction is a computer. Garfinkel's counsellor experiments indicate the pervasiveness of human sense-making procedures when faced with the most random behaviour from a co-participant (Garfinkel, 1967). In human–computer interactions, then, the rationality of any 'conversational' interaction will depend on the interpretative resources available for members for making that interaction 'conversational'. As human beings cannot switch off their sense-making procedures, even when they interact with computers, they are inevitably bound to make sense of that interaction. Thus, even in human–computer interaction, the human agent will have a range of inferential and interpretative resources by which to make sense of what a computer might be doing.

Obviously, prior to further research, we simply do not know whether these resources will be marshalled to such an extent that a 'conversational' interaction occurs, or does not occur. Only empirical examination of materials recorded from human–computer interactions will yield a verdict. And this point brings us to the final section.

HUMANS; AND THEIR INTERACTIONS WITH MACHINES

Consider the circumstances of the Surrey WOZ simulation. The subjects were led to believe that they were participating in an experiment to test a speaking machine; they were isolated in a room, provided with a set of scenarios and instructions, and asked to converse, through a telephone, with a person whose voice was disguised so that it sounded extremely robotic. Plainly, the actual exchanges between the users and the wizard were obtained in a contrived and artificial environment.

In the light of the circumstances from which the data were generated, it may seem odd to use an analytic methodology that emerged from the observation and description of naturally occurring interaction, in which the participants have no imposed or even agreed conversational agenda. However, despite the apparent incompatibilities of a conversation analytic investigation of partially orchestrated interaction, the WOZ simulation procedure furnishes a rich environment for the detailed description and analysis of the competencies that underpin human–computer exchanges.

Perhaps the most striking observation is the extent to which ordinary communicative competencies were deployed by the subjects in the experiment. A simple instance of this (although not one focused upon here) was the occurrence of politeness tokens such as 'please' and 'thank you'.

```
(1)     WOZ 3:8:M

14      W:    please (.) try (.2) pol(and) (.2) airlines
15            (1)
16      U:    thank you
```

It is by no means unusual to find subjects saying 'please' and 'thank you' in their exchanges with what they thought was a machine. In one sense this is comparable to thanking a kettle for boiling. This is not to mock the people who took part in the study, but to introduce the point that, on some occasions, the design of the subjects' turns was informed by the kinds of interpersonal concerns which pervade, and to some degree provide the motor for, the detail and arrangement of human–human interaction. This was particularly clear in the examination of turns which were designed, broadly, to constitute the user's alignment with what was inferred to have been the source of the system's difficulty.

In one respect this observation should come as no surprise, because the kind of competencies that appear to inform the users' turns are simply the kinds of cultural resources which in part stand as criteria of what it is to be 'human'. In this sense it would have been an unexpected result had the users demonstrated radically new sets of communicative competencies in their exchanges with what was supposed to be an intelligent artifact. But there is another point. It is not simply that we are claiming that the subjects behaved as if they were interacting with a human agent, for such an observation furnishes little insight to the detail of the users' conduct. Rather, we have tried to show that interactional resources, grounded in the everyday domain of face-to-face interaction, were deployed in the strategic pursuit of circumscribed goals, namely, flight information. It is the provision of this kind of understanding about the subjects' practical tasks which confirms the utility of a conversation analytic approach to the examination of simulated human–computer interaction.

Finally, perhaps the most salient point is that the use of a conversation analytic approach to the study of human–(simulated) computer interaction provides the kinds of insights which remain resolutely unavailable from more quantitative studies or intuition. This study has been a preliminary step in the analysis of those conversational resources, rooted in the domain of everyday talk-in-interaction, which are marshalled in exchanges with computerised artifacts and simulated versions of those artifacts. It is through the use of precisely these kinds of communicative resources that we may yet witness the emergence of distinctive forms of interaction between humans and machines.

APPENDIX A

Recognising and understanding spoken language

In previous chapters, there have been many examples of dialogues in which one party was a computer or a simulated computer. This appendix reviews in a fairly non-technical way the techniques that are now typically used to enable computers to understand spoken language (for a lengthier and more detailed review, see Holmes, 1988). We shall use one dialogue, reproduced below, as a running example to illustrate the problems that computer speech recognition and speech synthesis has to tackle. For the purpose of this illustration, the wizard will be referred to as the system (S) and the subject will be referred to as the user (U).

```
(1)     WOZ 4:6:F

S:   flight information
     (5)
U:   hello can you tell me the arrival time
     of bee ay (.) two nine six from chicago
     today
     (5.5)
S:   please wait
     (15)
S:   flight bee ay two nine six from
     chicago to london heathrow terminal four
     is running ahead of schedule
     (3.5)
U:   what time will it land
     (3.5)
S:   please wait
     (13)
S:   flight bee ay two nine six from chicago to london
     heathrow terminal four arrives at nine forty five
     (1)
U:   thank you (.5) bye
     (3)
S:   thank you good bye
```

REPRESENTING SPEECH

Because of the importance of written texts in the modern world, there is a tendency for speech to be regarded as a derivative and rather imprecise version of written language. But spoken and written language differ in many respects. Written language can be easily and naturally divided into words and sentences. In contrast, speech consists of an acoustic signal which is more or less continuous and lacking in natural sub-divisions equivalent to words. Spoken words normally join together without any clearly audible break between them. For example, spoken naturally within a sentence, there will not be any significant acoustic break between the two words 'six teenagers'.

Linguists have devised means of representing spoken language in written form so that it can be analysed. The basic unit is the *phoneme*, the smallest unit of speech where the substitution of one unit for another might make a distinction of meaning. For example, the words, 'saw' and 'law' differ in their initial phoneme, the first being /s/ and the second, /l/ (phonemes are conventionally written using the symbols of the International Phonetic Alphabet set between oblique lines). There are about 44 phonemes used in English, each of which encompasses some allophonetic variation. For example, the way that typical Scottish and southern England speakers pronounce the /r/ in 'roach' may differ considerably, although both are using the same phoneme. The particular manifestation of a phoneme is known as a *phone* and is represented by a symbol in square brackets.

The phones representing a specific phoneme may vary widely in acoustic properties, even when spoken by the same speaker. One important cause of variation is the influence of neighbouring sounds on the position of the tongue, a feature known as *co-articulation*. For example, the initial sound of the word 'you' changes when it is preceded by 'did', as in 'Did you'. More generally, articulations are modified by the phonetic context, with the result that the pronunciation of words spoken normally differs from the same words spoken slowly and deliberately. This is known as *adaptation* or *assimilation*. The consequence from the point of view of speech recognition is that the manifestation of each phoneme is not distinct and constant, but is highly context dependent, varying according to the preceding and following speech. This is one of the reasons why speech recognition is so difficult.

Recognition systems also have to contend with the hesitations, false starts and coughs, lip 'smacks' and other extraneous noise that are found in normal speech. Moreover, in fluent speech it is frequently the case that phones, especially in unstressed positions, are not articulated clearly enough to allow even human speakers to identify them with certainty. Often, whole syllables and words are omitted entirely. An example is 'bed and board', which when spoken at a normal speed sounds like 'bed'm bord'. Even if one does hear an unambiguous and complete sequence of phones, there can be ambiguity about the intended words (for example, Holmes, 1988: 8 cites the sentences 'It was a grey day.' and 'It was a grade A.').

Despite all these difficulties, people do manage to communicate by speech very effectively almost all the time. This is because listeners are able to use the linguistic context to aid in their understanding. This context includes prosody, syntax and semantics, as well as the content of the dialogue. *Prosody* refers to the pitch, intensity and timing variations in speech over the course of a phrase or utterance. In English, prosodic features are used to provide emphasis, to indicate the mood of the speaker, to distinguish interrogative utterances from exclamations (for example, 'Is that the time?' and 'Is that the time!') and, most importantly, to single out particular words and phrases as being the topic or focus of an utterance and to draw attention to words which introduce new ideas into the conversation. For example, the sentence 'London is in England.' can be spoken with prosody which emphasises 'London' (as in answer to the question, 'Which country is London in?') or 'England' (as in a correction to the statement, 'London is in France.').

The *syntax* of a sentence refers to its grammatical structure. Normally we assume that utterances do follow grammatical conventions (but there are important exceptions in practice, especially in speech). For example, it has been shown that when subjects hear the sentence 'Some thieves stole most of the lead off the roof', they can spot the word 'lead' much sooner than when they hear the sentence 'Some the no puzzle buns in lead text the off' (Marslen-Wilson and Tyler, 1980), indicating that the syntax is providing clues to help recognition. Similarly, semantics, the meaning of an utterance, has been shown to aid recognition and disambiguate speech. Thus human listeners use a range of contextual information to help with speech understanding and a computer system which is expected to have comparable performance will need to employ the same sources of knowledge.

SPEECH TECHNOLOGY

Although this book is not about the technology which is being developed to permit computers to recognise and synthesise speech, it is important to appreciate the technical problems which have to be overcome. Most of these technical problems stem from the variability and ambiguity of human speech referred to in the previous section. Further problems arise from the need to integrate knowledge about phonetics, vocabulary, syntax, semantics and dialogue together to arrive at the best possible understanding of an utterance. The latter problems pose some difficult design issues about the 'architecture', that is, the functional arrangement of computer speech systems. As speech understanding is still in its infancy, the systems which have been built exhibit some diversity in the design choices that have been made. However, there are emerging principles which have been learnt from experience of building prototypes. In this section, we will outline the main technical features shared to some degree by most current systems.

Most speech understanding systems currently being developed in research

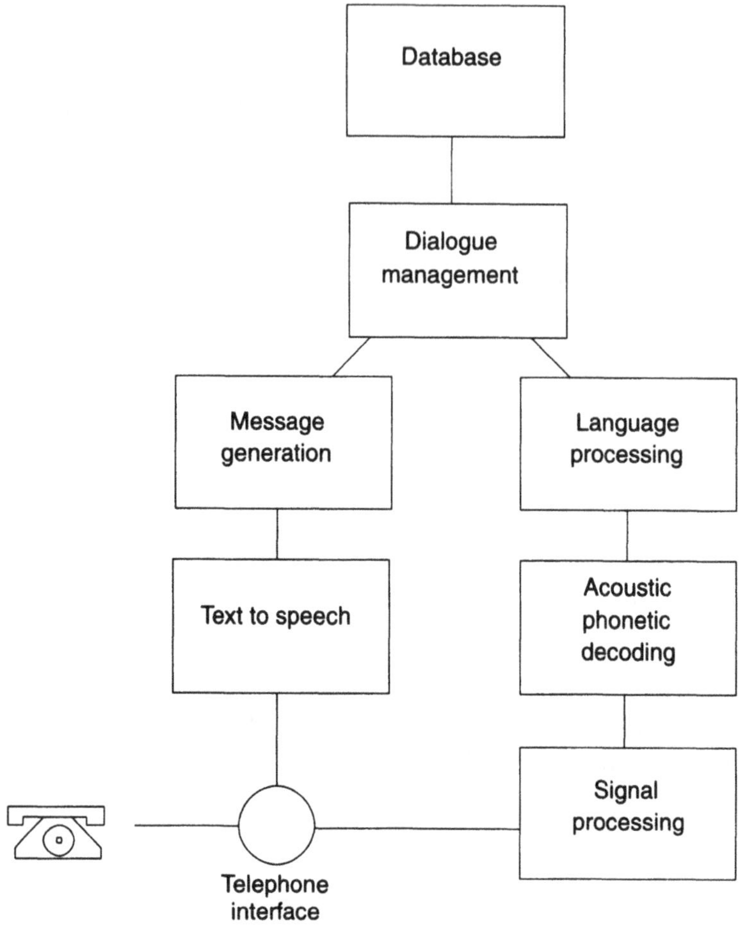

Figure 1 The architecture of a speech information system (after Peckham, 1990)

laboratories can be divided into a number of functional modules, as Figure 1 shows.

Electrical signals from a microphone or from the telephone line are conditioned to remove as much extraneous line noise ('crackles and pops') as possible and smoothed to eliminate major amplitude variations, such as might arise on the telephone when the speaker moves the handset nearer or further away from their mouth.

The analogue signal (Figure 2) is then converted into digital form and passed into an *acoustic-phonetic* module, often known as the 'Front End'. The major tasks of this module are to chop the continuous signal into segments, classify these segments into sub-word units, and then look up these units in a lexicon to identify the words they represent.

Figure 2 An analogue speech signal ('How are you today?')

THE FRONT END

The first step in phonetic processing is to extract the significant 'features' from the signal. It has been found that the amplitude and phase components in a speech signal can be discarded without much effect on phonetic recognition, but what must be retained is the frequency spectrum. One common method of extracting features is to pass the signal through a set of frequency filters, with bandwidths roughly equally spaced through the range 300 – 5000 Hertz. Each filter extracts the part of the signal within its own bandwidth. Usually, somewhere between ten and twenty filters are used. The output from each filter indicates the power of the input signal in its filter band over a short time span (10 to 20 milliseconds). The overall output from the whole filter bank is known as a *feature vector*.

In order to determine what has been said, the feature vector must be compared with *templates* stored in the system. For example, each word known to the system might have a corresponding template, consisting of the sequence of feature vectors which would be obtained if that word were spoken. In principle, the problem of recognition then reduces to the problem of comparing each of the stream of feature vectors obtained from the input against all the stored templates to find the closest matches. In practice, a more complex method must be used to allow for the effects of co-articulation, to compensate for timing differences arising from differences in the speed at which words are spoken, and to deal with differences between speakers. The most common approach is based on a technique known as Hidden Markov Modelling (HMM).

Hidden Markov Models

In order to understand the idea underlying HMMs, suppose that we had a (mathematical) model of a person's vocal tract. By exercising this model in appropriate ways, we could *generate* feature vectors corresponding to known, specific words. The model contains a series of *states*, each of which corresponds to one particular feature vector. In order to generate a whole word, the states are visited, one by one (with the possibility of looping back to the same state, or omitting some states, see Figure 3). Every time a state is

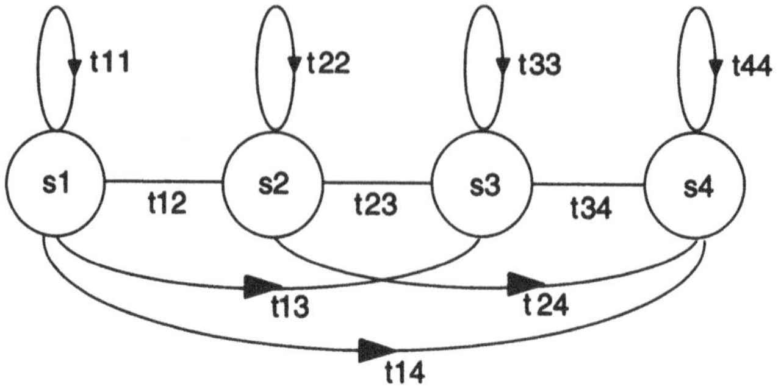

Figure 3 Structure of a four state Hidden Markov Model

visited, a feature vector is generated. These artificially generated feature vectors could then be compared with those spoken by the user. The principle is similar to the simple template matching procedure, except that instead of having stored templates, the model generates templates as required.

Now let us add a complication: that each transition between states (*s1* to *s4* in Figure 3) is associated with a *transition probability* (shown as the probabilities, *t* in Figure 3). This expresses the probability that generation will follow that particular path between states. The transition probabilities are set so that the most common sequence of feature vectors (i.e. the most common pronunciation of the word) is obtained by following the sequence of states with the overall highest probability, and other sequences are generated with probabilities corresponding to their occurrence in speech. The probabilities are obtained by 'training' the model with samples of the spoken word; a training algorithm iteratively refines the model's transition probabilities to maximise the fit of the model to the training data.

To reduce the number of models which have to be trained, HMMs are more commonly applied, not to words, but to smaller units. Phonemes are too small for the purpose because of the considerable variation in the way that they are spoken, depending on the speech context. Most systems therefore use 'context-dependent' phone models, with one model for each combination of two or three phones.

Once the models have been trained to set the transition probabilities, the recognition procedure amounts to determining, for every model in turn, the probability that this model will generate the observed sequence of feature vectors, and then choosing the model for which the probability is highest. Models can be linked together (with further transition probabilities) to produce composite models with which whole words can be recognised.

An advantage of the HMM approach is that the models can allow for differences between speakers by using training material from many speakers, thus making it possible to develop a recognition system which is to some degree 'speaker independent'. By means of context dependent phone modelling, the technique can deal with differences in the pronunciation of phonemes resulting from co-articulation and assimilation. Because sub-words are modelled, the system may be set up to ensure adequate coverage of the phonetic structure of the language, rather than attempting to model every word likely to be uttered by a speaker.

Neural networks

While HMMs are the most common technique used in present day systems, an alternative, *neural networks* (also known as parallel distributed processing or connectionist models), are becoming more popular. A neural network consists of three or more layers of interconnected nodes, each of which receives input from other nodes in the preceding layer and produces an output which is transmitted to the next layer. The output generated by a particular node depends on whether there are a sufficient number of signals arriving at its inputs. The output from the network as a whole depends on the signals presented to the inputs of the first layer and on the pattern of interconnections between the nodes. It is the pattern of interconnections (the *connection weights*) which causes the network to discriminate between inputs, yielding different outputs for each distribution of inputs. The connecting weights can either be designed into the network, or, more commonly, are automatically assigned by a training procedure in which the weights are adjusted so that a desired output is obtained from a known input, for each of a large sample of inputs and outputs.

The term 'neural network' comes from an analogy between the nodes of the network and neurons in the brain. However, while in the brain neurons work in parallel and each neuron can be regarded as a separate processor, almost all neural networks are simulated in a computer using one or a small number of processors. This imposes constraints on the size and speed of neural networks, which rarely have more than a few thousand nodes (compared with the estimated 100,000 million neurons in the human brain). In comparison with HMMs, neural networks are potentially capable of being trained to recognise more general types of structure and can process input more rapidly. In practice, however, these advantages have not yet outweighed the considerable knowledge and experience which has been gained with building and tuning systems based on HMMs and Hidden Markov Modelling is therefore still the predominant approach.

Lexical access

When the speech signal has been processed by an HMM, the result is a set of sub-word units corresponding to the speech input. Although it would be possible to process only the most probable sub-word units, this would mean rejecting other candidates which might have only a slightly lower probability.

Hence it is usual for speech recognition systems to produce, not just a simple sequence of the most probable sub-word units, but a more complex network showing all the units which can be detected with some probability over a given threshold.

The next step in processing is to move from sub-word units to words, by looking up sequences of sub-units in a lexicon. The lexicon contains, for each word known to the system, a standard pronunciation and possibly some variants. The look up has to be done for every probable combination of sub-units. For this reason, the output from the acoustic-phonetic module is not a simple sequence of words, but a 'word lattice' which gives the likelihoods of any of a large number of combinations of words being the ones which the user actually spoke (see Figure 4).

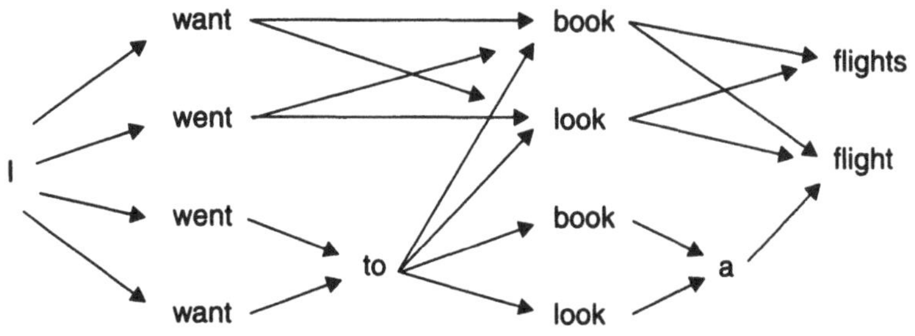

Figure 4 A simple word lattice

THE LINGUISTIC PROCESSOR

The word lattice is passed to a syntactic and semantic *parser*. This has the task of filtering the word lattice to reject those word combinations which are syntactically unlikely according to its rules of grammar (for example, 'Iron or how the says') or semantically unlikely (for example, 'I now hire vice ears'). The result is one or more 'parses' of the user's utterance which, for these examples, might have been 'I know who this is' (Phillips, 1988).

The parser acts according to a set of grammar rules. These rules both identify which sequences of words are recognised as comprehensible and assign some syntactic structure and meaning to the utterance. There are several fundamentally different designs for parsers and grammars (see, for example, Gazdar and Mellish, 1989); here we will describe only one, a unification grammar embedded in a lexicon.

We have already seen that a speech understanding system has to have a lexicon which indicates how every word known to the system is pronounced. In fact, short cuts can be made because English pronunciation follows some standard rules (barring numerous exceptions). Hence the lexicon can be primed with 'standard' pronunciations augmented with knowledge of exceptions. In order to make sense of utterances, the lexicon also needs to know about a number of 'features' of each word. First, it needs to have the basic syntactic characteristics of the word: for example, the part of speech (noun, verb, adjective, and so on), its number (is this the singular or plural form), gender (is this the male or female form) and so on. Second, it needs to know which other words will combine with this one. For example, the verb 'love' will combine with a noun or noun phrase which takes the role of the subject, and with another noun phrase taking the role of the object being loved. Of course, if the lexicon were to contain a full specification of all the grammatical categories which each word could be combined with, for every word in the lexicon, it would be enormous, even for a small vocabulary. Instead, words are arranged in classes (for example, 'love' is a simple transitive verb), and the grammatical knowledge is stored once for all words with the same classification. Some words will have several entries in the lexicon because they belong to several syntactic classes (for example, 'rule' can be a noun or a verb).

The third type of knowledge stored in the lexicon is semantic, that is, the meaning. For example, the meaning of the phrase 'the arrival time of bee ay two nine six' which occurs in the dialogue at the beginning of this chapter is composed from the meaning of its parts, so that the lexicon needs to know the meaning of 'time', that times can be qualified by words such as 'arrival', that flights have arrival times (and departure times) and so on. While there are various ways of storing this knowledge, one effective procedure is to use a hierarchical representation. For example, all journeys have arrival and departure times, and so this fact can be stored in the system along with the notion of a journey, and 'inherited' by flights, train journeys and all other kinds of journeys with entries in the lexicon.

The result of a semantic interpretation of 'the arrival time of bee ay two nine six' might resemble Figure 5, which consists of nested pairs of attribute-value expressions. The *attribute*, the first part of each pair (for example, 'carrier_id', the airline's identifying name) indicates the kind of object which is being mentioned and the *value* (for example, 'BA'), the object itself. As can be seen in Figure 5, the value may be a composite object, made up of a number of attribute value pairs, rather than a single object. The parser's task is thus to use the lexicon in order to discover a grammatical structure in the word lattice that it has obtained from the front end and to output a semantic interpretation. However, this interpretation is a literal one taking no account of the dialogue context. Dealing with contextual issues, that is, making a pragmatic interpretation of the utterance, is the task of the dialogue manager.

THE DIALOGUE MANAGER

The linguistic processor deals with utterances one at a time, with little or no notion of dialogue context or of the development of a dialogue over a series of turns. The next module in the system diagram shown in Figure 1, the

```
[type:s_time,
thedesc:
    [type:single_journey,
    thecarrier:
        [type:carrier,
        thecarrier_id:
            [type:carrier_id,
            value:BA],
        thecarrier_number:
            [type:number,
            value:296]
        ],
    thearrival:
        [type:arrive,
        thetime:
            [type:time_point,
            thetime: [type:s_time]
            ]
        ]
    ]
]
```

Figure 5 A semantic interpretation of the utterance 'the arrival time of BA296'

dialogue manager, superintends the computer's interaction with the user. It receives the output from the parser, interprets this in the light of the evolving dialogue, may interact with an external program such as a database to obtain answers to the user's queries, and replies to the user by sending instructions to a 'message generator' module. The latter has the task of translating these instructions into natural language for speech synthesiser, the module which 'talks' to the caller. The dialogue manager has to handle a number of functions as well as interacting with the parser, message generator and database: it manages the conversation as a whole, ensuring that the conversation opens and closes 'properly'; it determines the questions that the caller should be asked; and it keeps a history of the interaction so far so that, for example, a caller referring to 'the flight' can be understood in terms of the flight which was being discussed earlier in the dialogue.

Consider the processing which would be needed to generate the system utterances in the dialogue example shown at the beginning of this chapter. The interaction starts with the caller telephoning the flight enquiry service. A module in the front end detects that the phone is ringing and the dialogue manager instructs the speech synthesiser to generate a standard message of greeting:

S: flight information
(5)
U: hello can you tell me the arrival time
of bee ay (.) two nine six from chicago
today
(5.5)

The user responds with an initial enquiry. There are several problems which have to be dealt with at the dialogue level in this utterance. First, it consists of two pragmatically distinct parts: 'hello' and the rest. In a simple system, the 'hello' can be ignored, although as Chapter 5 demonstrates, a more sophisticated treatment would be preferable. The second part of the utterance is a question, 'can you tell me the arrival time . . .'. However, the question should not be treated 'literally'. The caller does not want to know whether the system is capable of providing the arrival time, but what the arrival time is. The phrase 'can you tell me' is apparently redundant, but, as we saw in Chapter 5, it is not irrelevant to the developing dialogue. From the fact that the user is asking for an arrival time, the system can identify the type of task it is being requested to engage in (for example, it is the arrival time, not the departure time, nor routing information which is wanted).

The caller then specifies the flight number, 'bee ay two nine six'. This flight number, together with the information that the flight is 'today' should be sufficient to look up the flight in a database to obtain its arrival time. However, the system must be prepared for the possibilities that: there is no flight BA296 (perhaps the system has mis-recognised one of the digits spoken by the caller); flight BA296 does not depart from 'chicago' (maybe the caller is confused or the system has mis-recognised the city name); there is no flight BA296 today ('today' can be ambiguous, especially if the enquiry is made late at night, when it is not clear whether the date referred to is the current day, or the next day), and so on. In any of these eventualities, the system needs to be able to make a graceful recovery from the apparent 'error'. This means that it must have some notion of what counts as an appropriate and polite dialogue, to tell the user about the problem and get the user to help overcome it.

The system in fact replies:

S: please wait
(15)
S: flight bee ay two nine six from
chicago to london heathrow terminal four
is running ahead of schedule
(3.5)

The user then asks:

U: what time will it land
(3.5)

In order to make sense of this, the system has to interpret the meaning of 'it'. This is not as easy as it might seem. The system needs to look back at the previous dialogue to see whether it can find something to which 'it' can refer. The most simple-minded approach would be to look for the most recently mentioned noun, but in this dialogue, since this is 'schedule', it is obviously not what the user meant. A more sophisticated procedure would be to note that 'it' must refer to something which can 'land' and look back to find the last such object, treating this as the reference for 'it'. Unfortunately, this will not work either, because it is *planes* which land, while previously only *flights* have been discussed. The search through the history of the dialogue would therefore fail to find anything which could be used as the referent of 'it'. The solution to this problem is for the dialogue manager to build a 'model' of the items referred to in the dialogue against which it can compare the information conveyed in each user's utterance. Thus, as soon as the user starts talking about flight BA296, it can start to construct a symbolic model of the flight, making standard assumptions about the normal features of flights (for example, they involve planes, they start and stop at airports, they have arrival and departure times, and so on). As the dialogue continues, the details of the model can be filled out with specifics, such as the city from which the plane departs. When, later, pronouns need to be interpreted, the model can be used to help.

This example (which only touches on the complexities of resolving reference in dialogues) illustrates some of the issues of pragmatics which need to be considered. Other features of ordinary conversation which a model of the objects being discussed can help resolve are *deixis* and *ellipsis*. Deixis means indirect references to items mentioned in the dialogue, for example, 'What time does *that* flight leave?', and ellipsis means the omission of part of a sentence, the assumption being that the omitted part will be understood from the context, for example, 'And the arrival time?'.

SPEECH SYNTHESIS

The remaining crucial components of a speech system are the message generator and speech synthesiser, the modules which 'talk back' to the user. The dialogue manager will construct a semantic representation of what the system wishes to say (for example, that BA296 arrives at 9.45 pm) and it is the task of the message generation component to translate this into a suitable sequence of words (for example, 'flight bee ay two nine six from chicago to london heathrow terminal four arrives at nine forty five') and the text to speech component to convert this into spoken form.

The translation from semantic representation to text can be done in two ways: by using pre-stored templates, or by using generation rules. The former method is more straightforward, although less flexible. If, for instance, the system is designed to provide flight arrival times the system can be given a template in which just the specific details relevant to the user's query have to be filled in. Such a template might look like this:

flight <airline> <flight number> from <departure airport> to <arrival airport> arrives at <arrival time>,

where the items in angle brackets are place holders to be replaced by the data to be conveyed to the user. The disadvantage of this technique is that it is rather inflexible. For example, when arriving at Heathrow Airport, it is helpful to know which of the four terminals the plane will land at. Thus for Heathrow arrivals, one should add <arrival terminal> to the template after <arrival airport>. But smaller airports have only one terminal, and the template for them should not include this parameter. The system could use two templates, one for the case with the terminal specified, and one for the case without. But this approach gets clumsy if the principle is extended to have a template for every different useful combination of parameters, and an approach which is based on a set of generation rules which define how to compose an utterance, given a semantic representation, can be more flexible and powerful. The pronunciation of individual words can be stored in the system's lexicon as a sequence of phonemes, in a similar way to a dictionary which records the pronunciation of the words. Alternatively, to save storage, the pronunciation of most words can be inferred from their spelling using a set of pronunciation rules. There still needs to be provision for exceptions, however, such as 'through', 'thorough' and 'rough'. Nevertheless, one set of 329 transcription rules has been estimated to convert successfully 90 per cent of a 50,000 words corpus of words. The result of this step is a sequence of phonemes which is then processed further to associate each phoneme with a sound, allowing for the fact that the pronunciation of phonemes differs according to the phonemes before and after.

A word-for-word transcription would produce very mechanical speech that would be hard to understand. A text to speech synthesiser needs to add prosody, that is, to apply stress (short variations of pitch) on particular words, to shorten or lengthen the duration of words, and to change the pitch across words. For example, in English, interrogative questions (those expecting an answer of yes or no) are usually asked with a rising pitch. Stress is placed on words to emphasise them; for example, in the interchange below, 'Dundee' should be stressed and lengthened in duration to emphasise the contrast with 'Dublin':

You want to fly to Dublin?
No, to *Dundee*.

In addition to these prosodic features, some words need to be stressed differently in order to create natural sounding speech. 'Function' words, which define the relationship between other words, for example, determiners such as 'the' and 'a', prepositions, conjunctions and auxiliary verbs, such as 'may', are all generally stressed much less than 'content' words in English.

Once the intended utterance has been composed, transcribed into phonemes and the prosody established, it needs to be converted into spoken form.

A stream of phoneme descriptors, annotated to show duration and pitch changes, is passed to an acoustic generator to create the spoken word. This is done with hardware which filters white noise through electronically controlled resonators that model the effect of the human vocal tract.

APPENDIX B
Scenarios in the WOZ simulation experiment

Scenario numbers are copied from the human–human dialogues from which they derive. Different scenarios having the same number (such as 2, 2a, 2b) are alternatively realised forms derived from a single source dialogue.

Scenario 1

Your boss is due to fly back from Germany tomorrow morning and you have to meet him off the plane. His flight number is BA 903 and the flight departs from Frankfurt and arrives at Heathrow Airport.

Scenario 1a

Find out what time the Frankfurt-Heathrow flight (BA903) gets in tomorrow morning. You'll have to meet your boss who's returning from Germany on it.

Scenario 2

You want to check the arrival time of tomorrow's flight from Warsaw. You think it will arrive at 9.30pm at Terminal 2 at Heathrow.

Scenario 2a

You want to check the arrival time of tomorrow's flight from Warsaw. You think it will arrive at 9.30pm at Heathrow Terminal 2.

Scenario 2b

You want to check the arrival time of tomorrow's flight from Warsaw. You think it will arrive at Heathrow Terminal 2 at 9.30pm.

Scenario 3

Your father is returning from a long vacation in the States and he expects you to meet him at the airport. Unfortunately you have lost the piece of paper with the arrival details: all you can remember is the flight number, BA 296, and that it departs from Chicago and arrives in London today.

Scenario 5

Your friends, John and Margaret, have just got married. Since you were unable to attend the wedding, you decide to see them off on their honeymoon to Spain. You know that they are leaving on a flight from Gatwick to Barcelona tomorrow morning.

Scenario 7

Later today, your brother is returning from a holiday in America and you want to meet him at the airport. You know that his flight number is BA 286 from San Francisco.

Scenario 8

You have just got married (congratulations!). Your honeymoon is to begin in a small village near to Turin in Italy. Your parents have agreed to pick you up from the airport when you return and they want to know when your return flight is scheduled to arrive. Unfortunately, you can't quite remember all the flight details: you know that the flight number is BA 584 but you don't recall exactly when it is scheduled to arrive.

Scenario 12

You have booked a flight from London Heathrow to Geneva leaving next Friday late in the morning. You have also arranged to rent a car there. Unfortunately the hire company needs your flight number in order to comply with local business regulations.

Scenario 13

Your daughter has just got married and you have agreed to pick up the happy couple when they return from their honeymoon in Crete. You know that their flight is scheduled to arrive at Gatwick at approximately ten o'clock this morning. However, you have just heard on the radio that Crete flight controllers are on a go-slow and that this might substantially delay flights.

Scenario 14

You have booked a seat on the BA flight 227 from Gatwick to Atlanta. You think, but are not sure, that the flight is scheduled to leave at 12.45pm today.

Scenario 14a

When is today's Gatwick–Atlanta BA227 scheduled to leave. 12.45 perhaps?

Scenario 18

Business calls you to New York. You've got a ticket for today's midday flight from Gatwick (BA 173). The small print says that flight details can be changed at short notice so you'd better check everything is still okay.

Scenario 18a

Business calls you to New York. You've got a ticket for today's noon flight from Gatwick (BA 173). Your ticket says that flight arrangements can be changed at short notice so you'd better make sure nothing has changed.

Scenario 19

After his big win on that TV game show, your brother has been sunning himself in Florida. He told you he was going to catch flight number BA 238 from Orlando, which was supposed to arrive at twenty-five to eight. He was going to come straight home to show you his tan but it's now eleven o'clock and he hasn't appeared.

Scenario 20

Find out when BA 481 from Barcelona is expected to arrive.

Scenario 21

Find out when Pedro's plane (flight 258 from Caracas) is going to arrive. Don't let them fob you off with an estimate; make sure the time is confirmed.

Scenario 22

You've got to meet your great uncle who is flying in on Hungarian Airlines' 6.10 flight. Nobody seems to be answering the phones at Hungarian Airlines. In desperation you call the world's favourite airline, British Airways. After all, your girlfriend/boyfriend works for them. But will they tell you about another airline? You're not optimistic . . .

Scenario 23

You're booked on the British Airways shuttle flight from London to Aberdeen tomorrow. You're not sure when you're going to be able to get to the airport so you'd better check whether or not you're tied to any one flight or if you can just turn up and get on the next plane.

Scenario 24

You want to find out about Gibraltar Airways. They don't seem to be in the phone book. Try British Airways – they might be able to help.

Scenario 26

Uncle Luigi has just called you up and invited you to a surprise party for cousin Vespasia being held in Rome this evening. You decide to take a couple of days off work and fly out this afternoon, if possible. Call British Airways and see what's available.

Scenario 35

You're going to fly to Zurich with British Airways. That's Terminal 4, isn't it?

Scenario 35a

Which terminal should you go to for BA flights to Zurich? Terminal 4 perhaps?

APPENDIX C
Transcription symbols

The transcription symbols used here are common to conversation analytic research, and were developed by Gail Jefferson. The following symbols are used in the data.

(.5)	The number in brackets indicates a time gap in tenths of a second.
(.)	A dot enclosed in a bracket indicates pause in the talk less then two tenths of a second.
·hh	A dot before an 'h' indicates speaker in-breath. The more 'h's, the longer the inbreath.
hh	An 'h' indicates an out-breath. The more 'h's the longer the breath.
(())	A description enclosed in a double bracket indicates a non-verbal activity. For example ((subject coughs))
-	A dash indicates the sharp cut-off of the prior word or sound.
:	Colons indicate that the speaker has stretched the preceding sound or letter. The more colons the greater the extent of the stretching.
( )	Empty parentheses indicate the presence of an unclear fragment on the tape.
(guess)	The words within a single bracket indicate the transcriber's best guess at an unclear fragment.
.	A full stop indicates a stopping fall in tone. It does not necessarily indicate the end of a sentence.
,	A comma indicates a continuing intonation.
?	A question mark indicates a rising inflection. It does not necessarily indicate a question.
*	An asterisk indicates a 'croaky' pronunciation of the immediately following section.
Under	Underlined fragments indicate speaker emphasis.
↑↓	Pointed arrows indicate a marked falling or rising intonational shift. They are placed immediately before the onset of the shift.

CAPITALS	Capital letters indicate a section of speech noticeably louder than that surrounding it.
° °	Degree signs are used to indicate that the talk they encompass is spoken noticeably quieter than the surrounding talk.
Thaght	A 'gh' indicates that word in which it is placed had a guttural pronunciation.
> <	'More than' and 'less than' signs indicate that the talk they encompass was produced noticeably quicker than the surrounding talk.
=	The 'equals' sign indicates contiguous utterances. For example:

```
14  A:  terminal four (.7) [heathrow=
15  C:                     [(four)
16  A:  =airport.
17      (.3)
18  C:  right.
```

[ ]	Square brackets between adjacent lines of concurrent speech indicate the onset and end of a spate of overlapping talk. For example:

```
15  A:  -yes it(ll) be ↑la:nding: ↓now: (.3) ahEAd
16       of ↑schedule=let me just check that for you?
17  C:  a↑head of ↓schedule, [bee  ay  two  ni]ne six.
18  A:                       [ahead of schedule] (.)
19  A:  yeah:(p), ↑hold on
```

A more detailed description of these transcription symbols can be found in Atkinson and Heritage (1984: ix–xvi).

NOTES

1 SOCIOLOGY AND HUMAN-MACHINE DIALOGUE

1 A brief introduction to the main aspects of speech systems technology can be found in Appendix A.
2 See also the critiques of cognitivist accounts of social action in Coulter (1985), and Bateman (1985).
3 Consequently, Button and Sharrock object particularly strongly to what they see as a claim by Frohlich and Luff (1990) to have done exactly what Button and Sharrock argue is impossible. (But see Fordham and Gilbert, forthcoming.)

2 INSPIRATION, OBSERVATION AND THE WIZARD OF OZ

1 We are referring here to the kind of discourse analysis which draws from linguistic theory and speech act analysis, rather than the more sociologically informed discourse analysis which has developed in social psychology (see for example, Potter and Wetherell, 1987; Edwards and Potter, 1992; Wetherell and Potter, 1992)
2 We provide empirical illustrations of these points in the chapter on conversation analysis, and in Chapter 8, when we discuss some repair strategies in the WOZ corpus.
3 We address these issues in more detail in Chapter 6 in our discussion of Sacks *et al.'s* (1974) analysis of turn-taking procedures in conversational interaction.
4 Other recent speech input/output WOZ simulations include Luzzati and Neel's (1989) train timetable information service simulation, those carried out as part of the ESPRIT Sundial project (Choukri, 1990; Ponamale *et al.*, 1990), and those carried out as part of the Danish Spoken Language Dialogue System Programme (Dybkjaer and Dybkjaer, 1993). These are concerned with flight reservation services, a hotel room booking service and the flight information service which forms the basis of the present volume.
5 As we report in the next chapter, subjects did complete two simple questionnaires about their experience of computers and the performance of the system. However, we did not treat information from these questionnaires as providing any important analytic insights. Indeed, many of the questions in the first questionnaire were included solely to predispose subjects to believe that the experiment involved 'intelligent' and 'conversational' computers, and were not designed to elicit substantive information.

3 THE SURREY WOZ SIMULATION PROCEDURE

1 In all, British Airways provided us with six cassette tapes taken randomly from their multi-tape recording equipment. Calls which were of a particularly poor quality were not transcribed. Also, on some occasions, there were two calls recorded simultaneously on the segment of the tape. In most cases, these overlapping calls were not transcribed. Those overlapping calls that were transcribed only had a portion of the exchange overlapping with another call. Apart from these simple considerations, there were no criteria for selecting which of the calls to transcribe: the transcriber started at the beginning of a tape and worked through both sides and then moved on to another tape until 100 calls had been transcribed.

2 A short note on the coding scheme for calls from the BA corpus: the number(s) in square brackets identifies the number of the call in the BA corpus (1 was the first call to be transcribed, 100 the last); the letters and numbers after the square brackets indicate which tape and which side the call comes from; and the two end capital letters identify the gender of the agent and the caller respectively.

3 The coding scheme accompanying the simulation data extracts refers to the subject and the trial. So, Dialogue 4:9 is the 9th trial of subject four; the letter after the trial number indicates the gender of the subject. Two different people were wizards during the experiment, one male and one female. However, we have not recorded the gender of the wizards in each trial for the following reasons. The vocoder ensured that the wizard's voice sounded entirely artificial and without gender characteristics. The subjects could not have known the gender of the wizard; and indeed, given that they all seemed to believe that they were talking to a computer, presumably the issue of the 'system's' gender did not even arise. Additionally, the people playing the part of the wizard to a large degree adopted identical speech delivery patterns. Consequently, we consider that the gender of the wizard had little or no effect upon the speech of the subjects.

4 In the social sciences there has been a long-standing concern about the use of questionnaires to elicit information about attitudes, opinions, thoughts, or whatever (Cicourel, 1964; Potter and Wetherell, 1987). While we are aware of these methodological arguments, we have elected to by-pass them on this occasion, as the information provided by the questionnaires does not form a central part of our analytic conclusions.

5 For clear rejections of strong artificial intelligence – the view that computers can support intelligence in a way analogous to the brain – see Dreyfus (1992), and Searle (1980). A robust attack on Searle's position can be found in Torrance (1984). For overviews of the debate see Boden (1987: 418–44), and Garnham (1988: 223–35).

4 CONVERSATION ANALYSIS

1 Collections of contemporary research papers can be found in Atkinson and Heritage, 1984; Button, Drew and Heritage, 1986; Button and Lee, 1987, and Drew and Heritage, 1992. Alternatively Psathas, 1979, Schenkein, 1978, and Sudnow, 1972, provide collections which contain some older papers. *Sociology*, 12, 1978, is a special edition devoted to the analysis of language use; while the papers in it are not purely conversation analytic, it is a useful introduction to ethnomethodologically informed examinations of language use. For an overview of major research findings, readers are referred to Levinson, 1983, Chapter 6; Heritage, 1989 gives an up-to-date perspective on recent developments within CA. For a more

general introduction to CA, however, readers should consult Harvey Sacks' transcribed lectures, published as Sacks, 1992. Other useful introductions can be found in Atkinson and Drew, 1979; Drew, 1994; Nofsinger, 1991; Wooffitt, 1990 and Wootton, 1989.

5 GETTING STARTED: OPENING SEQUENCES IN THE BA AND WOZ CORPORA

1 In his analysis of a single instance of a failure to remember someone from the past, Drew (1989) makes some relevant remarks about the relationship between the study of conversational organisation and the statistical manipulation of frequency counts of conversational practices.

2 Paul ten Have (1990) describes some methodological dilemmas in attempts to codify instances of conversational behaviour into categories for subsequent statistical analysis.

3 Of course, the agent does not actually hear a telephone ringing: rather, she or he has a panel in front of them which indicates when there is a call waiting to be answered, and they can access that line merely by flicking a switch. The flashing light on the panel thus acts as the summons in place of the ringing of the telephone. And in those cases where the service is receiving more calls than there are agents to deal with them, callers are placed in a queue system, the light is on permanently, and the summons then is continuous.

4 The actual situation is made somewhat complicated by the fact that British Airways acts as an agent for a number of different airlines, so queries about other companies may be warranted in some cases. Generally, however, members of the public do not appreciate that the BA flight information service can provide information about flights operated by other companies.

6 TURN-TAKING, OVERLAPS AND CLOSINGS

1 Button (1990) argues that, whereas computers are programmed such that the rules upon which they operate determine what they do, the rules (or 'procedures', 'methods', and so on) which people use are embodied in their conversational activities. He argues that whereas computers are driven by rules, people orient to them, and use them as the basis for inference and practical reasoning as to the moment-by-moment flow of the conversation

2 One consequence of the use of a vocoder was that the voice of the wizard seemed to merge seamlessly with the onset of the white noise in such a way as to make it very difficult to tell where one had stopped and the other had started.

3 This phenomenon, and its significance in the WOZ data, is discussed in detail in the second of our chapters on repair (Chapter 8).

4 Button (1987) analyses a number of strategies through which speakers may move out of closings into fresh topics.

5 In this solitary case the caller thanks the agent but does not go through the pre-closing and closing sequence identified by Schegloff and Sacks (1973).

```
[25] T1:SB:F:M
1    A:   flight information british airways
2         can I help you
3    C:   yeah have you got a flight coming in from
```

4 los angeles eleven fifty
5 A: arh heathrow or gatwick sir=
6 C: =heathrow
7 A: yes hold on a moment and I'll check
8 it for yo[u
9 C: ['kyou
10 (4.5)
11 A: yeah that's the two eight two
12 just a second I'll check it out fo[r you
13 C: [thank you
14 (2.5)
15 A: yeah that'll be landing at eleven thirty
16 C: eleven thirty
17 A: that's right sir terminal four heathrow=
18 C: =thanks a lot then
((end of inquiry))

6 It is noticeable also that compounded closing turns may occur as a consequence of the caller providing a first closing turn, the agent failing to respond sufficiently speedily, and the caller then producing the second closing turn.

[14] T1:SB:F:F

19 C: lovely (.) thanks very much indeed
20 (.)
21 C: b[ye
22 A: [thank you bye

[43] T3:F:F

10 A: yes the four three one from amsterdam
11 came in at thirteen oh five madam
12 (1)
13 C: thirteen oh five l[ovely thank you very
14 A: [that's right
15 C: much indeed for your help (.) [bye
16 A: [you're welcome
17 b'bye

7 However, the convention that once a caller has initiated a closing, then a closing sequence must be completed, is not unyielding. In the following extract, the caller appears to try to initiate a closing in lines 28, 31, and 46–7 before she is finally able to execute a closing sequence.

[2] T1:SA:F:F

16 A: ah (w'll) >yu've<=↑actually wro(t)-
17 rung the wrong ↑number=in future you need
18 tuh dial seven five ni:ne? (.7) one ↑eight (.5)
19 one ei:ght,
20 (.3)

```
21    C:    one (.) eight, (.) one ei[ght.
22    A:                             [(*ay) now ↑let me just
23          look for you? (.3) what time did you ha:ve?
24    C:    half past ni::n[:e.
25    A:                   [·h that's right
26          that's the ell oh two eight one.
27          (.3)
28    C:    a(h)r: >right< [I'll  (      )
29    A:                   [·h goes into terminal ↓two:
30          expEcted tomorrow: at oh nine ↓thi:rty:=
31    C:    =r:i:[gh(t) than[ks
32    A:         [·h        [they also have another
33          flight (.)  at ten ten,
34          (.)
35    C:    no this is: half past n[ine
36    A:                           [which may be:*
37          is an extra it looks like by the looks
38          of it [·h (i-)
39    C:          [what did you say=ell oh tee:
40    A:    ell oh: yeah ell oh tee is pol[ish airlines.
42    C:                                  [yeah
43    A:    b't the ↑flight number is ell oh: two
44          eight one.
45          (.)
46    C:    two eight (>right<)
47          ↑thanks ver[y much °indeed° ((sing song voice))
48    A:               [now when you've gotta ring
49          to↓morrow, ·hh you ring seven five ni:ne (.)
50          one ↑eight (.) one eight.
51    C:    ri:ght ok↑ay: thanks ↑very much in↓deed
52    ?:    thankyou
```

8 In the two remaining trials the callers were given the information, but then said nothing. After a certain amount of time the wizard initiated closing and the call was terminated without any further contribution from the subject. For example:

```
WOZ 5:5:F

1     A:    flight information may I help you
2           (.5)
3     C:    can you tell me what time the bee ay one seven
4           three to new york leaves please
5           (3.7)
6     A:    please wait
7           (23)
8           flight bee ay one seven three from london gatwick
9           to new york is scheduled to leave at twelve noon
10          (1.6)
11    C:    is it delayed
12          (4.2)
13    A:    please wait
14          (20.7)
15          there is a thirty minute delay (.7) but it may be
```

```
        corrected soon
        (1.5)
C:      can you repeat that please
        (16.5)
A:      There is a half hour delay (1.1) but this (1.3)
        will be corrected soon
        (17)
        thank you good bye
```

It was not always clear to the wizard whether or not the subject had replaced the handset. On such occasions, the wizard produced a terminal exchange just in case the subject was still on the line.

7 SOME GENERAL FEATURES OF THE ORGANISATION OF REPAIR

1 There are some notable exceptions to this. For example, Jefferson (1987) analyses two devices through which conversationalists correct co-participants.

2 Schegloff (1979) makes this argument with respect to sentences, but it applies more broadly to any utterance which occupies a topic initial position.

3 It is important to note that this is not third *turn* repair: third position repair can occur in third turn, but is not defined by such appearance. So, for example, third position repair can occur after an insertion sequence, but still be directed to the turn prior to that sequence.

4 Schegloff notes that one solution to the potential overlap problem is the use of pre-placed appositionals: 'yeah', 'but', 'so', and the like, which occur regularly at turn initial position, and which can be used to absorb some of the overlap generated when the prior speaker continues longer than expected. And, interestingly enough, when such appositionals are used in the next speaker's overlapped turn and the beginning of that turn is recycled, they are discarded. This is what would be expected if they were 'overlap absorbers', and the recycled part comes at the end of the overlap (Schegloff, 1987: 80–1).

5 This organisation is evidence of what might be called a second order orientation to the minimisation of gaps and overlaps between turns. For example: A and B are talking. B starts up, but A continues. B does not give up, but recycles the overlapped turn to coincide with the next anticipated end of A's turn, thus bringing off minimal gap and overlap (though organised with respect to the on-going overlap).

8 SOME REPAIR STRATEGIES ANALYSED

1 It is important to stress, however, that not all turns which follow a potentially problematic silence are designed to be heard as continuations of the turn prior to that silence.

WOZ 5:3:F (Simplified transcription)

```
W:      flight (.) information (.4) can (.) I (.)
        help (.) you
S:      (.3)
        ·hh can you tell me what time (.) bee ay five eight
```

```
5          four (.2) arrives please
6          (3.5)
7    W:    please (.) wait
8          (27)
9    W:    there (.) is (.) no (.) flight (.) number (.3)
           bee
10         (.) ay (.) five (.) eight (.) four
11         (.8)
12   W:    please (.) provide (.) more (.) information
13         (2.2)
14   S:    sorry hhh
15         (1.2)
16   S:    need more flight information hh
17         (.4)
18   S:    ·hhh uhm its
19         (1.2)
20   S:    it leaves at turin (.) leaves from turin
21         (4.5)
22   W:    please (.) wait
```

Here the subject produces a series of utterances in response to the system's request for more information. There are two instances in which the silences between these utterances approach the 1.2 second boundary, but in neither case is the utterance after the silence designed to be heard as continuing the prior. This is especially clear in the sequence in lines 18 to 20, where the utterance prior to the silence is '·hhh uhm its', an incomplete turn still in production.

2 This gradual release of information may be explicable by reference to data from the British Airways corpus. In the majority of calls, the callers preface their request with items such as 'can you tell me' or 'I'm enquiring about', and then go on to describe the flight and the specific information that they require. But there are cases in which the callers to the service merely state a minimal list of flight details in their first opportunity to formulate an explicit request. In every case in which this happens, the agent indicates that she is beginning to locate specific flight information, although there has been no specific request. For example,

```
[8] T1:SB:F:M 11-14

11   A:    YEs: ↑hello th [ere
12   C:                   [(ah)hhhh good (.3) er: the bee
13         ay five eight four from turin. love.
14   A:    five eight fou:r hold on please?
```

The agent's indication that she can proceed with the request indicates that she understands that the provision of even minimal flight information stands as a request for general information about that flight. With respect to extract (11), we may view the utterance in lines 20 to 24 as being informed by the subject's understanding that the provision of basic flight information can be sufficient to allow the recipient to deal with the request.

3 Remember that the scenarios were organised to encourage the subjects to experiment with the system and, if they felt so inclined, to discover if it could provide an alternative number for information which it could not provide.

4 It may be objected that these concerns are not relevant to subjects in conditions as contrived as those in the WOZ simulation. However, we consider that the WOZ

simulation is simply another environment in which culturally available, tacit practices and knowledge can become momentarily salient, and thereby inform in various ways subjects' conduct. Consequently, we consider it legitimate to explore this somewhat commercial dimension of cultural competence in our stimulation data.

5 We are not here proposing that the subject at this point believed that information about seat reservation was available by virtue of the system's presentation of related flight details. What the subject believed is not relevant. What we are pointing to are the ways in which the speaker designs the turn so that it comes off as one which 'pursues the kind of information it is appropriate to pursue when certain conditions have been established'.

9 CONVERSATION ANALYSIS, SIMULATION AND SYSTEM DESIGN

1 Button attributes this term to Wes Sharrock.

2 Fordham and Gilbert (forthcoming) provide a robust response to Button and Sharrock's claims about conversations, computers and rules.

3 And, as Fordham and Gilbert suggest, the arguments presented by Button (1990) and Button and Sharrock (1995) seem to promote the idea of a 'conversation police' who can demarcate what is conversation and what is not. (Fordham and Gilbert attribute the term 'conversation police' to Edmund Chattoe.)

REFERENCES

Allen, J. (1983) 'Recognizing intentions from natural language utterances' in M. Brady and R. Berwick (eds) *Computational Models of Discourse*. Cambridge, MA: MIT Press.

Atkinson, J.M. (1984a) *Our Master's Voices: the Language and Body Language of Politics*. London: Methuen.

Atkinson, J.M. (1984b) 'Public speaking and audience responses: some techniques for inviting applause' in J.M. Atkinson and J. Heritage (eds) *Structures of Social Action: Studies in Conversation Analysis*. Cambridge: Cambridge University Press, 370–409.

Atkinson, J.M. and Drew, P. (1979) *Order in Court: The Organisation of Verbal Interaction in Judicial Settings*. London: Macmillan.

Atkinson, J.M. and heritage, J. (eds) (1984) *Structure of Social Action: Studies in Conversation Analysis*. Cambridge: Cambridge University Press.

Bateman, J. (1985) 'The role of language in the maintenance of intersubjectivity: a computational investigation' in G.N. Gilbert and C. Heath (eds) *Social Action and Artificial Intelligence*. Aldershot: Gower.

Baum, F. (1974) *The Wizard of Oz*. London: Collins. (Originally published 1900.)

Bergmann, J.R. (1992) 'Veiled morality: notes on discretion in psychiatry' in P. Drew and J. Heritage (eds) *Talk at Work*. Cambridge: Cambridge University Press, 137–62.

Boden, M.A. (1987) *Artificial Intelligence and Natural Men*. Hassocks: Harvester Press.

Boguraev, B. (1985) 'User modelling in cooperative natural language front ends' in G.N. Gilbert and C. Heath (eds) *Social Actions and Artificial Intelligence*. Aldershot: Gower, 124–43.

Button, G. (1987) 'Answers as interactional products: two sequential practices in interviews', *Social Psychology Quarterly*, 50(2) 160–71.

Button, G. (1990) 'Going up a blind alley' in P. Luff, N. Gilbert and D. Frohlich (eds) *Computers and Conversation*. London: Academic Press, 67–90.

Button, G., Drew, P. and Heritage, J. (eds) (1986) *Human Studies* 9 (2–3). (Special Edition on Interaction and Language Use.)

Button, G. and Lee, J. (eds) (1987) *Talk and Social Organisation*. Clevedon and Philadelphia: Multilingual Matters.

Button, G. and Sharrock, W. (1995) 'On simulacrums of conversation' in P. Thomas (ed.) *The Social and Interactional Dimensions of Human-Computer Interaction*. Cambridge: Cambridge University Press.

Card, S.K., Moran, T.P. and Newell, A. (1983) *The Psychology of Human-Computer Interaction*. Hillsdale, NJ: Lawrence Erlbaum Associates.

Chapanis, A. (1981) 'Interactive human communication: some lessons learned from laboratory experiments' in B. Shackel (ed.) *Man-Computer Interaction: Human Factors Aspects of Computers and People*. Rockville, MD: Sijthoff and Noordhoff.

Chomsky, N. (1965) *Aspects of the Theory of Syntax*. Cambridge, MA: MIT Press.

Choukri, K. (ed.) (1990) 'Simulation studies' ESPRIT Project P2218 Sundial WP3 First Deliverable.

Cicourel, A.V. (1964) *Method and Measurement in Sociology*. London: Collier-Macmillan.

Coulter, J. (1985) *The Social Construction of the Person*. New York: Springer-Verlag.

Coupland, N., Wiemann, J.M. and Giles, H. (eds) (1991) *Miscommunication and Problematic Talk*. Newbury Park, CA: Sage.

Delomier, D., Meunier, A. and Morel, M.-A. (1989) 'Linguistic features of human-machine oral dialogue', *Eurospeech '89*, Paris.

Diaper, D. (1989) 'The Wizard's Apprentice: a program to help analyse natural language dialogues' in A. Sutcliffe and L. Macaulay (eds) *People and Computers: Designing for Usability. Proceedings of the 2nd Conference of the British Computer Society Human-Computer Interaction Specialist Group*. Cambridge: Cambridge University Press.

van Dijk, T.A. (1977) 'Semantic macro-structures and knowledge frames in discourse comprehension' in M.A. Just and P.A. Carpenter (eds) *Cognitive Processes in Comprehension*. London: Academic Press.

Drew, P. (1985) 'Analysing the use of language in courtroom interaction' in T. Van Dijk (ed.) *Handbook of Discourse Analysis*, vol. 3. New York: Academic Press, 133–48.

Drew, P. (1989) 'Recalling someone from the past' in D. Roger and P. Bull (eds) *Conversation: an Interdisciplinary Perspective*. Clevedon and Philadelphia: Multilingual Matters, 96–115.

Drew, P. (1994) 'Conversation analysis', *The Encyclopaedia of Language and Linguistics*, two volumes. Oxford: Pergamon Press and Aberdeen: Aberdeen University Press, vol. 2, 749–54.

Drew, P. and Heritage, J. (1992) *Talk At Work*. Cambridge: Cambridge University Press.

Dreyfus, H.L. (1992) *What Computers Still Can't Do: A Critique Of Artificial Reason*. Cambridge, MA and London: MIT Press.

Dybkjaer, L. and Dybkjaer, H. (1993) 'Wizard of Oz experiments in the development of the dialogue model for PI. Spoken Language Dialogue Systems', Technical Report, Roskilde University.

Edwards, D. and Potter, J. (1992) *Discursive Psychology*. London: Sage.

Erman, L.D. (1974) 'An environment and system for machine understanding of connected speech', unpublished PhD thesis, Carnegie-Mellon University, Pittsburgh, PA.

Erman, L.D. (1977) 'A functional description of the HEARSAY-II system', *IEEE International Conference on Acoustics, Speech and Signal Processing (ICASSP)*, Hartford, CT.

Fielding, N.G. (1992) 'Ethnography' in G. N. Gilbert (ed.) *Researching Social Life*. London: Sage, 280–300.

Finkelstein, A. and Fuks, H. (1990) in P. Luff, G.N. Gilbert and D. Frohlich (eds) *Computers and Conversation*. London: Acdemic Press, 173–86.

Fordham, A. and Gilbert, G.N. (forthcoming) 'On the nature of rules and "real" conversation', *AI and Society*.

Fraser, N. and Gilbert, G.N. (1991) 'Simulating speech systems', *Computer Speech and Language* 5, 81–99.

Frohlich, D. and Luff, P. (1990) 'Applying the technology of conversation to the

technology for conversation' in P. Luff, G.N. Gilbert and D. Frohlich (eds) *Computers and Conversation*. London: Academic Press, 187–220.
Garfinkel, H. (1967) *Studies in Ethnomethodology*. Eaglewood Cliffs, NJ: Prentice-Hall.
Garnham, A. (1988) *Artificial Intelligence: An Introduction*. London and New York: Routledge and Kegan Paul.
Garside, R., Leech, Ge. and Sampson, G. (1987) *The Computational Analysis of English: A Corpus-Based Approach*. London: Longman.
Gazdar, G. and Mellish, C. (1989) *Natural Language Processing in Prolog*. Wokingham: Addison-Wesley.
Gilbert, G.N. (1987) 'Cognitive and social models of the user' in H.-J. Bullinger and B. Schakel (eds) *Human-Computer Interaction – Interact '87*. Amsterdam: North-Holland, 165–72.
Gilbert, G.N. and Conte, R. (eds) (1995) *Artificial Societies: the Computer Simulation of Social Life*. London: UCL Press.
Gilbert, G.N. and Mulkay, M.J. (1983) 'In search of the action' in G.N. Gilbert and P. Abell (eds) *Accounts and Action*. Aldershot: Gower 8–34.
Gilbert, G.N. and Mulkay, M.J. (1984) *Opening Pandora's Box: A Sociological Analysis of Scientists' Discourse*. Cambridge: Cambridge University Press.
Greatbatch, D. (1988) 'A turn-taking system for British news interviews', *Language in Society* 17, 401–30
Greatbatch, D., Luff, P., Heath, C., *et al.* (1993) 'Interpersonal communication and human-computer interaction: an examination of the use of computers in medical consultations', *Interacting with Computers* 5 (2), 193–216.
Grice, P. (1975) 'Logic and conversation', in P. Cole and J.L. Morgan (eds) *Syntax and Semantics 3: Speech Acts*. New York: Academic Press, 41–58.
Grosz, B.J. (1977) 'The Representation and use of Focus in Dialogue understanding', unpublished PhD thesis, University of California, Berkely.
Guindon, R., Shuldberg, K. and Connor, J. (1987) 'Grammatical and ungrammatical structures in user-advisor dialogues: evidence for sufficiency of restricted languages in natural language interfaces to advisory systems', *Proceedings of the 25th Annual Meeting of the Association for Computational Linguistics*, Stanford, 41–44.
Guindon, R., Sladky, P., Brunner, H. and Connor, J. (1986) 'The structure of user-adviser dialogues: is there method in their madness?', *Proceedings of the 24th Annual Meeting of the Association for Computational Linguistics*, 224–30.
Guyomard, M. and Siroux, J. (1986a) PALABRE Phase 1 Experimental protocol CNET/TSS/RCP WP4 task 3. April.
Guyomard, M. and Siroux, J. (1986b) PALABRE Phase 2 Experimental protocol CNET/TSS/RCP WP4 task 3. May.
Guyomard, M. and Siroux, J. (1987) 'Experimentation in the specification of oral dialogue', *NATO-ASI Recent Advances in Speech Understanding and Dialogue Systems*, July.
Guyomard, M. and Siroux, J. (1988) 'Constitution incrémentale d'un corpus de dialogues oraux coopératifs', *Journal Acoustique* 1.
von Hahn, W. (1986) 'Pragmatic considerations in man-machine discourse', *COLING '86*, Bonn, 520–6.
Halliday, M. A.K. (1978) *Language as Social Semiotic*. London: Edward Arnold.
Hammersley, M. and P. Atkinson (1983) *Ethnography: Principles in Practice*. London: Routledge.
Hauptmann, A.G. and Rudnicky, A.I. (1988) 'Talking to computers: an empirical investigation', *International Journal of Man-Machine Studies* 28, 583–604.
ten Have, P. (1990) 'Methodological issues in conversation analysis', *Bulletin de Methodologie Sociologique* 27, 23–51.

Heath, C. (1984) 'Talk and recipiency: sequential organisation in speech and body movement' in J.M. Atkinson and J. Heritage (eds) *Structures of Social Action: Studies in Conversation Analysis*. Cambridge: Cambridge University Press, 247–65.

Heath. C. (1986) *Body Movement and Speech in Medical Interaction*. Cambridge: Cambridge University Press.

Heritage, J. (1984) *Garfinkel and Ethnomethodology*. Cambridge: Polity Press.

Heritage, J. (1988) 'Explanations as accounts: a conversation analytic perspective' in C. Antaki (ed.) *Analysing Everyday Explanation: A Casebook of Methods*. Newbury Park, CA and London: Sage, 127–44

Heritage, J. (1989) 'Current developments in conversation analysis' in D. Roger and P. Bull (eds) *Conversation: an Interdisciplinary Perspective*. Clevedon and Philadelphia: Multilingual Matters, 21–47.

Heritage, J. and Greatbatch, D. (1986) 'Generating applause: a study of rhetoric and response at party political conferences', *American Journal of Sociology* 92(1). 110–57.

Heritage, J. and Greatbatch, D. (1991) 'On the institutional character of institutional talk: the case of news interviews' in D. Boden and D. H. Zimmerman (eds) *Talk and Social Structure: Studies in Ethnomethodology and Conversation Analysis*. Cambridge: Polity Press, 93–137.

Hinds, J. (1979) 'Organizational patterns in discourse' in T. Givon (ed.) *Syntax and Semantics 12: Discourse and Syntax*. London: Academic Press.

Hirst. G. (1991) 'Does conversation analysis have a role in computational linguistics?' *Computational Linguistics* 17(2), 211–17.

Holmes, J.N. (1988) *Speech Synthesis and Recognition*. Wokingham: Van Nostrand Reinhold.

Hughes, J.A., Somerville, I., Bentley, R., *et al.* (1993) 'Designing with ethnography: making work visible', *Interacting with computers* 5 (2), 239–53.

Hymes, D. (1972) 'Models of the interaction of language and social life' in J.J. Gumperz and D. Hymes (eds) *Directions in Sociolinguistics: The Ethnography of Communication*. New York: Holt, Rinehart and Winston, 35–71.

Jefferson, G. (1983) 'Two explorations of the organisation of overlapping talk in conversation', *Tilburg Papers in Language and Literature* No. 28, Tilburg University, Tilburg, Netherlands.

Jefferson, G. (1984) 'Notes on the systematic deployment of the acknowledgement tokens "yeah" and "hm mm"', *Papers in Linguistics* (1) 7, 197–206

Jefferson, G, (1987) 'On exposed and embedded correction in conversation' in G. Button and J.R.E. Lee (eds) *Talk and Social Organisation*. Clevedon and Philadelphia: Multilingual Matters, 86–100.

Jefferson, G. (1989) 'Notes on a possible metric for a "standard maximum" silence of approximately one second in conversation' in D. Roger and P. Bull (eds) *Conversation: an Interdisciplinary Perspective*. Clevedon and Philadelphia: Multilingual Matters, 166–96.

Jefferson, G. (1991) 'List construction as a task and resource' in G. Psathas and R. Frankel (eds) *Interactional Competence*. Hillsdale, NJ: Lawrence Erlbaum Associates, 63–92.

Johansson, S. and Hofland, K. (1989) *Frequency Analysis of English Vocabulary and Grammar*. Two volumes. Oxford: Clarendon.

Lee, K. F., Hon, H.W., Hwang, M.Y., *et al.* (1990) 'Recent progress and future outlook of the SPHINX speech recognition system', *Computer Speech and Language* 4, 57–69.

Lehnert, W. and Ringle, M. (eds) (1982) *Strategies for Natural Language Processing*. Hillsdale, NJ: Lawrence Erlbaum Associates.

Levinson, S.C. (1983) *Pragmatics*. Cambridge: Cambridge University Press.

Lofland, J. (1971) *Analyzing Social Settings: A Guide to Qualitative Observation, and Analysis*. Belmont, CA: Wadsworth.

Lowerre, B. and Reddy, D.R. (1980) 'The HARPY speech understanding system' in W.A. Lea (ed.) *Trends in Speech Recognition*. Englewood Cliffs, NJ: Prentice-Hall, 340–60.

Luff, P., Gilbert, G.N. and Frohlich D. (eds) (1990) *Computers and Conversation*. London: Academic Press.

Luzzati, D. and Neel, F. (1989) 'Dialogue behaviour induced by the machine', *Eurospeech '89*, Paris.

McCorduck, P. (1979) *Machines Who Think: A Personal Inquiry into the History and Prospects of Artificial Intelligence*. San Francisco: W.H. Freeman Press.

Marslen-Wilson, W.D. and Tyler, L.K. (1980) 'The processing structure of spoken language understanding', *Cognition* 8, 1–71.

Mead, G.H. (1934) *Mind, Self and Society*. University of Chicago Press.

Meijs, W. (ed.) (1986) *Corpus Linguistics and Beyond*. Amsterdam: Rodopi.

Morel, M.-A. (1986) 'Computer-human interaction', NATO Research Study Group on ASP and CHI in Command and Control: Structures of Multimodal Dialogue Including Voice, Venaco, France.

Morel, M.-A. (1987) 'Computer-human communication' in M.M. Taylor, F. Neel and D.G. Bouwhuis, (eds) *The Structure of Multimodal Dialogue*. Amsterdam: North-Holland.

Murray, D.M. (1993) 'An Ethnographic Study of Graphic Designers', *ECSCW '93*, Milan.

Newell, A.F., Arnott, J.L., Dye, R. and Cairns, A.Y. (1987) 'A full speed simulation of speech recognition machines', *Proceedings of the European Conference on Speech Technology*, Edinburgh, 410–3.

Nofsinger, R.E. (1991) *Everyday Conversation*. Newbury Park, CA: Sage.

Norman, D.A. (1988) *The Psychology of Everyday Things*. New York: Basic Books.

Payne, S.J. and Green, T.R.G. (1986) 'Task-Action Grammars: A Model of the Mental Representation of Task Languages', *Human-Computer Interaction* 2(2), 93–133.

Peckham, J. (1990) Acoustic Bulletin.

Phillips, J.D. (1988) 'Using explicit syntax for disambiguation in speech and script recognition', University of Tübingen.

Pinch, T.J. and Clark, C. (1986) 'The hard sell: "patter merchanting" and the strategic (re)production and local management of economic reasoning in the sales routines of market pitchers', *Sociology* 20 (2), 169–91.

Ponamale, M., Bilange, E., Choukri, K. and Soudaplatoff, S. (1990) 'A computer-aided approach to the design of an oral dialogue system', *Proceedings of the Eastern Multiconference,* Nashville, Tennessee.

Potter, J. and Wetherell, M. (1987) *Discourse and Social Psychology: Beyond Attitudes and Behaviour*. London: Sage.

Psathas, G. (ed.) (1979) *Everyday Language: Studies In Ethnomethodology*. New York: Irvington.

Reilly, R. (1987) 'Ill-formedness and mis-communication in person-machine dialogue', *Information and Software Technology* 29, 69–74.

Richards, M.A. and Underwood, K.M. (1984a) 'Talking to machines. How are people naturally inclined to speak?' in E.D. Megaw (ed.) *Contemporary Ergonomics*. London: Taylor and Francis.

Richards, M.A. and Underwood, K.M. (1984b) 'How should people and computers speak to each other?', *Interact '84*, 33–6.

Robinson, H. (1990) 'Towards a sociology of human-computer interaction' in P. Luff, N. Gilbert and D. Frohlich (eds) *Computers and Conversation*. London: Academic Press, 39–50.

Sacks, H. Unpublished Lecture, Winter 1969, lecture 9: 15.

Sacks, H. (1979) 'Hotrodder: a revolutionary category' in G. Psathas (ed.) *Everyday Language: Studies In Ethnomethodology*. New York: Irvington, 7–14. (Edited by G. Jefferson from unpublished lectures: Spring 1966, lecture 18.)

Sacks, H. (1984) 'On doing "Being Ordinary"' in J.M. Atkinson and J. Heritage (eds) *Structures of Social Action: Studies in Conversation Analysis*. Cambridge: Cambridge University Press, 413–29. (Edited by G. Jefferson from unpublished lectures: Spring 1970, lecture 1.)

Sacks, H. (1992) *Lectures on Conversation,* Volumes I and II, edited by G. Jefferson and E.A. Schegloff. Oxford and Cambridge, MA: Basil Blackwell.

Sacks, H. and Schegloff, E.A. (1979) 'Two preferences in the organisation of reference to persons in conversation and their interaction' in G. Psathas (ed.) *Everyday Language: Studies in Ethnomethodology*. New York: Irvington, 15–21.

Sacks, H., Schegloff, E.A. and Jefferson, G. (1974) 'A Simplest Systematics for the Organization of Turn-Taking for Conversation', *Language* 50, 696–735.

Schegloff, E. (1968) 'Sequencing in conversational openings', *American Anthropologist* 70, 1075–95.

Schegloff, E. (1972) 'Notes on a conversational practice: formulating place' in D. Sudnow (ed.) *Studies in Social Interaction*. New York: Free Press, 75–119.

Schegloff, E. (1979) 'The relevance of repair to syntax-for-conversation' in T. Givon (ed.) *Syntax and Semantics 12: Discourse and Syntax*. New York: Academic Press, 261–88.

Schegloff, E.A. (1981) 'Discourse as an interactional achievement: some uses of "uh huh" and other things that come between sentences' in D. Tannen (ed.) *Analysing Discourse: Georgetown University Roundtable on Languages and Linguistics*. Washington, DC: Georgetown University Press, 71–93.

Schegloff, E.A. (1986) 'The routine as achievement', *Human Studies* 9 (2–3), 111–51.

Schegloff, E.A. (1987) 'Analysing single episodes of conversation: an exercise in conversation analysis', *Social Psychology Quarterly* 50, 101–14.

Schegloff, E.A. (1988) 'Presequences and indirection: applying speech act theory to ordinary conversation', *Journal of Pragmatics* 12, 55–62.

Schegloff, E.A. (1989a) 'Reflection on language, development and the interactional character of talk-in-interaction' in M.H. Bornstein and J.S. Bruner (eds) *Interaction in Human Development*. Hillsdale New Jersey: Lawrence Erlbaum Associates, 140.

Schegloff, E.A. (1989b) 'Harvey Sacks – lectures 1964–1965: an introduction/memoir', *Human Studies* 12 (Special Issue edited by G. Jefferson.), 185–209.

Schegloff, E.A. (1992) 'Repair after next turn: the last structurally provided defense of intersubjectivity in conversation', *American Journal of Sociology* 97 (5) 1295–345.

Schegloff, E.A., Jefferson, G. and Sacks, H. (1977) 'The preference for self-correction in the organisation of repair in conversation', *Language* 53, 361–82.

Schegloff, E.A. and Sacks, H. (1973) 'Opening up closings', *Semiotica 7*, 289–327.

Schenkein, J. (ed.) (1978) *Studies in the Organisation of Conversational Interaction*. New York: Academic Press.

Searle, R.R. (1980) 'The intentionality of intentions and action', *Cognitive Science* 4 (1), 47–70.

Searle, R.R. (1984) *Minds, Brains and Science*. Harmondsworth: Penguin.

Sinclair, J.M. and Coulthard, M. (1975) *Towards an Analysis of Discourse: the English Used by Teachers and Pupils*. London: Oxford University Press.

Smith, R.W. (1991) 'A computational model of expectation-driven mixed initiative dialogue processing', unpublished doctoral dissertation, Duke University.

Sorjonen, M.L. and Heritage, J. (1991) 'Constituting and maintaining activities across sequences: and-prefacing as a feature of question design', *Language in Society* 23 (1), 1–29.

Suchman, L. (1987) *Plans and Situated Actions: The Problem of Human-Machine Communication*. Cambridge: Cambridge University Press.
Sudnow, D. (ed.) (1972) *Studies in Social Interaction*. New York: Free Press.
Svartvik, J. and Quirk, R. (eds) (1980) *A Corpus of English Conversation*. Lund Studies in English 56. Lund, Sweden: Gleerup/Liber.
Terasaki, A. (1976) *Pre-Announcement Sequences in Conversation*. Social Science Working Paper 99, School of Social Science, University of California, Irvine.
Torrance, S. (1984) *The Mind and the Machine: Philosophical Aspects of Artificial Intelligence*. Chichester: Ellis Horwood Ltd.
West, C. and Zimmerman, D.H. (1985) 'Gender, language and discourse' in T. Van Dijk (ed.) *Handbook of Discourse Analysis Vol. 4: Discourse Analysis in Society*. London: Academic Press, 103–25.
Wetherell, M. and Potter, J. (1992) *Mapping the Language of Racism: Discourse and the Legitimation of Exploitation*. Hemel Hempstead: Harvester Wheatsheaf.
Whyte, W.F. (1955) *Street Corner Society*. Chicago: University of Chicago Press.
Winograd, T. and Flores, F. (1986) *Understanding Computers and Cognition*. Norwood, NI: Ablex Publishers.
Wolf, J.J. (1977) 'HWIM, a natural language speech understander', *IEEE Conference on Decision and Control*, New Orleans, LA.
Wooffitt, R.C. (1990) 'On the Analysis of Interaction: an Introduction to Conversation Analysis' in P. Luff, N. Gilbert and D. Frohlich (eds) *Computers and Conversation*. London: Academic Press, 7–38.
Wooffitt, R. (1992) *Telling Tales of the Unexpected: The Organization of Factual Discourse*. Hemel Hempstead: Harvester Wheatsheaf.
Wooffit, R. and MacDermid, C. (1995) 'Wizards and social control', in P. Thomas (ed) *The Social and Interactional Dimensions of Human–Computer Interfaces*. Cambridge: Cambridge University Press, 126–41.
Wootton, A. (1989) 'Remarks on the methodology of conversation analysis' in D. Roger and P. Bull (eds) *Conversation: An Interdisciplinary Perspective*. Clevedon and Philadelphia: Multilingual Matters, 238–58.
Young, R.M., Green, T.R.G. and Simon, T. (1989) 'Programmable user models for predictive evaluation of interface designs', *Proceedings of ACM CHI'89 Conference on Human Factors in Computing Systems: New Directions in Theory for Human-Computer Interaction*, 15–19.
Zimmerman, D.H. and West, C. (1975) 'Sex roles, interruptions and silences in conversation' in B. Thorne and N. Henley (eds) *Language And Sex: Difference and Dominance*, Rowley, MA: Newbury House, 105–29.

INDEX